Rethinking Capitalist Development

This volume honors the work of the late Josef Steindl (1912–1993). The chapters offer a critical examination of the major themes of Steindl's economics along with an appraisal of their relevance to the economic conditions of our times. The book thus centers on the particular connections which Steindl identified between the process of competition and the problem of macroeconomic stagnation.

Rethinking Capitalist Development discusses topics such as how Steindl's theory of microeconomic concentration and macroeconomic stagnation might be modified or extended to become even more thorough in its internal structure or in its applicability to historical phenomena. The question of how to take innovations and new products more adequately into account within Steindl's framework is explored.

Several of the chapters wrestle with both the formal and historical expositions of Steindl's theory, including consideration of the development of alternative mathematical models in which to present the dynamics of the macroeconomy and comparisons with or suggestions for alternative frameworks to capture historical developments in twentieth-century capitalism. The volume concludes with a posthumous contribution by Steindl himself, which addresses many of the major themes of the preceding chapters.

The Editors: **Tracy Mott** is Associate Professor of Economics at the University of Denver, Colorado. He is the author of *Kalecki's Principle of Increasing Risk and Keynesian Economics*, forthcoming from Routledge. He has written entries on Josef Steindl in *The Elgar Companion to Institutional and Evolutionary Economics* and *Business Cycles and Depressions: An Encyclopedia*. **Nina Shapiro** is Professor of Economics at Saint Peter's College, New Jersey. She is on the Managerial Board of Editors of the *Journal of Post Keynesian Economics*, and has numerous publications in both micro and macroeconomics. She has written the entry on Josef Steindl in the *Biographical Dictionary of Dissenting Economists*, and contributed to *A "Second Edition" of The General Theory* (1997).

The Contributors: Marcellus Andrews; Michael A. Bernstein; Harry Bloch; Keith Cowling; Amitava Krishna Dutt; Julie A. Hogeland; Marc Jarsulic; David P. Levine; Josef Steindl; Jan Toporowski.

Routledge frontiers of political economy

Rethinking Capitalist Development

Essays on the economics of Josef Steindl

Edited by Tracy Mott and Nina Shapiro

Routledge
Taylor & Francis Group

LONDON AND NEW YORK

First published 2005
by Routledge
2 Park Square, Milton Park, Abingdon, Oxon OX14 4RN

Simultaneously published in the USA and Canada by Routledge
270 Madison Ave, New York, NY 10016

Routledge is an imprint of the Taylor & Francis Group

Typeset in Times by Wearset Ltd, Boldon, Tyne and Wear
Printed and bound in Great Britain by MPG Books Ltd, Bodmin

British Library Cataloguing in Publication Data
A catalogue record for this book is available from the British Library

Library of Congress Cataloging in Publication Data
A catalog record for this book has been requested

ISBN 0–415–15959–8

Contents

Contributors

Marcellus Andrews, Professor, School of Public Affairs, Baruch College, The City University of New York, USA.

Michael A. Bernstein, Professor of History and Associated Faculty Member in Economics, University of California, San Diego, USA.

Harry Bloch, Professor of Economics, Curtin University of Technology, Australia.

Keith Cowling, Professor of Economics, University of Warwick, UK.

Amitava Krishna Dutt, Professor of Economics, University of Notre Dame, Indiana, USA.

Julie A. Hogeland, Dr., Agricultural Economist, Rural Business-Cooperative Service, US Department of Agriculture, Washington, DC, USA.

Marc Jarsulic, Dr., Attorney at Law, Clifford Chance US, LLP, Washington, DC, USA.

David P. Levine, Professor of Economics, Graduate School of International Studies, University of Denver, Colorado, USA.

Tracy Mott, Associate Professor of Economics, University of Denver, Colorado, USA.

Nina Shapiro, Professor of Economics, St. Peter's College, Jersey City, New Jersey, USA.

Josef Steindl, Dr., Austrian Institute of Economic Research, Vienna, Austria.

Jan Toporowski, Leverhulme Fellow and Reader in Economics at South Bank University, London, and Research Associate, Centre for Development Policy and Research, School of Oriental and African Studies, University of London, UK.

Introduction

Tracy Mott and Nina Shapiro

This volume of essays honors the work of the late Josef Steindl (1912–1993). The essays were originally solicited for a special issue of the journal *Social Concept*, and all but two of the essays began as submissions to that issue.[1] The project of collecting and editing the essays began in the Fall of 1991. Steindl himself was involved in the early stages of the project, and he encouraged its editors and commented favorably on its contents.

When it appeared in mid-1993 that *Social Concept* would not continue to be published, we decided to continue with the project as a book. We have been fortunate to be able even to publish in this collection an essay by Steindl himself, as we discovered in a set of unpublished papers left by him a piece which we believe fits remarkably well with the rest of this volume.[2] The fact that the volume was originally intended to be an issue of a refereed journal means that several of the essays were commented upon by scholars other than the editors. Most of these referees are also the authors of other essays in the volume, but two who did not make submissions to the volume and so must be acknowledged separately are Steve Fazzari and Duncan Foley.

The volume aims to illuminate Steindl's work through a critical appraisal of its central constructs, with their relevance to the economic conditions of our times as a special concern of the examination. That critical scrutiny of a body of thought is the highest tribute that can be paid it, and Steindl's work deserves the highest. It has the breadth of vision of the classical analysis, and precision ("rigor") of the modern one, representing the best of both schools.

The appraisal of Steindl centers on his magnum opus — *Maturity and Stagnation in American Capitalism* ([1952] 1976). This work sets out the relation between monopoly and stagnation that won him his renown. It relates the growth problems of the system to the structure of its markets, tying the stagnation of the 1930s, and the secular decline in the rate of investment that proceeded it to the concentration of industry and growth of oligopoly. In that book Steindl argues that the competitive process itself leads cost-differentials to develop among firms in an industry and that these differentials encourage price-cutting and further cost-cutting by the "progressive", lower-cost firms as a means of defeating their higher-cost rivals. Once the industry is dominated by the successful competitors who have no significant cost advantage over each other, however, the incentives to further price-cutting and to investment in additional productive capacity are considerably weakened.[3]

Maturity and Stagnation takes economics back to the long-run growth concerns of the classical school (Smith, Ricardo, Marx). It reopens the inquiry into the "wealth of nations", reconsidering the "nature and causes" of their opulence in the light of the insights of the macroeconomic contributions of Michał Kalecki and John Maynard Keynes. Its influence on Paul Baran and Paul Sweezy's *Monopoly Capital* and thus on the neo-Marxian school of "monopoly capitalism" is also well known and acknowledged.[4]

Various chapters in the present volume also discuss parts of Steindl's work outside of *Maturity and Stagnation*.[5] Some of Steindl's other work can be seen as leading into *Maturity and Stagnation* or as extending or modifying several of the ideas of that book. Others of his papers go into depth on particular topics in themselves, such as his work on the application of stochastic processes to the explanation of the size distribution of firms in an industry or to wealth or income distribution, though these matters are not totally unrelated to the concerns of *Maturity and Stagnation*.

The chapters in the present volume address Steindl's work as follows. There is a significant discussion of Steindl's theory of microeconomic concentration and macroeconomic stagnation and of how it might be modified or extended to become even more thorough in its internal structure or in its applicability to historical phenomena. In particular, there is a great deal of concern, not least in Steindl's own contribution to the book, with the question of how to take innovations and new products more adequately into account in Steindl's framework. There is a large amount of wrestling with both the formal and historical expositions of Steindl's theory here as well. These consist of the development of alternative mathematical models in which to present the dynamics of the macroeconomy and comparisons with or suggestions for alternative frameworks to capture historical developments in twentieth-century capitalism.

David Levine's contribution opens the volume by situating Steindl's work within the history of economic thought (Chapter 1). He identifies the problems in the classical attempts to develop a theory of value, distribution, and growth that is both internally consistent and adequate to the analysis of a market economy. He describes how Steindl's work offers ways to deal with the unfulfilled agenda of the classical economists, ultimately suggesting a break with that which limits the classical approach.

The two other chapters in Part I of the volume center even more on the microeconomics of Steindl's analysis. Steindl's theory of industrial concentration — the microfoundations of the stagnation thesis — is scrutinized in the chapters by Harry Bloch and Julie Hogeland. Bloch's contribution (Chapter 2) examines other parts of Steindl's work as well as *Maturity and Stagnation*. He asks whether Steindl's work leads to an adequate theory of industrial concentration. He suggests that adding new product development to Steindl's conception of industrial development solves a lot of the problems.

This connects well to Hogeland's chapter (Chapter 3), which focuses on the applicability of Steindl's theory of concentration to the nineteenth- and twentieth-century experiences of the US meat packing industry. Hogeland shows why and how this industry went through multiple phases of concentration and discusses how this calls for a modification of Steindl's theory along the lines suggested also in Bloch's and Levine's essays.

Part II of the book contains three chapters which seek to deal with some of Steindl's own frustrations regarding his macroeconomic model in *Maturity and Stagnation*. Amitava Dutt's chapter (Chapter 4) offers some modifications to Steindl's mathematical model which allow him to present a more tractable version of the model. He identifies Steindl's main theoretical contribution to be the first development of a formal model in which a shift in favor of profits tends to lead to lower growth, thus making clear what assumptions were necessary for this outcome, which had been suggested by Marx and other underconsumptionists. Dutt then proceeds to discuss an issue that has been raised regarding the internal consistency of Steindl's approach and to examine factors left out of the *Maturity and Stagnation* analysis, arguing that Steindl's framework there can successfully serve as a basis for incorporating these matters.

Marcellus Andrews's chapter (Chapter 5) takes a different approach to formalizing Steindl's theory. Andrews tackles the process of transition from competition to oligopoly. He constructs a model economy with sectors of large vs. small firms where the large firms initially have lower unit costs and so price-setting power. He then explores the consequences for concentration and capacity utilization of the likely strategic pricing reaction of the large firms at different existing levels of utilization. The result of increasing concentration and stagnation turns out to be rather sensitive to differences in the responsiveness of investment to profitability between the two sectors. If the smaller firms are more dynamically responsive, we can get a case in which the small firms grow faster than the large firms, reducing concentration and raising utilization. This case may well describe the periods of increasing competition due to innovations introduced by smaller, newer entrants at times in the history of the meat-packing industry, as described in Hogeland's chapter.

Dutt and Andrews both note the difficulties posed by Steindl's particular mathematical formulation of his model in *Maturity and Stagnation*, which takes the form of a mixed difference-differential equation system, which is known to be normally rather difficult to solve. Each of them develops an alternative formulation which produces a pure differential equation system. Marc Jarsulic's contribution (Chapter 6) also discusses this issue but furthermore wrestles with Steindl's later papers in which he modifies the restrictions on the role of innovations that he assumed in *Maturity and Stagnation*. In this later work Steindl argued that random shocks, with the positive shocks being more numerous than negative ones, could satisfactorily explain technical change, generating both cycles and long-run growth in a linear difference equation model. Jarsulic's chapter demonstrates that Steindl's original endogenous theory, with the internal accumulation of funds as the primary driver, can generate both cycles and growth if cast in a plausible nonlinear form.

The chapters in Part III focus on the applicability of Steindl's stagnation thesis to twentieth-century economic developments. Jan Toporowski's chapter (Chapter 7) begins by drawing out the methodological principles responsible for the distinctive value of Steindl's work. It then elucidates Steindl's understanding of the nature of business competition in some detail. Toporowski presents an alternative taxonomy for categorizing firms to that of Steindl, based on differences in the price elasticity of demand for output, which in turn arise from the degree of capital-intensity of production. Toporowski takes the increase in the percentage of industries which are less capital-intensive in the UK and USA today as having significant implications for the increasing problem that "Keynesian" macroeconomic stimulus programs tend to cause price inflation and balance of payment problems.

Michael Bernstein's chapter (Chapter 8) begins with a survey of other long-run theoretical explanations offered for the Great Depression of the 1930s in the USA to compare and contrast with Steindl's theory. He notes the difficulties in finding evidence in the 1930s' data able definitively to support or to question the applicability of Steindl's stagnation thesis. Bernstein then turns to an appreciation of Steindl's later additions to his *Maturity and Stagnation* analysis which illuminate how the US economy since the Depression has been able to overcome stagnation.

Keith Cowling's chapter (Chapter 9) continues the theme of the relevance of Steindl's ideas to history and adds a more global perspective. Cowling seeks to apply the stagnation thesis to the world of the transnational corporation. He identifies in significant detail the ways in which transnational oligopolistic competition aggravate, and in a few instances mitigate, the tendencies towards stagnation. He offers possible solutions to the problem by means of some sorts of democratic planning, but he also notes the obstacles this faces.

The book culminates with the chapter written by Steindl himself, "Trend and Cycle". This chapter (Chapter 10) touches on a number of the themes dealt with and issues raised earlier in the book, particularly of course the question of how to explain satisfactorily both the long-term upward trend with shorter cyclical movements around it that we observe in capitalist economies, but also the issues of how to treat innovative activity more adequately than was done in *Maturity and Stagnation*. This chapter also confronts the quandary over linear vs. non-linear cycle and growth modeling, raised in the mathematical chapters of Part II.

Kalecki ([1968] 1991, p. 435) called the problem of the trend and cycle "the *pièce de résistance* of economics". Steindl's approach here is to relate the long run and short run by realizing that business fixed investment is planned with a long-run perspective, while its implementation occurs in cyclical patterns as the optimism and pessimism of firms (cf. Keynes's "animal spirits") and the ability to obtain finance vary with overall changes in economic activity.[6]

In Chapter 10 Steindl holds that the way to treat innovations more adequately than he did in *Maturity and Stagnation* is to realize that they will normally give rise to the type of aggressive competition he described in that book as the pattern occurring in industries where large cost-differentials develop among the firms.[7] This fits rather nicely with the patterns presented in Hogeland's and Andrews's chapters, which describe conditions under which previously concentrated industries enter a phase of renewed competition due to adoption of a significant innovation by firms in what Andrews calls the "fringe" sector.

Steindl still maintains here that he is not convinced of the necessity of a non-linear cycle model.[8] He also raises the issue, discussed as well in Dutt's chapter, of the plausibility of postulating the existence of excess capacity in the long run. He argues that in the long run excess capacity will likely set up reactions that work towards eliminating it, mainly by leading to a revival of increased competition due to new entrants or existing firms which have developed innovations restoring cost-differentials as just described.

Steindl closes the chapter by arguing that long-run factors having to do with innovations or other sources of pressures on pricing or with pressures on wages from labor are indeed necessary for economic growth to occur in the face of the tendencies he identified in *Maturity and Stagnation* that work to raise the profit share. The key long-run element of the system then is the profit margin, or mark-up, which determines distributive shares.[9]

It might be worthwhile to conclude this Introduction with a remark about an aspect of the relation of the chapters in the volume to history. The developments in the US economy of the late 1990s and early 2000s are too recent to have been covered here, understandably and perhaps desirably, since history is normally better understood with passage of some time to allow deeper reflection and fuller compilation of evidence. Yet it might be remiss not to say something about the relevance of Steindl's theory to this period.

The post-millennium bust following the late 1990s' boom was the first since World War II not to be caused by policy tightening[10] but by the emergence of excess capacity, as a number of new aggressively competitive industries over-invested in various types of high-tech capacity and equipment. The rising productivity and increased cost-cutting competition lowered the fear of price inflation, encouraging policy-makers not to be as quick this time to raise the cost of credit to stop the boom. This, however, allowed the underlying stagnationist dialectic to re-emerge.[11] Competitors in the innovative industries cut prices and expanded production capacity, attempting to take market share from each other. The greater productivity from the newer technologies also enabled many older industries to be able to produce more with less labor and capacity, at the same time as the capacity of the newer industries was continually running ahead of the demand available to cover overhead and direct costs. The mounting losses began to sink the weaker competitors in the younger industries. Capacity began rapidly to become redundant, the profitability of further investment plunged, and we are now seeing massive shakeouts and consolidations in the newer industries, as the relatively stronger firms eliminate the weaker ones. These developments seem surely to demonstrate once again the relevance of Steindl's theory of competition leading to excess capacity, industrial concentration, and macroeconomic troubles.

Notes

1 These two essays are the one by Keith Cowling and the one written by Steindl himself. Cowling's essay is also the only one previously published. It was prepared for the 1994 Steindl Memorial Issue of the *Review of Political Economy*, and while it was inadvertently left out of that issue, it has been published in a subsequent issue.

2 We want to thank Julio López for drawing our attention to Steindl's unpublished papers and to Alois Guger for providing us the opportunity to publish this particular paper. We also wish to thank Prof. Guger and Claudio Milazzo for their editorial work on the paper.

3 Each of us has written appreciations of Steindl's work. See Mott (1994, 1997) and Shapiro (1988, [1992] 2000).

4 See Baran and Sweezy (1966, p. 56). See also Cowling (1982) and Mott (1992).

5 See Steindl ([1979] 1990) for a compendium of his most noted work outside of *Maturity and Stagnation*.

6 Cf. Levine (1981, Chap. 6) and Andrei Shleifer (1986).

7 Cf. Shapiro (1981, 1988).

8 See Steindl (1989) for an earlier statement of this position.

9 Cf. Mott (2002).

10 Steindl ([1979] 1990) calls this "stagnation policy".

11 "Stagnation theory" in Steindl's ([1979] 1990) terminology.

References

Baran, Paul and Sweezy, Paul (1966) *Monopoly Capital*, New York: Monthly Review Press.

Cowling, Keith (1982) *Monopoly Capitalism*, New York: John Wiley and Sons.

Kalecki, Michał (1991 [1968]) "Trend and the Business Cycle", in Jerzy Osiatyński (ed.), *Collected Works of Michał Kalecki*, vol. II, Oxford: Clarendon Press, pp. 435–450.

Levine, David (1981) *Economic Theory*, London: Routledge and Kegan Paul.

Mott, Tracy (1992) "In What Sense Does Monopoly Capital Require Monopoly? An Essay on the Contribution of Kalecki and Steindl", in John Davis (ed.), *The Economic Surplus in Advanced Economies*, Cheltenham: Edward Elgar Publishing, pp. 114–129.

Mott, Tracy (1994) "Josef Steindl", in Geoff Hodgson, Warren Samuels and Marc Tool, (eds), *The Elgar Companion to Institutional and Evolutionary Economics*, Cheltenham: Edward Elgar Publishing, pp. 301–304.

Mott, Tracy (1997) "Josef Steindl", in David Glasner (ed.), *Business Cycles and Depressions: An Encyclopedia*, New York: Garland Publishing, pp. 650–652.

Mott, Tracy (2002) "Longer-Run Aspects of Kaleckian Macroeconomics", in Mark Setterfield (ed.), *The Economics of Demand-led Growth: Challenging the Supply-Side Vision of the Long Run*, Cheltenham: Edward Elgar Publishing, pp. 153–171.

Shapiro, Nina (1981) "Pricing and the Growth of the Firm", *Journal of Post Keynesian Economics* vol. 4, pp. 85–100.

Shapiro, Nina (1988) "Market Structure and Economic Growth: Steindl's Contribution", *Social Concept* vol. 4, pp. 72–83.

Shapiro, Nina ([1992] 2000) "Josef Steindl (1912–1993)", in Philip Arestis and Malcolm Sawyer (eds), *A Biographical Dictionary of Dissenting Economists*, Cheltenham: Edward Elgar Publishing, pp. 629–636.

Shleifer, Andrei (1986) "Implementation Cycles", *Journal of Political Economy* vol. 94, pp. 1163–1190.

Steindl, Josef ([1952] 1976) *Maturity and Stagnation in American Capitalism*, New York: Monthly Review Press.

Steindl, Josef ([1979] 1990) "Stagnation Theory and Stagnation Policy", in *Economic Papers 1941–88*, New York: St. Martin's Press, pp. 107–126.

Steindl, Josef (1989) "Reflections on Kalecki's Dynamics", in Mario Sebastiani (ed.), *Kalecki's Relevance Today*, New York: St. Martin's Press.

Steindl, Josef (1990) *Economic Papers 1941–88*, New York: St. Martin's Press.

Part I

Concentration and development

1 Reproduction and transformation in the theory of the market

Observations on Josef Steindl's theory of capitalist dynamics

David P. Levine

Introduction

Theories of the market take it more or less for granted that their work remains incomplete so long as they fail to arrive at theoretically determinate relative prices. This means that they must show how prices vary quantitatively with the magnitudes of specified parameters. This approach to price theory has the important characteristic that it begins with a fixed structure. For neoclassical theory this is a structure of resource constraints and preference orderings, each capable of specification in quantitative terms. For the classical theory, in its modern versions, the structure is one of reproduction, also specified in quantitative terms. Here I will be concerned only with the classical theory, and the potential impact the approach suggested by Josef Steindl's work might have on it.

Thinking about price theory along the lines suggested above creates difficulties for the classical theory. I begin by indicating what those difficulties are, then briefly outline an alternative way of approaching the problem, one that treats price determination as an element of structural transformation rather than reproduction. I take this shift in perspective to be implied in Steindl's analysis of capitalist dynamics.

The core of the classical theory

Modern accounts of the classical conception of the economy focus on the reproduction and expansion of a production structure (Sraffa 1960; Walsh and Gram 1980). In this view, a system of technical interdependence constitutes the core of the economic process. A market economy consists of a set of legally independent private producers, each dependent on others for production of inputs necessary to their own reproduction, and each providing labor, means of production, or means of consumption needed by others.

The most elementary account of the logic of the classical theory assumes that the system of needs and technical conditions (or methods) of production does not change. This makes the economic process one of reproduction in the strong sense since it replicates a fixed structure. Piero Sraffa uses the term self-replacement to depict reproduction in this strong sense. The classical theory, in its most elementary form, is a theory of an economy in a self-replacing state.

While the concept of a self-replacing state constitutes the analytical backbone of the classical idea, when used as the basis for the determination of a system of prices, it lacks one crucial element. The theory provides a method for valuing products in commodity (or numeraire) units, but it provides no reason for doing so. If, indeed, the system merely reproduces itself at a fixed level, the peculiar concerns of a market disappear (Hayek 1945; Levine 1981, Ch. 7).

Value becomes significant due to the necessity of measuring output independently of those units relevant to its use (or use value in the classical terminology). This necessity arises when the value and not the use of output is the end of production. It only makes sense, however, to make value the end if we need to measure it relative to something else expressed in the same units. The ideas of profit-making and capital accumulation do just that; they require measuring the value of capital and output today against their value in the past (or possibly in the future).

The classical theory assumes that the production structure yields output exceeding that just adequate to replace used up inputs and necessary consumption. This excess has come to be termed the "surplus". When a production structure enables an economy to produce at a level that both replaces used up inputs (including "necessary" consumption) and generates a surplus, that production structure has a potential for growth.

A problem arises in determining this potential due to the inclusion of labor as an input. Unless we can specify the necessary costs of producing labor, the labor input makes reproduction costs ambiguous. As important as it is, I will not explore this matter here.

In the classical theory, the economy produces a surplus to make possible its own expansion. Since the economy has the capacity to produce more output than it needs to reproduce itself at a given level, it can increase the level of production each period by reinvesting (or productively consuming) the surplus. The classical treatment of accumulation begins with a theory of expanded reproduction. Expanded reproduction differs from reproduction only in magnitude. The structure of production remains fixed, while its components increase.

Fixity of the structure of production in the context of growth means that (1) the additional workers who enter the production process do so with the same needs as those of the original group; and (2) the technical rules for transforming inputs into outputs apply for varying levels of production (as would be assured by constant returns to scale). The assumption that the technical rules for transforming inputs into outputs do not change when we change the scale of production invokes the idea of a period of time long enough to make expanded reproduction possible but short enough that "changes in technical knowledge can normally be neglected" (Pasinetti 1977, p. 69).[1]

For the classical theory the (expanded) reproduction of a fixed structure is the logical core of the economic process. All analysis of structural change treats the logic of self-replacement as its foundation (Marx 1967, Vol. I, p. 566; Pasinetti 1981, p. 29). The logical core of the classical theory provides an initial formulation for the historical mission of capitalist accumulation: the extensive growth of the production structure. Through extensive growth, the capitalist economy exploits opportunities available to increase what Marx refers to as society's material base.

What, from the standpoint of social progress, does extensive growth accomplish? Classical theory provides two answers to this question. First, extensive accumulation transforms labor into wage labor. Second, extensive accumulation assures the full exploitation of labor's productive potential under given (technical) conditions. The first answer comes to us from Adam Smith, who saw capital accumulation as the transformation of unproductive into productive labor. The second comes from Ricardo, who saw capital accumulation as the process of exhausting available fertile soil. The classical theory of extensive growth depicts a process of transition by which all labor becomes wage labor and all available fertile land is brought under cultivation. In doing so, the analysis incorporates two important inconsistencies.

The first of these has to do with the wage. On one side, because of its impact on the demand for labor, capital accumulation implies a higher wage. Assuming that capital intensity is more or less constant, and the supply of labor inelastic, the demand for labor grows with the accumulation of capital and eventually encounters a limit in the supply of labor. As the economy approaches this limit, wages tend to rise. While the classical analysis of this problem is not as secure as we would like, the major classical theorists all assumed that rapid accumulation would imply a tightening of the labor market and rise in wages.[2]

Rapid accumulation increases demand for labor, tightens conditions in the labor market, and presses up the wage. On the other side, capital accumulation implies a lower wage because the worker must, in Smith's word, "share" his product with the capitalist in order to finance the accumulation process (Smith 1937, p. 65). So long as accumulation proceeds on the basis of fixed technical know-how, labor productivity remains the same (or deteriorates in the face of diminishing fertility of the soil), and investment requires a lower level of consumption than would be possible in its absence.

The second important inconsistency has to do with the underlying purpose or historical mission of the growth process. Accumulation leads to no improvement in per capita consumption. It is hard, then, to see what social purpose is served by organizing our economic lives around markets and private ownership of the means of production.[3]

The two inconsistencies in the classical argument call into question the fundamental claim of the classical project that reproduction constitutes the core of the growth process of capitalist economy. Marx's apparently innocent claim that "every social process of production is, at the same time, a process of reproduction" (1967, Vol. I, p. 566) in fact requires us to reconcile the logic of capitalist accumulation with that of self-replacement. Doing so turns out to raise some difficulties.

The classical analysis of structural change

Important features of the classical argument were left out of the foregoing discussion, in part to identify its logical core, in part to link up with modern versions of that theory. These features have to do with structural change. The classical economists do conceive of structural change. At a minimum, they consider increasing productivity due to the extension of the division of labor. Beyond this, Smith and Marx consider the emergence of modern forms of economic organization and some of their implications. Does the classical analysis confirm the claim that reproduction sets the foundation for structural change? To answer this question, I begin by briefly summarizing the classical account of structural change.

To make labor produce profit, the capitalist reorganizes the production process. This reorganization proceeds in three steps: (1) The capitalist brings workers together in a single place of work. Marx refers to this as cooperation; it is a simple concentration of labor implied by the original division of society into workers and capitalists. (2) Because the workers now work together in a single location, the labor they do can be allocated more efficiently among them. Specialization through division of labor increases productivity. (3) Concentration and division of labor set the foundation for mechanization to reduce the part played by labor, and increase profitability.

We can interpret concentration and division of labor as changes in form. Smith's famous example of the division of labor in the production of pins interprets the division of labor as an organizational change. As Smith describes it, division of labor leaves the component parts of the production process unaltered, changing only the allocation of those parts among the workmen. Marx tends to treat mechanization as a logical extension of division of labor from the distribution of work originally done by a single workman among a group to its further distribution between workers and machines. The original division of labor suggests this further division, since it eliminates the necessity for a unifying intelligence in the form of a craftsman, while transforming a complex labor process into a series of simple tasks appropriate to the use of machinery. Again the components and product of the process remain unaltered.

This quality of the production process continues a basic theme of the classical conception of economic growth. For this reason, we are not surprised to find it reappearing in those modern classical theories seeking to incorporate technical change (Pasinetti 1981, pp. 206, 231). While the classical theory may no longer treat growth as a purely extensive process, since it brings with it a change in the productivity of labor, growth still means the expansion of a structure that remains fixed in certain of its essentials. The wealth produced as a result of the division of labor and technical change can be treated as if it consists of the same things produced before any change in the production process.

The division of labor does help account for the surplus that makes growth possible. It also helps establish a rationale for valuing output and thus for the price system. By attaching values to the components of the social product, we can calculate productivity at the level of the individual unit of production. By so doing, we make it possible to define a goal for the unit other than reproduction: its own expansion as measured by its ability to produce more value than it needs for reproduction.

In the elementary model of reproduction, wages, profits, output, and employment remain constant. In the model of extensive growth, wages rise temporarily to a level above subsistence due to tightness in the labor market. In the model of accumulation with technical change, the net product tends to increase with the growth of capital and productivity. The disposition of a growing net product poses a problem which, while at the heart of classical theory, is not explicitly addressed by classical theorists.

Two strategies allow classical thinkers to avoid explicitly dealing with the tendency for the surplus to rise. The first defines the temporal structure of the process so as to suppress the problem altogether. The second introduces counter-forces that limit the growth in the net product as accumulation proceeds. Smith adopts the first strategy, Ricardo and Marx the second. It is in developing a strategy for dealing with the rising surplus that Kalecki and Steindl help resolve a core problem of the classical theory.

Smith does not directly pose or address the question how a growing economy deals with increasing productivity. Instead, he addresses a different question. Smith treats the increase in productivity due to division of labor as a part of the transition from barbarism to civilized society, from poverty to wealth. Rather than acting as a determinant of the magnitude of profit, the division of labor helps to explain the origin of profit. In effect, Smith avoids the problem of a growing surplus by defining the temporal framework in a way that leaves it out of account. When we consider the contrast between two states of society, the process that takes us from one to the other becomes an event. When we treat capital accumulation as an event, its importance stems from the difference it creates between the state of society before and after. This difference has to do with the distribution of property rights in society's capital stock and with the productivity of labor. As Marx puts it, it is "the effect of capital and its process ... to conquer all of production and to develop and complete the divorce between labor and property" (1973, pp. 511–512). The redistribution of property establishes the basis for the true mission of capitalist accumulation as Marx conceives it, to act as "a historical means of developing the material forces of production and creating an appropriate world market" (1967, Vol. I, p. 250). The identification of the historical mission of capitalism with the development of the "material forces of production" underlies the logical structure of Marx's theory of accumulation. The introduction of machinery enhances the productivity of labor and gradually replaces labor as the primary basis of production, eventually making labor superfluous (1973, pp. 705–706). Marx's claim is arguably central to any classical theory of structural transformation.

Marx did not much elaborate on the meaning and significance of the creation of the world market. I think this is largely because the analytical framework he took over from Smith and Ricardo was ill-suited to the task, focusing as it does on conditions of production and distribution. In thinking about how the economy responds to the tendency for the surplus to rise, Marx followed his classical predecessors. He attempted to show how changes in capital intensity offset the impact of technical change on profitability.

Marx's famous law of the tendency for the rate of profit to fall would solve the problem if it were analytically satisfying. But, it has not proven a sound foundation for thinking about the process of capitalist expansion. We are left, then, with two agendas: (1) completing the account of capitalist expansion by treating more explicitly the process of the creation of a world market, and (2) responding to the tendency for the surplus to rise implied in growing productivity. Steindl's work helps us with both agendas.

Competition and stagnation

Steindl sets out from a tendency for profit margins to increase due to technical change (Steindl 1952; see also Levine 1981). The technical change he has in mind is predominantly of the sort that improves productivity given the product. He also assumes that the market for the product grows at a rate fixed by the overall rate of growth of the economy taken as a whole. This sets up a conflict between the internal rate of accumulation of the firm, set by its capacity to finance investment out of profit, and the rate of growth of the market for its products, set by aggregate conditions.

In the classical theory, the firm more or less automatically reinvests its profit. Thus, were profit margins to rise, the rate of investment would also rise as would the rate of growth of output (assuming no systematic rise in capital intensity). Demand would keep pace with capacity. To do so, of course, it must increase at an accelerating rate.

Had the classical thinkers explored this implication more systematically they would have had to come to terms with the problem of market growth and what Marx refers to as the "realization of surplus-value". They avoid doing so by assuming either diminishing fertility of the soil or increases in capital intensity of a magnitude adequate to offset, and more than offset, increases in profit margins.

In place of fertility and capital intensity, Steindl suggests we look to the market as the first limit to accelerating accumulation. For the market to limit investment, investment cannot simply follow current profitability. The additional consideration is the current and expected demand for the product. This consideration appears through Steindl's inclusion of the degree of capacity utilization as a determinant of investment. Capacity utilization depends on the current rate of market growth. To the extent that investors treat that rate as a parameter, it limits investment.

Within this framework, it is easy to generate two results. First, as profit margins rise, given the rate of market growth and thus level of investment, aggregate demand must fall. Paradoxically, improving the productivity of labor tends to have a dampening effect on output and employment. The second result has to do with the firm's response to this situation. The firm experiences a problem of demand for its products. But, since it cannot affect the overall level of demand, it focuses its attention on its market share. Accumulation leads to competition over market shares, and ultimately takes place through competition.

Steindl's main concern is to develop a theory that might help account for situations of economic stagnation. He treats competition over market shares as a possible solution to the problem of market constraints on investment and economic growth. Investment in new capital stock and possibly in a sales effort, both associated with competition over market shares, stimulates demand. If competition takes the form of price competition, it directly offsets the tendency for profit margins to increase. The structure of the accumulation process tends to limit profit margins.

This means, of course, that the benefits of technical change accrue, at least to some extent, to workers, whose real wages rise as prices fall with the competition of capitals. Thus, Steindl has pinpointed a mechanism by which capitalism brings about an improvement in welfare, though as an unintended consequence. There is here a recognition that the wage is not only a cost of production, and thus a limit to profitability, but also a component of demand, and thus a stimulus to profitability. Recognition of wages as a component of demand bears on the exploration of the creation of the market emphasized, if not analyzed, by Marx.

Yet, the picture Steindl draws is not in the end a very rosy one. True, real wages rise with the competition of capitals, but only for the employed part of the labor force. As competition exhausts itself with the concentration of capital and the creation of oligopoly structure in industry, it loses its ability to stimulate investment. As a result, the tendency for profit margins to increase no longer translates into rising real wages, but instead expresses itself as a tendency for stagnation of output and employment. Steindl argues that exhaustion of competitive pressures paved the way for the great depression of the 1930s.

The theory of stagnation incorporates some of the strengths and weaknesses of the classical approach discussed above. Steindl's argument indicates how we might reconcile the implications of technical change for profitability with the expectation that profit margins will not rise without limit, and indeed tend to be more or less stable. It also indicates how capitalism translates rising productivity into improving living standards. This opens up a revision of the classical conception of the nature and mission of capitalism, and begins to flesh out Marx's notion that the creation of the world market is part of capitalism's social purpose.

At the same time, the theory conceives capital accumulation as a process that works itself out within the confines of a given structure. While change takes place in industrial organization with shifting market shares and concentration of capital, the distribution of output across industries remains the same. Indeed, it must remain fixed for the tendency toward stagnation to hold.

Marx's treatment of mechanization alluded to above has relevance here. Mechanization is a form of structural change. Yet Marx conceives it to leave the structure of production unaltered in certain fundamentals. The nature of the product (or set of products) does not change, even though the productive inputs do. The logical core of the classical theory remains in force in Steindl's work since he focuses on changes in productivity rather than changes in the nature, composition, and distribution of output. To this extent, accumulation remains a process of expanded reproduction. It is a much more complex process, with some paradoxical results. But, it is still expanded reproduction rather than transformation.

Reproduction and transformation

Steindl discovers a mechanism by which capitalist accumulation creates the world market and transforms the nature and composition of output. In doing so, I think, his theory suggests a break with the core of the classical approach, a break he did not explore.

As I argue above, at its core, the classical theory is a theory of reproduction and expanded reproduction. Yet, as Marx in particular was well aware, capitalism is fundamentally a system of transformation. The effort to conceive the transition from the savage state to civilization as a reorganization and redistribution of parts was attractive to Smith, and so it seemed to Marx when he went about analyzing the accumulation process. Yet it hardly captured the essence of the matter, which is not reorganization and reproduction, but transformation and structural change.

The difficulty arises in attempting to think about structural change as a concretization of reproduction, and thus to think of reproduction as an ongoing process within the process of transformation. The classical theory intends to do just this; and Steindl follows that theory when he assumes that the composition of output remains fixed. This method impairs our understanding of the market system including the nature and determination of value.

It has always proven difficult for economics to treat price determination as an expression of transformative forces. Thinking of price as a part of reproduction allows for quantitative solutions to questions about price determination not available when we assume that price expresses the transformation of a structure and not renewal within the framework of its parameters. Clearly, of course, any theory of price must make price determination an element of a larger framework of economic relations. Whether this is a framework of fixed parameters depends, however, on what we mean by price determination. In manufacturing, price depends on prime costs and profit margins (as emphasized by Kalecki). Profit margins express the transformative process that creates and alters market structure, and the distribution of demand across products, existing and new. That is, margins do not simply move with change in structure, their magnitude at a point in time measures and expresses ongoing structural transformation. If margins measure and express forces of transformation, we cannot root them in an underlying process of reproduction.

Reproduction prices vary with changes in the structure of reproduction. Each set of prices corresponds to a regime of reproduction parameters that express a given structure. Those prices do not contain or express the forces for change except in the limited sense that they allow for profit. Steindl's theory carries a different message. Margins express the dynamics of competition and of the reorganization of market structure. Both their trend and their level express the transformative processes, in his case of competition over market shares.

If we take the next step and allow not just the distribution of market shares within an industry, but the distribution of output across industries and the industries themselves, to vary, that variation should express itself in the level of price, not simply in its movement over time (see Levine 1981, Part III). Doing so fully emancipates value from the ideas of self-replacement and expanded reproduction. The difficulty is that, in emancipating value from the ideas of self-replacement and reproduction, we will also make value depend on forces other than those of technology and distribution, particularly forces loosely subsumed under the heading of demand or, more generally, of the market. The result is to undermine the idea that price is a purely or essentially "objective" phenomenon. Resistance to doing so, including that resistance incorporated in the special assumptions of Steindl's theory, indicates how powerful are the ties much contemporary non-neoclassical thinking has to the classical methodology, and how strong is the associated fear of giving in to the subjective approach to value that took over at the end of the last century. Yet, while resistance to the subjectivism of post-classical economics keeps alive the idea that value, in the words of Ricardo, is "intrinsic and not arbitrary", too great an adherence to the classical methodology will lead us to develop our theory along lines that leave out of account the fundamental dynamic processes of capitalist economies.

Conclusion

I suggest above that reproduction of a structure is the logical core of the classical theory. Yet, making this idea the logical core of the theory of value creates problems, problems centering on the trend of wages and the disposition of an increasing surplus. What accounts for the classical procedure and for the attraction it has had in economics over the past two or three decades?

The answer to this was clearly identified by Marx. The classical theory in its Smithian form, and in the form adapted from Smith by Marx, contains two conflicting themes, each built into the structure of its argument. According to one, the logic of capitalism is that of economic development. Smith speaks of the transition from the savage state to civilized society; Marx speaks of the historical mission of capitalism. According to the second theme, the logic of capitalism is that of the extraction and appropriation of a surplus. Here, Smith speaks more benignly about the worker sharing his product with the capitalist while Marx speaks of the exploitation of labor. These are two very different themes that lead the analysis of capitalism in very different directions.

Steindl stands at their intersection point. Because he takes the composition of demand to be given, his argument is amenable to a formulation in the language of surplus appropriation. Yet, because his theory focuses our attention on the transformation of the market and the role of demand, it suggests that we move away from the second classical theme in the direction of the first. Much, of course, is at stake. Emphasis on the notion of surplus extraction demands that we develop a framework for speaking of the amount and distribution of the aggregate net product; and this means that we must have a theory of value capable of measuring aggregate surplus. The aggregate surplus must act as a determinant of aggregate profit and of the profit realized by the particular producer. This framework directs our attention toward aggregate profits and aggregate wages, their distribution and redistribution. The theory of value can only help us here if it helps us speak of magnitudes varying within a fixed structure.

Emphasis on transformative forces makes it difficult to conceive of the amount of surplus and profit as a whole prior to the operation of the market forces that govern determination of prices and profit margins. Transformation works through the agency of the units of the system. This does not imply that the whole is reducible to the prior determination of the parts, as in the neoclassical theory. Rather, it means that when we conceive of the whole we do not do so as an aggregate structure given independently of its elements. Structure and agent emerge simultaneously, and the transformative forces operate at both levels. Steindl's theory begins to conceive this dialectic. Prices and profits depend on competition of capitals. The competitive process is framed within a larger structure of market growth. To complete the picture, we only need to consider that larger structure of market growth (the scale and rate of increase of aggregate demand) as something that results from the development of the competitive process itself.

Doing so might return us to the classical notion of the historical mission of capitalism as Marx formulates it. It would also help redirect our attention to the temporal structure favored by Adam Smith, a broader and longer view within which the local and more limited processes can begin to make sense. Economics needs the longer view of Smith and Marx. Unfortunately, the analytical framework that has attracted those interested in a classically inspired theory is one that tends to set the longer view aside rather than make it central to the understanding of the economic process.

Acknowledgments

I would like to thank Harry Bloch, Tracy Mott and Nina Shapiro for comments on an earlier draft of this chapter.

Notes

1 We may, of course, question what meaning this has other than in justifying the desired abstraction.
2 The classical theory did not clearly distinguish the impact of this process on money wages from its impact on real wages and the wage share. Classical thinkers generally assume that the wage bargain determines the real wage.
3 In a narrower Marxist vision, the mission of capitalism would be the provision of surplus from the exploitation of labor in the form of profit to the capitalist class. This is a narrow view, certainly more restricted than Marx's own.

References

Hayek, Friedrich (1945) "The Use of Knowledge in Society", *American Economic Review* (September), pp. 519–530.
Levine, David (1981) *Economic Theory*, vol. II, London: Routledge & Kegan Paul.
Marx, Karl (1967) *Capital*, vol. I, New York: International Publishers.
Marx, Karl (1973) *Grundrisse*, Harmondsworth: Penguin Books.
Pasinetti, Luigi (1977) *Lectures on the Theory of Production*, New York: Columbia University Press.
Pasinetti, Luigi (1981) *Structural Change and Economic Growth*, New York: Cambridge University Press.
Smith, Adam (1937) *The Wealth of Nations*, New York: Modern Library.

Sraffa, Piero (1960) *Production of Commodities by Means of Commodities*, Cambridge: Cambridge University Press.

Steindl, Josef (1952) *Maturity and Stagnation in American Capitalism*, Oxford: Blackwell.

Walsh, Vivian and Gram, Harvey (1980) *Classical and Neoclassical Theories of General Equilibrium*, New York: Oxford University Press.

2 Steindl's analysis of firm growth and the tendency toward industry concentration

Harry Bloch

Introduction

A recurring theme in Steindl's analysis of firm growth is the tendency toward industry concentration. His earliest writings examine the influence of risk on firm growth (Steindl 1941, 1945a and 1945b).[1] He then turns his attention to the influence of technical progress (Steindl 1976), and, finally, to the influence of random processes (Steindl 1965). In each of these analyses there emerges a tendency toward the concentration of industry.

Steindl takes the concentration of industry to be an established fact of mature capitalism and sees his analysis as providing an explanation for this fact. The same analysis provides the basis for the behavior patterns attributed to oligopolistic firms. He then examines the implications of the oligopolistic pricing and investment behavior for macroeconomic performance (Steindl 1976, 1979 and 1989). The analysis of firm growth thus provides the foundation for Steindl's understanding of mature capitalism. The present chapter examines Steindl's analysis of firm growth and evaluates his explanation of industry concentration.

Risk

Steindl analyzes the impact of risk on the growth of firms in two papers in *Oxford Economic Papers*, Steindl (1941) and (1945a), and in his monograph, *Small and Big Business* (1945b). The return on investment in this analysis is uncertain, but the firm is assumed to be able to estimate the variance of the return (Steindl 1941, pp. 43–44). Entrepreneurs demand a risk premium on investments to compensate for exposure to bankruptcy and loss of control that comes with the variance in return. The risk premium rises more than proportionately with the variance in return. At any point in time there exists a limited range of investments that yield a sufficient risk premium and this determines the equilibrium level of investment for the firm (Steindl 1945a, pp. 21–23).

Steindl argues that there is a difference in the opportunities for risk and return facing small and large firms. Economies of scale tend to raise the return to large units of capital above that of small units of capital (Steindl 1945b, pp. 13–18). This advantage is somewhat offset by the difficulties of expansion in an imperfectly competitive market, but is reinforced by a reduced cost of borrowing for larger firms (Steindl 1945b, pp. 18–21).

Steindl argues that the firm has limited access to capital. In the first instance this limit is set by the private wealth of the entrepreneur. This may be supplemented by borrowing, but the corresponding rise in the gearing ratio increases the variance of the firm's rate of return and the risk premium required on investment (Steindl 1945b, pp. 42–44). Share issuance in a joint stock company allows opportunity for increasing investment without very much additional risk, but this opportunity is only available to entrepreneurs whose personal wealth is above a certain level (Steindl 1945a, p. 42). Thus, the concentration of personal wealth provides the basis for a scarcity of firms controlling large units of capital.[2]

The scarcity of firms controlling large units of capital ensures that the returns on those opportunities available only to large units of capital are not competed down to a normal rate of return. There is no such scarcity of firms controlling small units of capital. Entrepreneurs who control large units of capital are therefore able to earn differential rents (Steindl 1945a, p. 44).

Steindl assumes in the simplest case that firms expand their capital over time only through internal accumulation, i.e. by saving and reinvesting profits earned in excess of interest payments and dividends. He further assumes that firms have an equal propensity to save (Steindl 1945a, p. 33). When large firms earn a higher rate of return than small firms, they grow relative to small firms through a faster rate of internal accumulation. This leads to relative concentration of industry in the absence of entry of new firms.

Alternatively, large firms use their advantageous position to choose a lower risk exposure than that of small firms (Steindl 1945a, pp. 32–33). In this case the rate of disappearance of large firms due to bankruptcy will be less than that for small firms. The disappearance of small firms leads to absolute concentration of industry. Absolute concentration is further encouraged if the rate of profit for the whole economy is constant or declining. In this case, the rate of profit for small entrepreneurs will definitely be falling leaving more of them exposed to bankruptcy (Steindl 1945a, pp. 37–39).

The differential rents obtained by large units of capital provide the basis for a concentration of capital in the economy. Whether the concentration occurs in relative or absolute form depends on the trend in the profit rate for the economy as a whole. At the level of the individual industry there is a tendency for the rise in overall concentration to be reflected in a rise in industry concentration due to a preference by entrepreneurs to invest in their established business to achieve the economies of scale. The only limit suggested to the tendency toward a rise in industry concentration is that concentration leads to the imperfection of competition. With imperfect competition, if an entrepreneur wishes to increase its market share at the expense of a competitor "he has to incur such advertisement expenditure, or to make such price cuts, as to draw some of the latter's customers over to himself" (Steindl 1945a, p. 35). Presumably, concentration in the economy as a whole continues as firms are free to diversify into other industries.

Technical progress

Steindl expands his analysis of firm growth to examine the influence of technical progress in *Maturity and Stagnation in American Capitalism* ([1952] 1976). He continues with the argument noted above that there is a general advantage to large firms due to economies of scale. This combines with improvements in productivity that occur at an uneven pace across firms in the same industry to yield differences in the level of production cost even among firms in the same size class. These differential costs are the basis for differential rents applying to firms within an industry (Steindl 1976, pp. 37–40). Steindl then analyzes the impact of the cost differences on firm growth and on the concentration of the industry.

Firms with differing levels of production cost can coexist in the same industry in Steindl's analysis due to imperfect competition. He argues that industrialists assume, probably correctly, that the price elasticity of demand for the product of their industry is quite low, so that a reduction in price would not greatly expand sales. Furthermore, they are concerned that raising price would attract new entry into the industry. Thus, with imperfect competition there is a general tendency to price rigidity (Steindl 1976, pp. 14–17).

When prices are rigid, cost-reducing innovations lead in the first instance to an increase in the gross profit margins of the innovating firms. If the level of excess capacity for the firms with lowest unit production cost is within acceptable limits, these "progressive" firms have no incentive to cut prices. This allows high-cost firms to survive, even when these "marginal" firms do not gain access to the cost-reducing technology.

Steindl maintains the argument from his analysis of risk that investment by firms is tied to their internal accumulation. The higher profits earned by progressive firms therefore lead to expansion of their productive capacity relative to marginal firms. Eventually, the progressive firms become the largest firms in the industry. If the number of marginal producers is constant, the industry is subject to relative concentration in the sense of a faster rate of growth and growing market share for the limited number of largest firms (Steindl 1976, pp. 40–42).

When technical progress raises the profits of progressive firms, there is an increase in the rate of internal accumulation for the whole industry and a resulting increase in the rate of growth of industry capacity. Eventually, the rate of growth of industry capacity exceeds the exogenously given rate of expansion of industry demand, so that unplanned excess capacity emerges. Progressive firms initially react to this unplanned excess capacity by engaging in aggressive price or selling competition. The marginal firms can not match the aggressive competition due to their smaller gross profit margins, so that they are forced to cede market share to the progressive firms and in some cases become bankrupt and exit the industry. The decline in the number and size of the marginal firms results in the absolute concentration of industry in the sense that the total sales of small firms as a group decline at the same time as the total sales of large firms as a group rise (Steindl 1976, pp. 42–43).

Random processes

Random influences are implicit in Steindl's analyses of the effects of both risk and technical progress on firm growth. Probabilistic returns to investment are the source of the risk that impacts unevenly on firms of different sizes. Also, different degrees of technological innovation across firms contribute to the cost differentials that are the basis for differences in rates of internal accumulation and growth. Yet, neither the analysis of risk nor the analysis of technical progress formally models the mechanics of random influences.

Formal models of random influences on firm growth are examined in Steindl's *Random Processes and the Growth of Firms* (1965). Here, Steindl treats a firm's growth in any period as a random event. He assumes the random events for each firm are identically and independently distributed in each period, so that the movement of the distribution of firm size over time is modeled as a stochastic process. He then examines the properties of such models as providing insights into the distribution of firm sizes and the level of industry concentration.

Steindl's basic model of stochastic firm growth is a birth and death process. The abstraction Steindl uses in explaining this process is the firm as a population of customers (Steindl 1965, Chapter 2). Customers enter (are born) and leave (die) the firm's population of customers randomly in proportion to the firm's pre-existing population. For a firm of any given age there is a probability distribution of the number of customers. New firms are assumed to enter the market at a fixed rate, leading to a mixed distribution of firms of various ages and sizes. If the process has been going on for a long time, there is a steady state of the stochastic process provided the parameters of the birth and death process and the rate of entry of firms are within certain limits.

Steindl considers the factors that influence industry concentration in the steady state of the birth and death process of customers. He suggests that either a rise or a fall in the industry growth rate, as given by the difference between the birth rate and death rate for customers, can increase concentration in a new steady state (Steindl 1965, p. 70).[3] While there may be off-setting changes in the rate of net entry of firms, he concludes that 'the tendency toward concentration is to some extent endemic' (Steindl 1965, p. 72). This is particularly the case when concentration is measured by the share of the few largest firms. For this share continues to grow through time even when there is a steady state in the sense that the mean size of firms in the industry has a constant expected value.

Comments

A consistent theme in Steindl's analysis of firm growth is the importance of diversity among firms. Diversity in the analysis of risk arises from inequality in the distribution of the wealth of entrepreneurs. In his analysis of technical progress, diversity arises from an uneven pattern of technological innovation and the existence of economies of scale. Finally, in the analysis of random processes, diversity is the outcome of a stochastic process of customer allocation.

The centrality of diversity across firms distinguishes Steindl's work from that in the Marshallian tradition of the representative firm. The distinction is quite purposeful, as *Small and Big Business* opens with an attack on this Marshallian tradition (Steindl 1945b, chapter 1). Thus, the following evaluation of Steindl's contribution to the analysis of firm growth and industry concentration emphasizes his treatment of diversity among firms.

By formalizing his analysis of random events as the source of diversity in the process of firm growth, Steindl is able to distinguish the steady state for the distribution of firm size from the diffusion process leading to that steady state. Diffusion occurs as a movement from an initial state in which there may or may not be differences in size across firms to the steady state in which the distribution of firm size is stabilized. He argues that diffusion can lead to a rise in the inequality of firm size and an associated rise in measured industry concentration, but that analysis of the process of diffusion does not provide an alternative to an economic theory of concentration (Steindl 1965, p. 69).

An economic theory of concentration, according to Steindl, concerns either the forces determining the distribution of firm size in the steady state or the reasons why a steady state is not achieved. In the case of a formal model of a random process of firm growth, whether or not a steady state is achieved and the distribution of firm size associated with any such steady state are both determined by the value of parameters of the random process. There is no formal model of a random process in Steindl's analysis of firm growth based on risk or technical progress, but the analysis does focus on factors that influence the rate of growth of individual firms, the rate of entry of new firms and the rate of exit of marginal firms.

The distinction between the determinants of the distribution of firm size in the steady state and the determinants of the distribution in a diffusion process is relevant to the evaluation of the analysis of industry concentration based on each of the three approaches to firm growth used by Steindl. A first question is whether in each analysis he provides an economic theory of concentration as opposed to simply a description of diffusion occurring within a random process of firm growth. A second question is the extent to which each of the analyses provides a coherent basis for his proposition that there is a tendency toward increased concentration in capitalism.

Steindl's theory of industry concentration

The analysis of concentration with a change in the industry growth rate in the customer allocation model satisfies Steindl's requirement for an economic theory of concentration. There is a clear separation of the analysis of the impact of the industry growth rate on concentration in the steady state from the analysis of changes in measured concentration that occur in the process of diffusion associated with a change in the growth rate. Steindl uses a comparison of steady states when he evaluates the impact on concentration of changes in the industry growth rate as the difference between the customer birth and death rates. The intermediate diffusion process is relevant to this comparison *only* to the extent that the associated changes in profitability and survival of firms may impact on the rate of entry of new firms in the new steady state.

Customer birth and death rates are exogenously determined and independent of the firm's size in the customer allocation model (Steindl 1965, pp. 46–47). This means that the rate of entry of new firms is the only parameter of the stochastic firm growth process than can adjust to ensure the existence of a steady state. The achievement of a steady-state solution to the random process both before and after the change in industry growth rate requires that the rate of entry of new firms adjust within certain limits.

Steindl's discussion of the influence of industry growth rate on the rate of entry of new firms focuses on the competitive environment facing new firms (Steindl 1965, pp. 70–72). Conditions are more promising for entry when the industry growth rate is higher and less promising when the industry growth rate is lower. These changes are in the right direction to allow existence of a steady state, but there is nothing in the discussion that ensures the changes will be sufficient to guarantee a steady state will be established.

Steindl acknowledges that the analysis of the growth of firms as a birth and death process for customers is limited because it "cannot describe the competitive advance or decline of firms in detail *except as random changes*" (Steindl 1965, p. 47). The competitive environment only has an influence on the rate of entry of new firms as noted above. Neglect of competitive advance and decline of established firms removes variation in customer birth or death rates across firms as an alternative method for obtaining a steady state for the stochastic process of firm growth.

Differential competitive strengths of firms are central to Steindl's analysis of risk and his analysis of technical progress. Favored firms grow in size relative to those in the disadvantaged group.[4] This difference in relative growth rates combines with the net rate of exit or entry of firms to determine movement in the distribution of firm size and the level of measured concentration in an industry in a manner similar to that in the analysis of stochastic firm growth.

In the analysis of risk the larger firms are the favored firms, while in the analysis of technical progress the favored firms become the larger firms because they have lower costs and higher rates of internal accumulation. Steindl argues that there is little or no entry into the group of favored firms.[5] The result is that the expected size of firms in this group tends to increase over time. This increase in expected firm size applies to the whole industry when the number of small firms declines with exits exceeding entry in the process of absolute concentration.

Steindl argues that his analysis of the pattern of competition leading to absolute concentration with either risk or technical progress "provides us with a theory of concentration" (Steindl 1976, p. 51). Yet, in this pattern of competition the expected size of firms grows without limit. When the expected size of firms grows without limit, there is no distinction between concentration that results from the process of diffusion and concentration that might occur in a steady state. Without this distinction being possible or an explanation for absence of a steady state, the conditions that Steindl requires for an economic theory of concentration in his discussion of formal models of random processes are not met.

An economic theory of concentration begins to emerge in *Maturity and Stagnation in American Capitalism* only when Steindl addresses the impact of increasing concentration on firm behavior.[6] He argues that as the dominance of favored firms increases they come to recognize their interdependence and break the link between their rate of profit and their rate of growth. When the firms recognize their interdependence, they reduce their investment to match the rate of growth of market demand (Steindl 1976, pp. 53–55). The conditions for a steady state in the random process generating the distribution of firm size may then be met.[7]

Unfortunately, the shift in investment behavior that occurs with increasing dominance by favored firms is not well developed. Neither the level of concentration in the steady-state distribution of firm size nor the determinants of this distribution are explained. This means that there is an inadequate basis for formalizing the analysis of technical progress along lines similar to Steindl's model of customer allocation. Thus, substantial work remains if Steindl's analysis is to be completed to yield an economic theory of concentration as opposed to a description of a diffusion process.

The tendency toward industry concentration

If Steindl's analysis does not provide an economic theory of concentration, what sense can be made of his proposition that there is a tendency toward the concentration of industry in capitalism? One response is that Steindl is referring to the diffusion associated with disequilibrium of a random process of firm growth. The process of absolute concentration that is part of the analysis of firm growth with both risk and technical progress represents such a disequilibrium process. However, this interpretation does not fit well with Steindl's use of the concept of industry maturity.

The analysis of Steindl's theory of concentration above suggests that there is a shift in investment behavior with maturity. Prior to maturity, firms expand through internal accumulation, investing in their existing industry an amount proportional to their profit. After maturity, firms refrain from further expansion when their internal accumulation would otherwise result in undesired capacity.[8]

The shift in investment behavior with maturity obstructs the working of the tendency toward concentration. If favored firms refrain from expansion through internal accumulation, there is no longer a basis for their growth relative to firms that do not earn differential rents. The increasing dominance of favored firms associated with disequilibrium in the process of absolute concentration comes to an end.

The association of maturity with an end to disequilibrium fits a particular interpretation of the meaning of the tendency toward increasing concentration in capitalism. In this interpretation it is the increase in industry concentration, following the process of absolute concentration that leads to maturity. Maturity and the tendency toward industry concentration don't coexist, rather, they follow sequentially as part of a dynamic of the pattern of competition.

If the disequilibrium preceding maturity is characterized as diffusion in a random process, then achievement of maturity may be viewed as the outcome of the random process with constant parameters. Steindl implies that maturity is an irreversible condition that occurred in historical time, specifically in the period leading up to the Great Depression. There seems no reason why the random processes working on the growth of firms in various industries in the American economy or any other established industrial economy should have resulted in a substantial number of industries crossing the threshold to maturity in the period leading up to the Great Depression. Furthermore, if random processes continue to operate after maturity is achieved, concentration in a mature industry may occasionally drop below the critical level required for mature behavior causing a reversion of the maturation process.[9]

An alternative way in which the achievement of maturity may be viewed is that the historical evolution of the institutions of capitalism alters the parameters of the random process of firm growth. It would need to be shown that as capitalism evolves the parameters of the random process shift in such a way as to generate more inequality of firm size or a smaller number of firms. This may be due to the effects of differing levels of risk or innovation or changes in the differential advantages of large firms. Unfortunately, Steindl's analysis of risk and technical progress is not well enough developed to indicate the types of changes that would lead to higher concentration in the steady state.

Rethinking Steindl's theory of industry concentration

What are the essential components of Steindl's analysis of industry concentration? Three candidates stand out from the above discussion as being present in each of Steindl's approaches to the analysis of the growth of firms. These are diversity among firms, continuity in the firm's circumstances across time and the influence of the pattern of competition on the entry and exit of firms. In addition, the modification of firm behavior in response to the pattern of competition is a feature that occurs only in his analysis of firm growth with technical progress.

The role of diversity among firms in each of Steindl's three approaches to the analysis of firm growth is discussed above. Continuity over time in the firm's position is also recognized in each approach. Continuity in the analysis of risk and the analysis of technical progress is achieved through growth by means of internal accumulation, so that the size of the firm in any time period depends on both size and profitability in the previous period. Continuity in the customer allocation model is achieved through treating the firm's customers as each subject to an independent growth and death process, so that size in any time period depends on both prior size and a random shock that is proportional to prior size.

Diversity and continuity interact in each approach to produce a diffusion process in which relative concentration occurs without limit when the number of firms in the industry is constant and the behavior of firms is unaffected by increasing concentration. The pattern of competition provides the potential limiting force to the tendency toward industry concentration by either influencing the net rate of entry of firms into the industry or by influencing the behavior of firms already in the industry. Thus, the influence of the pattern of competition on the net rate of entry or the behavior of established firms can provide the mechanism for converting the analysis of a diffusion process into an economic theory of concentration that includes an explanation of the transition to a steady state.

As noted in the discussion of Steindl's theory of concentration above, the pattern of competition has a very restricted role in his analysis of firm growth as a random process. Firm behavior has no effect on the growth or decline of its own or its rivals' population of customers. Instead, Steindl relies on the industry growth rate influencing the rate at which new firms enter the market to explain how a steady state distribution of firm sizes may be re-established following a change in the rate of industry growth. He acknowledges this limitation, but apparently is unable or unwilling to broaden the role of the pattern of competition in this analysis.

Steindl provides a somewhat broader role for the pattern of competition in limiting concentration in an industry in his analysis of firm growth with risk. Here, Steindl (1945a, pp. 36–37) suggests that firms choose to diversify when the imperfection of competition limits the opportunity for further expansion within their original line of business. This brings the process of concentration within the industry to a halt, presumably before the industry has become a monopoly. However, there is no equivalent process operating at the level of the economy as a whole.[10]

The analysis in which Steindl most fully develops the role of the pattern of competition is that of technical progress as set out in *Maturity and Stagnation in American Capitalism*. There is a discussion of the prospects for diversification, but the conclusion is reached that the flow of funds into other industries is impeded (Steindl 1976, pp. 54–55). Instead, the emphasis is on the shift in investment behavior as the pattern of competition in the industry shifts from competition to oligopoly. With oligopoly comes the possibility that funds will be accumulated without being invested in the expansion of productive capacity in any industry. This provides the basis for the tendency to stagnation in mature capitalism as developed in Part II of the treatise.

As noted above, the shift in investment behavior accompanying the change from competition to oligopoly in Steindl's analysis is not very fully developed. Also, when the link between concentration and maturity is interpreted as a sequence with increasing concentration leading to mature (oligopoly) behavior, ambiguity arises as to the timing of the emergence of maturity and the possibility of reversion to competition. Addressing these points provides a possible avenue for a reconstruction of Steindl's analysis that would meet the criteria he sets for an economic theory of concentration.

One way forward is to adopt the vision of the firm as a self-expanding unit of capital. This would locate the change in firm behavior that occurs with maturity in the firm's inherent purpose. This is the approach pursued by Levine (1981) and Shapiro (1988). Both consider firms, particularly the progressive firms that earn differential rents in Steindl's analysis, to have broader horizons than a particular product market.

The broader horizon of the firm in the analysis of Levine and Shapiro extends beyond the type of diversification into other established lines of business that Steindl considers. In particular, they focus on new product development as a direction of expansion for a firm impeded by a limited market for established products in its original line of business. The opportunities for new product development are not limited by concentration at any level of aggregation. Indeed, these opportunities are not limited by aggregate demand of the Keynesian type. The development of new products can generate new wants that alter the propensity to consume in the economy. Also, the development of new products can lead to the premature obsolescence of existing capital stock, removing the shackles of a limited replacement demand for capital.

Suppose one accepts the broader horizon of the firm and considers the implications of new product development. What becomes of the economic theory of concentration? In particular, what happens to the notion of a tendency toward industry concentration as capitalism matures?

First, the concept of maturity becomes firm and industry specific. An individual firm shifts its behavior from expanding capacity in its original line of business to engaging in new product development as a response to the constraint on expansion imposed by a limited market for established products. This applies only in industries that have completed a process of absolute concentration and have become oligopolistic. Maturity applies to the bulk of the economy only by coincidence. Steindl may have become sympathetic to this position as he recognizes the possible importance of technological long waves in the introduction to the reprinting of *Maturity and Stagnation in American Capitalism* (1976, pp. xv–xvi).

Second, new product development provides the basis for a reversion from mature oligopoly to competition. This is raised as a general possibility in the discussion above of how maturity might occur stochastically in a random process of firm growth when diffusion during disequilibrium results in concentration rising above a certain level. Continuation of the random process could then result in concentration falling below the critical level. Success in new product development is very much a random event, so the shift in behavior with maturity becomes the seed of the process that eventually can undermine maturity. The experience of the computer industry worldwide shows the possibility of reversion from mature oligopoly to competition following the development of personal computers as a new product.

Finally, the specificity of maturity and the prospects for reversion to competition provide an economic theory of concentration that is both dynamic and stochastic. Maturity and the accompanying oligopolistic behavior are a moment in a progression that neither starts nor ends with maturity. While the notion of a cycle is probably too regular to fit the likely evolution of the pattern of competition, the stochastic nature of the outcome of efforts on new product development are such as to always leave open the possibility of a competitive transformation in any mature industry. Indeed, the shift to maturity and the associated shift to efforts on new product development increase the probability of significant innovations that would provide the basis for a reversion to competition.

Conclusions

Steindl's analysis of firm growth contrasts favorably with the static approach to the determination of firm size in neoclassical theory of the firm. The latter provides no explanation for the observed spread of firm size within industries, depending instead on the notion of a representative firm. Furthermore, there is no explanation for the growth of firms in the balance of economies and diseconomies of scale that determine the size of the representative firm.

The insights contained in Steindl's analysis provide a starting point for the development of an economic theory of concentration. It is argued that his own analysis is inadequate to this purpose, but that modifications to his approach can be made that would yield such a theory. Suggestions are put forward for a theory in which maturity is a moment in a dynamic and stochastic pattern of competition.[11] While this theory might have revisionist implications for Steindl's analysis of a stagnationist tendency in mature capitalism, the overall thrust of the theory would seem to be compatible with the spirit of Steindl's seminal work.

Acknowledgments

Earlier versions of this chapter were presented at the Seventh History of Economic Thought Society of Australia Conference, as well as at seminars at the University of New South Wales and the University of Tasmania. Comments from participants were useful in revising the chapter. Helpful comments have also been received from John King, David Levine, Tracy Mott, John Nightingale and Nina Shapiro. The usual caveat applies. Some material in this chapter was previously published in Bloch (2000a). Permission from Blackwell Publishing Limited on behalf of *Australian Economic Papers* to republish this material is gratefully acknowledged.

Notes

1 All references to Steindl's work are to the original publication, except for *Maturity and Stagnation in American Capitalism* for which references are given from the more widely available 1976 edition. Many of the other papers cited here and below are reprinted in Steindl (1990).
2 Steindl's argument concerning the relationship between the variance of return and the risk premium closely follows Kalecki's principle of increasing risk (Kalecki 1937).
3 Steindl argues that either a rise or fall in the industry growth can lead to increase in the mean size of firm. An increase in the growth rate without affecting entry leads the mean size of the firm to grow indefinitely. This movement is enhanced if there is a decrease in the mortality of firms with the increase in industry growth. In the case of a decline in industry growth, the mortality of firms rises leading to a decrease in the number of firms. Mean firm size rises if the net growth in the firm population declines more than industry growth.

4 The higher growth rate for favored firms is due to their higher profit rate, which leads to a higher rate of internal accumulation.

5 In his analysis of risk Steindl argues that entry into the favored group of large firms is restricted due to the scarcity of large units of capital. In his analysis of technical progress, he argues that entry into the favored group of progressive firms is restricted because marginal firms cannot raise the capital through internal accumulation or external finance to innovate.

6 In the analysis of firm growth with risk, Steindl (1945a, pp. 35–37) suggests that the tendency toward concentration in an industry may be limited by the imperfection of competition. However, the only suggested modification in the behavior of large firms resulting from this limitation is that they diversify into other lines of business. While concentration in the individual industry may abate, concentration for the economy as a whole continues.

7 If the rate of growth of market demand is zero and the expected rate of growth of firm size is limited to the rate of growth of capacity, the expected size of progressive firms remains constant under the condition that their growth of capacity is equal to the growth of market demand. Steindl (1976, pp. 50–51) argues that the rate of net entry of marginal firms adjusts to maintain a zero expected profit for each marginal firm. This implies that their expected size remains constant and that any disappearance of marginal firms is exactly offset by new entry.

8 Shapiro (1988) argues that the shift in investment behavior occurs as an industry switches from being competitive to being oligopolistic. The role of the increase in concentration in a shift from competitive to oligopolistic behavior is consistent with conventional views on the role of market structure as a determinant of firm behavior. However, the conventional view generally only links pricing behavior, rather than both pricing and investment behavior, to different levels of concentration.

9 Steindl acknowledges the possibility of innovation by a new entrant upsetting the steady state of a mature industry in a recent paper (see Steindl 1987).

10 The influence of the pattern of competition on the economy as a whole occurs through the average rate of profit in the economy. As the average profit rate falls the probability of bankruptcy rises for firms of all sizes. The effect on small firms is particularly severe, given their higher exposure to this risk, providing the basis for absolute concentration with a falling average profit rate. The only limit that Steindl suggests for the average profit rate is on the upside rather than the downside, leading him to the conclusion that 'the absolute concentration is an essential feature of capitalist development' (Steindl 1945a, p. 39).

11 The parallels and contrasts between Steindl's approach and that of Joseph Schumpeter are discussed in Bloch (2000b).

References

Bloch, Harry (2000a) "Steindl's Contribution to the Theory of Industry Concentration", *Australian Economic Papers*, vol. 29 (March), pp. 92–107.

Bloch, Harry (2000b) "Schumpeter and Steindl on the Dynamics of Competition", *Journal of Evolutionary Economics*, vol. 10, pp. 311–328.

Kalecki, Michał (1937) "The Principle of Increasing Risk", *Economica*, vol. 3, pp. 440–447.

Levine, David P. (1981) *Economic Theory*, vol. II, London: Routledge and Kegan Paul.

Shapiro, Nina (1988) "Market Structure and Economic Growth: Steindl's Contribution", *Social Concept* vol. 4 (June), pp. 72–83.

Steindl, Josef (1941) "On Risk", *Oxford Economic Papers*, no. 5 (June), pp. 43–53.

Steindl, Josef (1945a) "Capitalist Enterprise and Risk", *Oxford Economic Papers*, no. 7 (March), pp. 21–45.

Steindl, Josef (1945b) *Small and Big Business: Economic Problems of the Size of Firms*, Oxford: Blackwell.

Steindl, Josef [1952] (1976) *Maturity and Stagnation in American Capitalism*, New York: Monthly Review Press, reprint of 1952 edition published by Blackwell.

Steindl, Josef (1965) *Random Processes and the Growth of Firms*, London: Griffin.

Steindl, Josef (1979) "Stagnation Theory and Stagnation Policy", *Cambridge Journal of Economics*, vol. 3 (March), pp. 1–14.

Steindl, Josef (1987) "Kalecki's Theory of Pricing: Notes on the Margin", in G. Fink, G. Poll and M. Riese (eds) *Economic Theory, Political Power and Social Justice*, Vienna: Springer Verlag.

Steindl, Josef (1989) "From Stagnation in the 30s to Slow Growth in the 70s", in M. Berg (ed.) *Political Economy in the Twentieth Century*, Oxford: Phillip Allan.

Steindl, Josef (1990) *Economic Papers, 1941–88*, London: Macmillan.

3 An application of Steindl's theory of concentration to the US meat packing industry, 1865–1988

Julie A. Hogeland

Introduction

The path of industry evolution proposed by Josef Steindl in *Maturity and Stagnation in American Capitalism* (1976) has been explored and clarified from a theoretical standpoint in recent literature (Shapiro 1981, 1988; Levine 1975). Evaluating Steindl's ideas against the backdrop provided by a specific industry offers yet another perspective, the subject of this chapter. The century-long process of concentration, break-up, and re-concentration of the meat packing industry is used as a case study of the applicability of the concepts of absolute concentration and mature capitalism introduced in *Maturity and Stagnation*.

The meat packing industry meets the fundamental condition of structural change proposed by Steindl: increases in industry concentration were triggered by a cost-saving innovation embodied in new plant and equipment. The industry diverges from *Maturity and Stagnation* by demonstrating *multiple* phases of concentration. Yet the innovations triggering each phase of concentration – "the refrigerated rail car" and "boxed beef" – were unified by a common principle, to ship meat as free of waste fat and bone as possible. Consequently, Steindl's ideas cannot be simply accepted or rejected in the context of the meat packing industry.

Steindl's paradigm

Maturity and Stagnation explains how profit margins in an industry are determined over the long term through the forces of technical change. In turn, profit margins trigger changes in market structure. Steindl's model of this process is based on the assumption that capital is self-expanding value through a process he calls "internal accumulation": firms routinely retain part of their profits for reinvestment *in their own industry*. This industry is assumed to grow at a predictable and stable rate, which, coupled with the restriction on investment, allows the process of competition among firms to be unambiguously revealed through changes in market share. The difficulty of gaining sufficient expertise to enter a new market and gain customer acceptance ("goodwill") argue against investment in other industries.

Steindl locates his theory at a point in the development of capitalism where technical innovations create the possibility of lower costs and firms selectively adopt such innovations. Early adopters of innovations are not necessarily the largest firms. As Steindl goes on to describe a process of increasing concentration, the *initial* industry structure is probably more competitive, in the neoclassical sense, than oligopolistic.[1] Nevertheless, the result is large firms with cost advantages over smaller, less visionary, or less flexible firms.

The source of the initial innovations is unclear: do they emerge exogenously within a specifically favorable historical setting, i.e., Joseph Schumpeter's "epoch-making innovations", or are they based on early efforts at research and development by entrepreneurs? As will be shown, the history of the meat packing industry supports the latter interpretation, which seems to be the interpretation favored by Steindl.

We may also infer that he presupposes a "base line" rate of ongoing technical change which, as he describes, culminates in methods of significantly lowering production costs, notably scale economies.[2] At this point, the industry appears to be defined in terms of large firms and small firms, owing to the presence of scale economies. In this context, only large firms are called "progressive" by Steindl, since only these firms innovate. The reduction in costs resulting from scale economies give progressive firms above normal profit margins which increases their internal accumulation. Progressive firms then automatically expand their degree of capacity use and output capacity in an effort to increase their market share. This turning point in the industry is reached once the internal accumulation of progressive firms gives them a growth rate surpassing the overall growth rate of the industry.

Consequently, a hierarchy of firms emerges in the industry based on production cost differentials. The initial dichotomy between small marginal firms and large progressive firms implicitly set forth by Steindl is disrupted. The industry becomes volatile and unstable as new competitive relationships among firms emerge.

The target of expansionary drives are firms who operate with older technology. Steindl thought that such "marginal" firms would generally be small, their possibilities for renovation and growth constrained by lower ("normal") profits.

When the progressive firms expand, they must differentiate themselves from marginal firms by making a special "sales effort": changing their image, improving their product, or cutting prices. Steindl observes that product differentiation may increase both production costs and the sales costs per unit of sales, thereby offsetting to some degree the cost savings accruing from innovations. Through their impact on profit rates, sales efforts determine the scope of changes in market structure.

The general definition of sales efforts used by Steindl can be expanded to explicitly cover the possibility of multiple efforts, i.e., cutting prices and simultaneously improving product quality. This introduces the potential for an interaction effect magnifying the impact of each form of sales effort, a modification which will be useful in analyzing the meat packing industry.

As progressive firms expand to their potential, their market share grows and the industry becomes more concentrated. High cost or financially weak firms, typically found among the marginal firms, are forced out of business. Their disappearance defines the phenomenon of *absolute concentration*, and represents what Steindl called the "ideal pattern" of competition.

The erosion of profit margins begun with the special sales effort accelerates as the process of absolute concentration proceeds. Sales efforts simultaneously generate increases in market share and reductions in profit margins. Eventually profit margins shrink to the point where the remaining firms do not have sufficient resources (internal accumulation) to continue eliminating competitors, and the industry stabilizes at a higher level of concentration. The rate of internal accumulation of the survivors again corresponds to the industry's growth rate.

The process of absolute concentration is signalled by increasing concentration coupled with decreasing profit margins. The reverse situation not considered by Steindl would be increasing profit margins in the context of decreasing concentration. Both situations are important in analyzing fluctuations in concentration in the meat packing industry.

Dean Worcester (1957) used the mid-century condition of the meat packing industry to explain in a neoclassical context why dominant firms decline. He argues that dominant firms opt for short-run profit maximization when they have no cost advantage over entrants. Therefore, the dominant firms have decided their optimal, i.e., long run, strategy is to decline. In a Steindlian context, the "dominant" firms can be thought of as large marginal firms. In his theory, Steindl observes that oligopolistic industries, where a few producers make up the market, can contain marginal firms who are clearly not small firms. Such firms operate on a substantial scale, are capital-intensive, and receive abnormal profits. Absolute concentration will occur in this situation only when the cost advantage of the progressive firms grows to the point where a sufficient sales effort can be mounted against marginal firms. Steindl calls this "the case of an industry where entry is difficult" (1976, p. 52).

Throughout *Maturity and Stagnation* progressive firms are regarded as established firms. Although Steindl uses the term "entry" in the context of industries that are already oligopolistic, the ramifications of entry are not an important dimension of Steindl's theory, for, as Nina Shapiro (1981) states:

New firms enter the industry through the door of its marginal group. The members of this group are the ones whose markets can be invaded with the capital available to new entrants. It is because new entrants can meet the capital requirements of producing at the scale of the industry's marginal firms that the marginal firms earn, as a group, only "normal profits".

(ibid., p. 75)

In the nineteenth century, the capital intensity of a meat distribution system built around railroads acted as a barrier to entry, thereby supporting Steindl's position that only established firms were capable of innovation. After the early twentieth century, the gradual development of a highway network and refrigerated trucks eroded the competitive advantages of rail distribution. This reduction in the capital requirements for distribution, itself an innovation, made entry easier. At the same time, the large established packers, the "progressive" firms of the nineteenth century, were locked into a costly capital-intensive distribution system, as they had built their plants and distribution facilities around railroad hubs or terminals. The entrants gradually reduced the market power of the established firms, reflected in a prolonged period of deconcentration within the industry.

To cover situations like this, an important theoretical extension would be the concept of innovation-through-entry. As a more detailed examination of meat packing will demonstrate, the fundamental dynamic of Steindl's theory – cost reductions accruing from innovations, the erosion of profit margins through sales efforts intended to gain market share, and the resulting growth in industry concentration – continues to operate irrespective of this modification.

After *Maturity and Stagnation*, Steindl, (1990) recognized that innovation through entry could be triggered by high profit margins within an industry. In such cases, he anticipated the high fixed costs required to increase industry capacity using new technologies would force the absolute concentration process to proceed by fits and starts (ibid.: p. 313).

In predicting that the process of absolute concentration would be discontinuous, Steindl implicitly assumed that once an industry has high fixed costs, so will subsequent technologies. In contrast, the innovations which paved the way for boxed beef were either size-neutral or favored small firms. Consequently, the decline in four-firm concentration ratios during the twentieth century was steady and continuous.

Steindl's observations about meat packing

In *Maturity and Stagnation*, Steindl briefly assessed the meat packing industry of the mid-1930s, and noted the presence of competition despite a "fairly high degree of concentration", a four-firm concentration ratio of 56 percent (ibid.: p. 89). He attributed the presence of competition to "a special technical development", the growth of medium-sized rural packers who

> competed strongly with the four big centralised meat packers of Chicago. This explains why the industry follows "the competitive pattern." In the long run this may prove again a temporary phase: "the big four" have been buying up country meat packers and the process of concentration is renewed.
>
> (ibid., p. 89)

A "temporary phase" would support the static viewpoint of *Maturity and Stagnation*: industries remain concentrated once the absolute concentration phase has eliminated marginal producers, resulting in the entrenched oligopolistic state Steindl termed *mature capitalism*. Irreversible concentration is a condition of his theory because the price-cost relations established during the initial concentrating phase are viewed as permanent and therefore do not permit the entry of atavistic firms. New innovations could result in yet another round of concentration, but under no circumstances will concentration fall. Therefore, the "country packers" were unlikely to develop new innovations that would position them as a new generation of progressive firms.

In fact, the "temporary phase" lasted a long time: the market shares of the Big Four (or their predecessors) declined from 85 percent in 1887 to 21 percent in 1971. Steindl could not have foreseen that his special case of difficult entry was unfolding during the mid-twentieth century, and would, as he predicted, eventually culminate in a more concentrated industry. In 1977, four-firm concentration ratios among cattle slaughterers began a sustained rise from 22 percent to 57 percent in 1988. Four firm concentration levels among firms slaughtering steers and heifers, the type of cattle generally used for boxed beef, went from 29 percent in 1972, the first year tabulated, to 70 percent in 1988.

This historical pattern of concentration, deconcentration, and re-concentration suggests the paradigm presented in *Maturity and Stagnation* should be recast to incorporate cycles of competition and concentration as part of the evolution of an industry in response to technical change. This adjustment was proposed by Steindl (1990) in terms which correspond to the meat packing industry:

> You have to consider *change* if you want to say something about the *formation* of prices and profit margins. You want to study the disruption of equilibrium by new entry and by technological change … An essential feature of a dynamic theory will be that it has to consider not one type of firm, but two or more types according to their role in the disruption—defensive or aggressive, conservative or innovative.
>
> (ibid., p. 312).

Development of the initial oligopoly

The oligopolists of the first wave of concentration, the "Big Four" – Swift, Armour, Cudahy, and Wilson – were not those of the second wave of oligopoly. Yet the "Big Three", of the 1980s, IBP,[3] ConAgra, and Cargill, followed much the same path to industry prominence as their predecessors.

In the mid-1800s, the perishability of meat made the industry diffuse and unconcentrated. Mary Yeager (1981) comments:

> Packing required no huge investments or sophisticated technology, only a supply of meat and a good curing recipe. ... Neither the packer's role nor functions were clearly defined. Slaughtering, butchering, and packing activities were disintegrated. Relationships between those in the industry were fluid and unsystematic, depending largely upon local conditions, the weather, availability of supplies, and distances to market.
>
> (ibid., p. 1)

Then, as now, transportation defined the scope of the meat packing industry. As steamboats, canals, and railroads developed, the growing demand for food in the eastern cities of New York, Boston, Baltimore, and Philadelphia led to the emergence of specialized processors and slaughterers. Although the industry quickly became one of the nation's largest, its growth was constrained by the perishability of meat.

As Chicago became a railroad hub, it also emerged as a leading livestock market for cattle shipped in from Iowa, Indiana, and even Texas, culminating in the construction of the gigantic Union Stockyards in 1865. The stockyards facilitated the development of specialized and systematic relationships between local packers and the marketing agencies (middlemen) selling livestock on behalf of farmers and ranchers. Yet even as meat packing became more defined as an industry, it still remained "unconcentrated, disintegrated, and non-oligopolistic" (Yeager 1981, p. 17). By themselves, railroads did not revolutionize the meat packing industry.

Heavy capitalization requirements quickly converted the railroad industry into an oligopoly highly vulnerable to excess capacity. To minimize the impact of freight wars and retain their lucrative trade in live animals, railroads shipped beef carcasses ("dressed beef") at a rate equivalent to livestock. Thus, collusion through rate fixing and livestock pooling was an early feature of the meat packing industry.

Gustavus Swift, a cattle dealer and meat wholesaler, recognized the inefficiency of paying freight on the inedible portions of the animal and the costs accompanying an excessive number of middlemen. He wanted to develop a streamlined, centralized distribution system for cattle and meat. As railroads were not interested in developing a refrigerator car, Swift used his own funds to develop a prototype car in 1878. Swift then found a railroad line that had a minimal trade in livestock and gave it a monopoly on dressed beef shipments.

Swift continued to perfect the refrigerator car to enable the quality of chilled dressed beef to be on a par with fresh beef. The perishability of his product forced Swift to implement price competition and high volume sales as part of his marketing strategy. Growth, not profitability, was his target.

> "If you did not sell, then you stood no chance to make it." "As long as a manager sold plenty, G.F. Swift stood by him," explained his son Louis, "even if he made no money." Forced to economize and cut costs wherever he could, Swift was not content simply to keep goods moving just fast enough to avoid being spoiled. On the contrary, he worked to develop a technique "which kept his goods moving at a rate far faster than was needed." Part of that technique was more effective sales methods. Swift always told his salesmen to "cut [the meat] and scatter it out". He reasoned that wholesalers would be more willing to distribute his meat and customers more willing to buy if they were not forced to buy the whole carcass but were allowed to choose only those cuts they knew would sell.
>
> (Yeager 1981, p. 62)

Swift reinvested any profits in plants, cars, sales outlets, and cooling facilities, as well as ongoing experiments with refrigeration. His trade expanded rapidly. By the early 1880s, his strategy of vertical integration began making money, and attracted like-minded competitors, Philip Armour, Nelson Morris, and George Hammond. In the early 1890s, Cudahy & Co., and Schwarschild & Sulzberger (later Wilson & Co.) also entered the industry. Unlike Swift, each of these firms began shipping dressed beef as an extension of other livestock or meat enterprises because the large scale and scope of Swift's business demanded a similar investment.

This capsule of the origins of oligopoly in meat packing reveals themes introduced by Steindl: a cost-reducing innovation developed by an entrepreneur, which is copied only by large firms; scale economies resulting from continuous processing ("disassembly" lines for slaughtered cattle); a goal of expanding market share through specific sales efforts; and at least for Swift, reinvestment of profits back into the beef business. The concept of boxed beef, a (further) innovation inducing yet another round of concentration in the industry, was latent in Swift's emphasis on "cutting the meat and scattering it out". The technological focus of Steindl's theory corresponds to the production-driven orientation of the meat packing industry.

The path of industry development predicted by Steindl also differs in key respects from the meat packing industry. Theoretically, inter-industry coordination plays no role in the process of absolute concentration.

In meat packing, railroads made a coordinated system of livestock pro-
curement, slaughter, processing, and distribution possible. The potential
impact of vertical integration on concentration levels was also not considered by Steindl. Using meat packing as an example, Alfred Chandler
(1977) saw that efficient, high volume throughput within plants needed
vertical integration to realize the scale economies of capital-intensive technologies.

Steindl's theory emphasizes price competition and sales efforts. If vertical integration is added to the theory, other strategic weapons need to be
considered, for, as Kathryn Rudie Harrigan (1983) remarks, "Vertically
integrated competitors use foreclosure in lieu of price competition to
squeeze out nonintegrated firms by denying them access to materials,
markets, innovations, or other competitive advantages" (ibid., p. 31).

By focusing on price competition and sales efforts, Steindl may have
overemphasized the importance of markets for finished goods (output)
relative to equally important inputs. Labor and livestock are the primary
inputs in the meat packing industry. These inputs exerted a decisive influence on the market power of the Big Four once domestic markets for beef
became saturated at the end of the nineteenth century.

A saturated market, underutilized capacity, temporary shifts in market
power resulting from price competition, irregular product flows, and
increased costs led the Big Four to cooperate in setting prices and maintaining product flow. These firms had reached the stage of mature capitalism insofar as small or marginal firms had already been eliminated from
the industry. Yet Steindl's theory lacks a mechanism whereby the oligopolists of mature capitalism protect and consolidate the gains in market share
achieved during absolute concentration. If entry can occur during mature
capitalism, the need for a protective strategy is paramount. For the meat
packing industry, the answer was collusion. What collusion has in common
with Steindl's concept of mature capitalism is a refusal, on the part of the
oligopolists, to cut prices to eliminate unwanted excess capacity. The oligopolists then initiate their decline in the manner described by Worcester
by operating at a higher cost than entrants.

Market sharing at terminal markets,[4] where each packer bought the
same percentage of livestock year after year, was one of the forms of collusion readily documented by the newly-established Federal Trade Commission. With market sharing, each participant expanded only at the rate at
which the overall market was expanding – a twist on Steindl's proposal
that absolute concentration ends when the growth rate of the progressive
firms equals the growth rate of the industry.

Decline of oligopoly

Overcapacity in distribution facilities during the early 1900s encouraged
the Big Four to attempt to increase market share by handling a wide array

of foods. At this point, the Big Four broadened the scope of their industry from "meat packing" to "food processing". This extension corresponds to the horizontal integration Steindl associated with mature capitalism.

The result of the FTC investigation was a 1920 Consent Decree compelling the Big Four to divest themselves of any direct or indirect financial interest in livestock marketing, terminal railroads, market news publications, and the handling of some 145 commodities, including vegetables, condiments, cigars, and grape juice. These restrictions basically limited the Big Four to meat marketing. Another Consent Decree in 1935 forced the Big Four to stop both market sharing and the "test cost" system of maintaining uniform costs, prices, and profits among themselves. Industry concentration began to decline in the mid-1930s.

The impact of the Consent Decrees on the Big Four is hard to assess because the rest of the industry was decentralizing, developing in the opposite direction pursued by the Big Four. A highway system and the use of trucks to transport livestock or chilled meat led to more rural markets (auctions[5]) for livestock, as well as new rural packing plants. Whereas the Big Four operated multi-story, multi-species (i.e., pork, beef, lamb) plants, entrants built single-story, specialized, beef-only plants. This was the beginning of a streamlined production process that eventually culminated in the scale economies offered by steer and heifer slaughter for fabrication into boxed beef.

The introduction of federal grading in 1906 undermined the brands established by the Big Four, by standardizing evaluations of beef quality across all plants, large and small. The Big Four responded by putting more emphasis on pork products like sausage where branding continued to be profitable. However, they continued to be the largest slaughterers of cattle, in terms of volume, throughout most of the twentieth century. In fact, their emphasis on branding may have distracted them from scale economies. Steindl raises this point in *Small and Big Business* (1945), the foundation for ideas expressed in *Maturity and Stagnation*: "Each firm or plant tries to supply the whole gamut of varieties and thus ... only succeeds in conducting small scale operations" (p. 18). Steindl's observation implicitly suggests marketing acumen may be important as size in directing the course of an industry.[6]

In the nineteenth century, the leading packers strenuously sought ways to reduce labor costs. This was followed by the perception that a skilled labor force could be a source of stability, complementing the efforts of the Big Four to maintain the status quo in prices and profits. Multi-species plants also required cross-trained highly skilled butchers. In the twentieth century, the urban and unionized plants of the Big Four eventually had wage rates twice the level of many competitors. Not surprisingly, from the mid-1930s through 1971, the Big Four consistently had lower profits than smaller competitors.[7] The substantial scale and capital intensity of the Big Four qualify them as marginal firms in terms of Steindl's case of difficult entry. Their lower profits made them even more "marginal", and therefore they are a composite of both the "ideal pattern" and "difficult entry" cases of competition.

The impact of decentralized livestock markets and urban/rural wage differentials might have been reduced had the Big Four not decided to let urban plants fully depreciate before relocating into areas closer to cattle supplies (feedlots). Richard Arnould (1971) concluded that nonfood diversification into pharmaceuticals, sporting goods, animal feeds, fertilizers, and finance "probably saved the economic lives" of some of the Big Four firms" (ibid., p. 32). This conclusion is open to question insofar as the Big Four were not free to invest in other areas of food processing, whereas competitors were.

The closing of the Chicago Union Stockyards in 1970 signalled the demise of the Big Four, for the new decade brought takeovers and spin-offs that completely altered the identities of these firms. Only in 1981, after repeated appeals by the packers, was the Consent Decree lifted by the Courts on the basis of the significant changes in the industry which had occurred since 1920.

The era of boxed beef

In *Small and Big Business*, Steindl remarks:

> If there are economies open to small plants – and a technical develop-
> ment may sometimes favor small scale equipment – then any bigger
> firm may make use of them just as well as a smaller firm, because there
> is nothing to prevent it from investing in a number of smaller plants.
> From this asymmetry it follows that small firms can never (in the long
> run) earn higher profits than big firms.
>
> (1945, p. 10)

These expectations are not fulfilled in the case of meat packing. The differences in profitability have already been indicated. What remains to be demonstrated is the responsiveness of large firms to innovation. The fact that boxed beef was a concept pioneered by Safeway and Armour would seem to support Steindl, but:

> Safeway, in essence, designed the system to use in their central fabri-
> cation plants. However, Iowa Beef was the first one to develop facili-
> ties close to the feedlot that were adequate and large enough to
> handle a large volume of boxed beef over an extended period of time.
>
> (Cook 1981, p. 34)

In *Maturity and Stagnation*, Steindl presumes that the oligopolists will continue to innovate, but not necessarily apply new innovations because the industry no longer has the same potential for growth in market share as it did during the absolute concentration phase. The meat packing industry shows that an innovation must be split into concept and application, each considered in the context of potential entry.

Currier Holman, the founder of Iowa Beef, opened the first major boxed beef plant in 1968. At that time, his competitors were not other packers, but national and regional retail chains that typically bought carcasses from packers, and used their own cutting (breaking) facilities to put the meat into merchandisable form. (McCullough 1990, p. 6) Boxed beef was not readily accepted by retailers. A government study concluded:

> the traditional method of cutting carcasses in the store [was] the most expensive per pound, with boxed beef close behind it. The cheapest method by far ... was shipping carcasses to a large, centralized warehouse of a retail chain and preparing the fresh meat cuts there for delivery to the chain's outlets.
>
> (Duewer and Crawford 1977)

Cutting and packaging meat to retard spoilage probably made boxed beef cost somewhat more than the traditional carcass beef. (Kwitny 1979, p. 286) Nevertheless, within a decade boxed beef was fast becoming the industry norm. Where the savings from boxed beef were realized was in the elimination of unionized butchers' jobs in supermarket warehouses and stores, in replacing skilled labor with less-skilled packinghouse butchers who received rural pay rates. IBP reduced its own wage bill by breaking the power of the meat packing unions' "master contracts" which established wages for plants across the industry.

In *Maturity and Stagnation*, Steindl focused on the savings emerging directly from an innovation, which, in his theory, were captured by the innovating firm itself. Boxed beef saved retailers money, not packers. Packer costs were reduced by eliminating or minimizing unions. Perhaps to emphasize the main features of his argument, Steindl treats progressive firms and their industry as if this was all that mattered during the concentrating phase. A more comprehensive view suggested by meat packing would recognize that progressive firms are part of a marketing chain. Thus, the impacts of an innovation could be felt upstream or downstream, and still enable the progressive firms to restructure their industry as described by Steindl.

Both boxed beef and chilled dressed beef were new products. Steindl recognized that new products could, like cost-reducing technological changes, stimulate investment to bring on absolute concentration, Shapiro (1981) observes how product variation can allow entrants to:

> break the existing firms' monopoly of the market. This is particularly clear where the manufacture of the new product necessitates the

utilization of a fundamentally different technical apparatus and, there-fore, capital structure than that currently employed. Established con-cerns will be reluctant to switch over to the new product, since this switch involves the devaluation of the capital sunk in their presently running equipment.

(ibid., p. 92)

Her observations correspond to the meat packing industry insofar as the Big Four held on to outdated plants and production methods and there-fore did not position themselves to produce the new product, boxed beef, before competitors.

Shapiro further argues that modifying Steindl's theory by introducing product development during absolute concentration subordinates the emphasis Steindl accorded pricing in favor of market development for new products or commodities. Industry accounts emphasize the market devel-opment needed for boxed beef to succeed. To have a national market commensurate with the huge output from its plants, IBP needed to capture the New York market, and to that end, accommodated some of the demands made by organized labor. (Steindl points out that one of the prerequisites of the absolute concentration phase are markets correspond-ing to the output of the progressive firms.) Although IBP used an uncon-ventional approach to market development, the end result was the same as more traditional sales efforts might have been in another setting: boxed beef was purchased by New York supermarkets. Price effects were indi-rect, realized through lower costs for retailers. Both price and market development were components of the strategy used by IBP to establish boxed beef in the industry

Was boxed beef a new industry or was it simply a new product? Con-centration in the beef industry is now measured not only in terms of cattle slaughter, the historical reference point, but also in terms of steer and heifer slaughter and boxed beef production. This adjustment suggests steer and heifer slaughters and boxed beef producers – the companies are the same – are in a different league than cattle slaughterers. They produce dif-ferent products: table beef versus ground beef or beef used for processed foods. This argument leaves Steindl's original position intact: two separate industries each experienced absolute concentration.

Alternatively, chilled carcass beef and boxed beef can be regarded as successive refinements of a single commodity, beef. The potential for further refinements of this commodity through elimination of yet more fat and bone supports the concept of a single industry which went through multiple cycles of concentration in the course of product development.

Conclusion

The evolution of the US meat packing industry over the 1865–1988 period reveals important parallels with the concepts of absolute concentration and mature capitalism introduced by Steindl in *Maturity and Stagnation in American Capitalism*. In the "ideal pattern" of competition envisioned by Steindl, an innovation developed by an individual entrepreneur generates scale economies, which in turn lower production costs and increase profit margins. By adopting this innovation, "progressive" firms are positioned to eliminate smaller or financially weaker "marginal" firms, a process Steindl called "absolute concentration". Progressive firms use profits to finance special sales efforts to boost market share. Eventually, the cost of continued sales efforts erode the profits accruing from the innovation, thereby ending the process of absolute concentration. Having reached maturity, the industry then stabilizes at a permanently higher level of concentration.

Although the resulting oligopoly may continue to innovate, it is no longer driven by the growth possibilities of the absolute concentration phase. Within the scenario depicted by *Maturity and Stagnation*, the oligopoly may choose to stagnate, enjoying higher profit margins without fear of competition from entrants.

The meat packing industry diverges from the static model set forth in *Maturity and Stagnation* by demonstrating two phases of concentration separated by a prolonged period of deconcentration. Yet the particulars of the absolute concentration process described by Steindl correspond to each phase of oligopoly. Each was initiated by an entrepreneur introducing a technical change that resulted in cost-reducing scale economies. In the late nineteenth century, Gustavus Swift's refrigerated rail car enabled chilled carcass beef to displace fresh beef from local slaughter. In the late twentieth century, decades of technological change in the meat packing industry culminated in the possibility of scale economies, which Currier Holman realized in transforming carcass beef into boxed beef.

Each oligopoly developed from circumstances predicted by Steindl: scale economies arising from a technological innovation embodied in plant and equipment, and extensive sales efforts to develop nascent markets. Although Steindl thought such sales efforts would be rooted in price competition and product differentiation, the latter can be extended to include entirely new products, as manifested in the differences between fresh beef, chilled beef, and boxed beef. These differences required unique methods of market development, i.e., striking a bargain with organized labor as a precondition for market access and therefore, price competition. In this context market development then represents a confrontation between the institutional infrastructure associated with each product. This, Steindl would agree, is the basis for converting the static model of *Maturity and Stagnation* into a dynamic theory.

In *Maturity and Stagnation*, Steindl focused on a single point in the production process, expressed in terms of a single industry. The experience of the meat packing industry suggests Steindl's theory should be broadened to consider the impact of vertical integration or institutions like organized labor on the supplies and quality of inputs. Adequate cattle supplies were the pivotal factor determining whether an established firm or an entrant could capture the scale economies associated with boxed beef.

Moreover, the emphasis Steindl accorded the production process implicitly minimized the market power of buyers, be they individual consumers or institutions. Steindl's theory considers the cost advantages of an innovation only in terms of the manufacturing process, whereas in meat packing, these advantages were primarily realized by the retail sector, a necessary condition for the success of boxed beef.

The oligopoly established in the nineteenth century, the "Big Four", eventually came to represent Steindl's concept of mature capitalism. In the static model depicted in *Maturity and Stagnation*, Steindl expected the success of the progressive firms would protect their profit margins indefinitely. In the meat packing industry, entry, which Steindl did not consider until later writings, was precluded by collusion. Steindl predicted mature capitalism would be associated with high prices; collusion represents a unique expression of that tendency.

As subsequent anti-trust policy eliminated the possibility of horizontal integration, but *did not affect concentration levels within meat packing*, the Big Four could have chosen to maintain their dominant position by using innovation as a barrier to entry. Because the cost of writing off outmoded facilities appears to have been unacceptable, and unlike competitors, the Big Four could not eliminate excess capacity by investing elsewhere in the food sector, they chose to become marginal firms within meat packing. Steindl's theory focuses on firms who respond to technical change and are therefore, "progressive". Only in his "case of difficult entry" did he allude to situations where large, capital intensive firms might choose not to innovate, and therefore, become "marginal" firms.

Consequently, the meat packing industry of the nineteenth and twentieth centuries represents a composite of Steindl's "ideal pattern" of competition and "case of difficult entry," as presented in *Maturity and Stagnation in American Capitalism*. The period between oligopolies represented the break-up of the initial oligopoly through entry, a process which took most of the twentieth century. In his "case of difficult entry", Steindl predicted an extended period of time would be needed for innovative firms to build a cost advantage sufficient to break up an oligopoly containing large, capital-intensive, inflexible firms. When Steindl wrote *Maturity and Stagnation*, he believed entrants would never upset an established oligopoly, and therefore, did not explore the ramifications of entry through innovation. Cycles of absolute concentration were possible, in theory, but would never result in a less concentrated industry. Yet the experience of the meat packing industry indicates that innovation can occur through entry, and result in cycles of competition and concentration. These industry characteristics create the basis for an important extension of the theory.

Acknowledgments

Although the ideas expressed here are those of the author, comments from Tracy Mott and Nina Shapiro, the encouragement of Robert M. Feinberg and Robert Blecker and the support of the Agricultural Cooperative Service were instrumental in preparing this chapter.

Notes

1 Competitive industries possess marginal producers with normal profits according to Steindl.
2 This interpretation of Steindl is based on the continuous innovations in packing plant layout and machinery and cattle feeding that occurred in the meat packing industry during the nineteenth and twentieth centuries (Reimund, Yeager). These innovations undoubtedly contributed to the impact made by the refrigerated rail car and boxed beef but were not sufficient by themselves to restructure the meat packing industry. The impact of these secondary innovations will be considered more fully in the section on the meat packing industry.
3 Formerly Iowa Beef Processors, Inc.
4 "Terminal" refers to large livestock markets like Chicago's Union Stockyards which were established at the end or "terminus" of a railroad line.
5 Terminal markets are served by several marketing agencies. Auctions are run by a single agency. An alternative to either of these is "direct marketing", where the livestock producer individually negotiates a price with a packer, and ships the cattle direct to the plant. This has become the predominant form of livestock marketing in the twentieth century.
6 Consider this excerpt from the June 22, 1992 issue of the *National Provisioner*: "ConAgra has a history of entering established markets, reshaping and dominating them. It is one advantage of being big. But ConAgra also wields its market acumen as much as its size" (p. 11).
7 After 1957, Cudahy was no longer one of the four largest meat packers.

References

American Meat Institute (1948–1955) *Financial Results of the Meat Packing Industry*. Chicago, IL: American Meat Institute.
American Meat Institute (1956–1971) *Financial Facts About the Meat, Packing Industry*, Chicago, IL: American Meat Institute.
Arnould, Richard J. (1971) "Changing Patterns of Concentration in American Meat Packing, 1880–1963", *Business History Review*, Spring, 45, 18–34.
Chandler, Alfred (1977) *The Visible Hand*, Cambridge, MA: Belknap Press.
Cook, James (1981) "Those Simple Barefoot Boys from Iowa Beef", *Forbes*, 22 June.

Duewer, Lawrence and Crawford, Terry (1977) *The Dallas Morning News*, 14 August.

Harrigan, Kathryn Rudie (1983) *strategies for Vertical Integration*, Lexington, MA: Lexington Books.

Hogeland, Julie A. (1992) "The Tendency Toward Oligopoly in the Meat Packing Industry", PhD diss., American University.

Kwitny, Jonathan (1979) *Vicious Circles: The Mafia in the Marketplace*, New York: W.W. Norton & Co.

Levine, David P. (1975) "The Theory of the Growth of the Capitalist Economy", *Economic Development and Cultural Change*, October, 23, 47–74.

McCullough, Kevin (1988) "Keynote Address", in Wayne D. Purcell and Teresa Altizer (eds), PROCEEDINGS, Key Issues in Livestock Pricing: A Perspective for the 1990s, Blacksburg, VA: Virginia Polytechnical Institute, Research Institute on Livestock Pricing, May.

Perry, Charles R. and Kegley, Delwyn H. (1989) *Disintegration and change: Labor Relations in the Meat Packing Industry*, Philadelphia, PA: University of Pennsylvania, Wharton School.

Reimund, Donn A. *et al.* (1981) *Structural Change in Agriculture: The Experience for Broilers, Fed Cattle, and Processing Vegetables*, Washington, DC: U.S. Department of Agriculture, Economics and Statistics Service, April, Technical Bulletin No. 1648.

Shapiro, Nina (1981) "Pricing and the growth of the Firm", *Journal of Post Keynesian Economics*, Fall, 4, 85–100.

Shapiro, Nina (1988) "Market Structure and Economic Growth: Steindl's Contributions", *Social Concept*, June, 4, 72–83.

Steindl, Josef (1945) *Small and Big Business*, Oxford: Basil Blackwell.

Steindl, Josef (1976) *Maturity and Stagnation in American Capitalism*, New York: Monthly Review Press.

Steindl, Josef (1990) "Kalecki's Theory of Pricing: Notes on the Margin", in Josef Steindl, *Economic Papers 1941–88*, New York: St. Martin's Press.

Worcester, Dean A., Jr. (1959) "Why Dominant Firms Decline", *Journal of Political Economy*, August, 65, 338–347.

Yeager, Mary (1981) *Competition and Regulation: The Development of Oligopoly in the Meat Packing Industry*, Greenwich, CT: JAI Press, Inc.

Part II
Distribution and growth

4   Steindl's theory of maturity and stagnation and its relevance today

Amitava Krishna Dutt

Introduction

Steindl's book, *Maturity and Stagnation in American Capitalism*, which explained the stagnation in US economic growth in the 1930s in terms of the rise of oligopoly in US industry, appeared in 1952.[1] As Steindl (1976, p. ix) later noted, the timing of the publication of this book "could not have been less propitious for its success". The advanced industrialized nations of the world embarked on a long phase of rapid growth, and stagnation was not the crying issue of the day.[2] Moreover, despite the so-called "Keynesian revolution", neoclassical economics increasingly came to dominate the economics profession, and few could be expected to take much notice of a Marx-inspired self-professed follower of Kalecki.[3] Although Steindl's work in this book has had some impact on some Marxist writers,[4] it has largely been neglected in the economics profession.[5]

The purpose of this chapter is to argue that Steindl's book deserves much more attention than it has received thus far. The main element of this argument is that Steindl has developed in this book a valuable theoretical model with which a variety of currently important questions concerning the macroeconomics of growth and distribution in both advanced and less-developed countries can be usefully examined – and in fact a start in this direction has already been made. This theoretical model, rather than its specific explanation of stagnation in the US in the 1930s, will be the lasting contribution of this book.[6]

This argument is made in two stages. First, an exposition of a simplified version of Steindl's model of growth, amended to make its logic transparent, is provided. Next, using this model to understand the nature of Steindl's contribution, we examine the current relevance of Steindl's contribution.

It should be stated at the outset that the objective of this chapter is not to review all aspects of Steindl's theoretical analysis contained in his book. There is much in the book regarding the microeconomic behaviour of firms – for instance, on why firms hold excess capacity, and on the pricing policies of firms under different market structures – and on other macroeconomic issues such as the role of borrowing by firms in the growth process (see below); the focus of this chapter is on the macroeconomics of monopoly power and stagnation, undoubtedly a central aspect of the book.

Steindl's model of growth

Steindl (1976, p. xvi) wrote of his 1952 work that the "attempt at mathematical formulation (Chapter XIII) leaves me deeply dissatisfied, because it does not reproduce my theory adequately. Most readers may prefer to skip it." For Steindl the problem is not so much with mathematical modelling as such, though he (see Steindl, 1984, pp. 246–248) is acutely aware of the dangers of the sterility of using mathematics in economics solely for rigour and losing touch with social and institutional substance. This is clear, first, from his statement that "the mathematical formulation of the underlying theories has considerable advantages in checking the logic of the argument, and making the assumptions explicit (Steindl 1952, p. 226), and second, from the fact that he tried, several times after his 1952 attempt, to set out his theory in mathematical form (see Steindl 1979, 1985a, 1989). But it is fair to say that his efforts did not do justice to his theory. This section develops a simplified model which follows Steindl's *Maturity and Stagnation* model of Chapter XIII as closely as possible, making only two major changes in it.

One change relates to Steindl's portrayal of lags in his investment function. Steindl took into account lags using Kalecki's method of assuming that current variables affected investment several periods later. This treatment gives rise to a mixed difference-differential equation, and serves to complicate and perhaps even obfuscate the analysis. The model of this chapter introduces lags into investment behavior by assuming that firms have a desired investment function, and that they adjust current investment to this desired investment through time according to an adjustment coefficient.[7] This formulation has the advantage of producing a pure differential equation system which allows the economy's dynamics to be portrayed in a simple and transparent manner.

The other change relates to neglecting the effects of changes in what Steindl calls the reciprocal gearing ratio (or the ratio of the firms' own capital to total capital). While this allows us to simplify the model considerably, it has a cost: our model cannot analyze the implications of changes in the firms' debt position its interaction with the growth process. However, this issue, while certainly of great interest, is not central to Steindl's analysis of the interaction between growth and distribution that is at the basis of his analysis of stagnation. Indeed, in two of the three subsequent formal presentations of his analysis, Steindl (1979, 1989) has abstracted from this issue himself.[8]

The structure of the model

Following Steindl, consider a closed economy with no government fiscal activity, which produces one good with labor and capital.[9]

Investment behavior is captured in the model by assuming that the firms have a desired rate of investment as a ratio of capital stock given by

$$g^d = \alpha_0 + \alpha_1(S_f/K) + \alpha_2(u - u_0) \tag{4.1}$$

and that they adjust their actual rate of investment as a ratio of capital stock according to

$$dg/dt = \Theta (g^d - g) \tag{4.2}$$

where g denotes investment as a ratio of capital stock and g^d its desired level, S_f the flow of internal saving of firms, K the stock of capital, $u = Y/K$, the ratio of output, Y, to capital stock, and a measure of the rate of capacity utilization, u_0 the planned rate of capacity utilization of firms (the rate which makes the term involving α_2 disappear), $\alpha_i > 0$ and $\Theta > 0$ are parameters, and t denotes time.[10] These equations capture Steindl's assumptions that the level of investment (after a lag) depends positively on the level of internal firms' saving (following Kalecki's (1971) discussion of capital market imperfections and the principle of increasing risk), and that investment as a ratio of capital stock (after a lag) depends positively on the gap between the rate of capacity utilization and its desired level.

The rest of the equations are identical to Steindl's. First, the level of gross profits depends positively on the level of output and negatively on the level of capital stock, so that

$$R = m_1 Y - m_2 K \tag{4.3}$$

where R denotes gross profits and $m_i > 0$ are fixed parameters and $m_1 < 1$. Steindl took this to be a generalization of Kalecki's distribution theory, and in later work (see Steindl 1979, pp. 110–111) clarified that m_1 depends on Kalecki's markup on prime costs (on variable or direct labor), while m_2 depends on overhead labor requirements assumed to be proportional to the stock of capital. The constancy of the markup denotes the presence of oligopolistic firms in the economy (more of which below). Second, the level of net profit, P, is obtained by subtracting interest payments from gross profit, so that

$$P = R - i(K - K_f) \tag{4.4}$$

where i is the rate of interest which is paid on the firms' debt, and assumed to be given and K_f the stock of capital internally owned by the firms.[11] Third, firms pay dividends, D, according to

$$D = a_1K_f + a_2(P - a_1K_f) \tag{4.5}$$

where $1 > a_i > 0$ are constants, which shows that dividends paid increases with the firms' own capital (denoting that the firm is more secure), and with the level of net profit. The difference between net profit and dividends represents firms' savings, S_f, so that

$$S_f = P - D. \tag{4.6}$$

Fourth, household savings is a fraction, s, of its income, so that

$$S_h = s(Y - S_f). \tag{4.7}$$

Finally, we assume away depreciation, so that we get

$$dK/dt = I, \tag{4.8}$$

where I is the level of real investment and

$$dK_f/dt = S_f. \tag{4.9}$$

Taking into account depreciation gives rise to interesting questions concerning the difference between gross and net capital which Steindl discusses at length (see Steindl 1952, pp. 175–191; Steindl 1979, pp. 109–110, 115–116), but because these issues are not central to Steindl's analysis of the effects of monopoly power on growth, and because he ignored the issue in his treatment in chapter XIII, they are not considered here.

Steindl examined the properties of his model by solving his difference-differential equation system for the endogenous variables, by examining the behavior of these variables as time approached infinity, and by examining how such behavior changed with changes in some key parameters. The analysis here proceeds somewhat differently, and addresses the issue of change over time more carefully. First, I analyze the short-run behavior of the economy in which the goods market adjusts, given the stocks of capital and the growth rate of capital. Second, I consider how the economy moves over time in the long run due to changes in the growth rate; this analysis allows a clear discussion of the possibility of instability in the economy, an issue which was verbally emphasized, but not formally analyzed, by Steindl. The effects of some parametric changes are considered, both in the discussion of the short and long runs.

The economy in the short run

In the short run, assume that the stocks of capital, K and K_f are given, as is g, the rate of capital accumulation, but that output, and hence the rate of capacity utilization, u, varies to clear the market for goods. In short-run equilibrium, the goods market clears through variations in output and capacity utilization with the price being fixed by cost plus markup; equilibrium output is thus demand-determined.

In short-run equilibrium, therefore, we require that the excess demand for goods is zero, so that

$$C + I - Y = 0, \tag{4.10}$$

where C is the level of real consumption, which is by definition given by

$$C = Y - S_f - S_h. \tag{4.11}$$

Substituting from equations (4.11), and (4.3) through (4.7), and dividing by K (and noting that $g = I/K$ and $u = Y/K$), we get

$$\begin{aligned} g - [(1-s)(1-a_2)m_1 + s]u + [(1-s)(1-a_2)(m_2 + i)] \\ - [(1-s)(1-a_2)(i-a_1)]k = 0 \end{aligned} \tag{4.12}$$

where $k = K_f/K$, the share of capital owned by firms, that is, what Steindl calls reciprocal gearing ratio. The short-run equilibrium value of u can be solved from (4.12) and is given by

$$u = \frac{\{g + [(1-s)(1-a_2)(m_2 + i)] - [(1-s)(1-a_2)(i-a_1)]k\}/}{[(1-s)(1-a_2)m_1 + s]} \tag{4.13}$$

Assume that in the short run output adjusts at a rate proportional to the excess demand in the goods market, which (as a ratio of capital stock) is given by the left-hand side of equation (4.12). Since a rise in u reduces excess demand, the adjustment of output in the short run is seen to be stable.

The short-run equilibrium effects of changes in various parameters and state variables can be easily seen from equation (4.13). A rise in g increases aggregate demand and hence u along standard Kaleckian lines with a multiplier given by the denominator of the equation; a fall in s has a similar effect by increasing aggregate demand. A rise in k, the ratio of capital owned by firms, has an ambiguous effect, depending on the sign of $i-a_1$. The rise in k implies a redistribution of capital from households who consume a part of its income to firms which do not consume. The effect of this on aggregate demand depends on what this asset redistribution does to the distribution of income. The interest rate measures what firms pay households for borrowing their capital, while a_1 measures to what extent firms increase dividends (thus transferring income to households) when their capital stock increases. If the interest rate is higher than a_1, the redistribution of capital stock from households to firms is accompanied by a similar redistribution of income flows, and there is therefore a fall in aggregate and hence u; in the opposite case the reverse happens. Steindl (1952, p. 217) assumes that $i = a_1$, which implies that the change in k leaves u unchanged. Following him, and for reasons of simplicity, I will make this assumption in what follows. Changes in distributional parameters which shift income from firms, which do not consume, to households, who do, obviously raise aggregate demand and u: this happens when m_1, the share of marginal income going to gross profits, falls, and m_2, which depends on payments to overhead labor, rises. A rise in a_2, the dividend payout parameter, has an ambiguous impact. In the case in which $i = a_1$ it is given by

$$du/da_2 = (1 - s)[m_1g - s(m_2 + i)]/[(1 - s)(1 - a_2)m_1 + s]^2. \qquad (4.14)$$

Finally, a rise in the rate of interest, i, increases u. This somewhat unusual result is explained here by the fact that a higher interest rate redistributes income from firms who do not consume to households who consume and thus adds to aggregate demand, while there is no adverse impact on investment which is given in the short run.[12]

Long-run dynamics and equilibrium

In the long run we assume that the economy is always in short-run equilibrium (or that the goods market clears) and K, K_f, and g move through time according to (4.8), (4.9) and (4.2), respectively.

The equation of motion for g can be obtained by substituting equations (4.3) through (4.6) into (4.1) and substituting this into (4.2), which yields,

$$dg/dt = \Theta\{\alpha_0 + \alpha_1(1 - a_2)[(m_1u - (m_2 + i)) + (i - a_1)k] + \alpha_2(u - u_0) - g\}.$$

which, given our assumption that $a_1 = i$, can be written as

$$dg/dt = \Theta\{(\alpha_0 + [\alpha_1(1 - a_2)m_1 + \alpha_2]u - \alpha_1(1 - a_2)(m_2 + i)$$
$$- \alpha_2u_0 - g\} \qquad (4.15)$$

Since in the long run u is given by equation (4.13), which makes it depend only on g (but since $a_1 = i$, *not* on k) and the other parameters; equation (4.15) represents a self-contained dynamic system which shows how g changes over time depending on values of g and the parameters of the system. We may examine the behavior of this system with the use of a phase diagram, as shown in Figures 4.1 and 4.2, which shows values of dg/dt for different values of g.[13]

Long-run equilibrium is established when $dg/dt = 0$, that is, where the function in (4.15) crosses the horizontal axis. The stability of this equilibrium depends on the slope of this function at this equilibrium. For

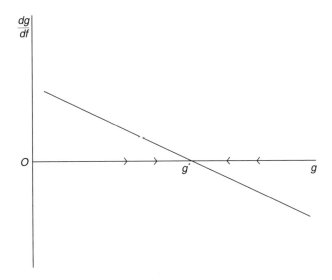

Figure 4.1 The case of stable equilibrium.

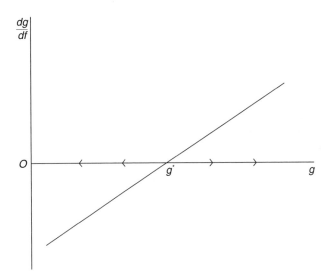

Figure 4.2 The case of unstable equilibrium.

stability, we require that its derivative evaluated at this equilibrium is negative.

From equations (4.13) and (4.15) it follows that this derivative is given by the expression

$$\tau_g = \Theta \{[\alpha_1(1-a_2)m_1 + \alpha_2]/[(1-s)(1-a_2)m_1 + s] - 1\}. \tag{4.16}$$

This will be negative if

$$(1-s)(1-a_2)m_1 + s > \alpha_1(1-a_2)m_1 + \alpha_2 \tag{4.17}$$

and positive if this inequality is reversed. A rise in g raises the desired rate of accumulation by increasing the rate of capacity utilization (by equation (4.13)), through its effects on the firms' internal savings (the term involving α_1) and the direct effect of capacity utilization (α_3). If condition (4.17) is satisfied, the rise in g will be greater than the rise in g^d, and dg/dt will fall; otherwise it will increase. Condition (4.17) is thus the stability condition for long-run equilibrium.

It should be noted that the left-hand side of (4.17) shows the increase in the saving rate (or actual rate of accumulation, g) due to a change in the rate of capacity utilization (it is the denominator of equation (4.13), the reciprocal of which is du/dg at short-run equilibrium), while the right-hand side shows the change in the desired rate of investment (or desired rate of accumulation, g^d) due to a change in the rate of capacity utilization. This means that if inequality (4.17) is satisfied, the response of savings to the capacity utilization rate is greater than the response of investment. Thus the long-run stability condition is the usual macroeconomic stability condition (though it is usually a short-run stability condition) that saving is more responsive to changes in the relevant decision variable than is investment.

Figure 4.1, with a downward-sloping dg/dt curve represents the case of stable equilibrium at g^*, while Figure 4.2, with an upward-rising dg/dt curve, represents the unstable case.[14] Steindl described both cases informally. The instability portrayed in Figure 4.2 has to do with a divergence between the actual rate of capacity utilization and the desired rate of capacity utilization which, according to Steindl (1952, pp. 135, 137), *may* result in a downward or upward spiral in which a higher (lower) degree of capacity utilization results in a higher (lower) rate of investment which in turn leads to a higher (lower) rate of capacity utilization.[15]

Finally, we turn to the long-run effects of parametric changes. We confine our attention to the effects on the variable which interested Steindl, the long-rate of growth of capital, g^* (and output), in the case of the stable equilibrium of Figure 4.1. These effects can be found either by examining their effect on the dg/dt curve, noting that if it shifts it up (down) given g, we can conclude that g^* increases (decreases); or by using equations (4.13) and (4.15) at $dg/dt = 0$ to directly compute its value given by

$$g^* = (1/D)\{\alpha_0 - \alpha_1(1 - a_2)(m_2 + i) - \alpha_2 u_0 \tag{4.18}$$
$$+ [(\alpha_1(1 - a_2)m_1 + \alpha_2)(1 - s)(1 - a_2)(m_2 + i)]/[(1 - s)(1 - a_2)m_1 + s]\}$$

where

$$D = \{1 - [\alpha_1(1 - a_2)m_1 + \alpha_2]/[(1-s)(1 - a_2)m_1 + s]\}.$$

Steindl's primary concern was with the effects of increases in m_1 and u_0, which represented to him a rise in industrial concentration. In a Kaleckian manner, this would increase profit margins and hence m_1; moreover, if oligopolistic firms were more wary of excess capacity, u_0 would increase. From equation (4.18) it is obvious that $dg^*/du_0 < 0$: fear of excess capacity will reduce desired investment and the rate of growth of the economy. Concerning dg^*/dm_1 it can be shown by differentiating (4.18) that its sign depends on the sign of the expression

$$A = \alpha_1 s - (1 - s)\alpha_2.$$

A rise in the profit margin has two contradictory effects: it increases the internal savings of firms and raises their desired rate of accumulation through the second term of the investment function (1), while by redistributing income away from households it reduces consumption demand, capacity utilization and the desired rate of investment through the third term of the investment function. Since the strength of the first effect depends on α_1 while that of the second depends on α_2, a large α_2 relative to α_1 will make A negative, and therefore reduce the rate of growth.[16] It may be noted that a lower value of s increases the depressive effect on demand of the income redistribution away from households, and increases the chances of $dg^*/dm_1 < 0$. This is the case in which Steindl's result that a rise in concentration reduces the long-run rate of growth is obtained; it is not a certainty.

It can also be seen from (4.18) that $dg^*/d\alpha_0 > 0$, that is, a rise in autonomous investment raises desired investment both directly and through the multiplier effects on internal saving and capacity utilization. The signs of dg^*/dm_2 and dg^*/di are seen to depend on A. If $A < 0$, which is Steindl's case in which $dg^*/dm_1 < 0$, both these derivatives are positive: the negative effects of higher payments to households due to interest payments and payments to overhead labor are more than offset by the positive, demand creating, effects of these payments.[17]

The effects of the remaining parametric changes are best seen by examining the effect on the dg/dt curve. A rise in s reduces the short-run equilibrium value of u, as seen above, and thus shifts the dg/dt curve down; thus $dg^*/ds < 0$. The paradox of thrift prevails, and the long-run effect on u is greater than in the short run because of the fall in g over time. The sign of $dg^*/d\alpha_1$ is positive if $m_1 u - (m_2 + i) > 0$ at long-run equilibrium; since this expression is positive if the gross rate of profit exceeds the interest rate, which we may assume to be the case in long-run equilibrium, the effect of a higher responsiveness of desired investment to internal saving by firms is positive. The sign of $dg^*/d\alpha_2$ depends on the sign of $(u - u_0)$ at long-run equilibrium; if unplanned excess capacity persists at long-run equilibrium, $dg^*/d\alpha_2 > 0$. Finally, it can be shown that the sign of dg^*/da_2 is equal to the sign of the expression $-[g^*m_1 - s(m_2 + i)]A$. It can be shown that if firms have a non-zero share of total capital in long-run equilibrium, $g^*m_1 > s(m_2 + i)$. Thus, in the case in which $A < 0$, we have $dg^*/da_2 < 0$: a higher dividend rate, by redistributing income to households, will increase aggregate demand, capacity utilization, and the rate of growth.

The relevance of Steindl's theory

Having provided a formalization of Steindl's model of growth and his theory of stagnation, I now turn to the issue of its current relevance. Steindl (1976, p. ix) has noted that the atmosphere of confidence following the publication of his book has ended, and "the worms have been creeping out of the welfare state", and this may make his analysis more appealing now. However, Steindl (1989, p. 166) writes that

> after 1975 I was sometimes commended for having shown foresight. This made me smile because, on the one hand, I did not think that the experience of post-war prosperity had necessarily disproved my ideas, on the other hand, I did not think that these ideas were directly applicable to the new problems of the seventies.

Nevertheless, Steindl (1979, pp. 107–108]) appears to believe that his theoretical apparatus can serve in dealing with the problems of the post-war scene. How relevant is Steindl's analysis today?

To examine this question I will proceed in four stages. First, I will consider the nature of Steindl's contribution, as reflected in the model of the previous section; we need a clear idea of the precise nature of this contribution to assess its current relevance. Second, I will discuss an issue regarding the internal consistency of Steindl's analysis: if it is internally inconsistent it is never relevant. Third, I will discuss the factors left out of Steindl's analysis which are relevant in the discussion of current economic problems; since Steindl himself has discussed this issue in his subsequent work, I will make that the basis of my comments. Finally, I will argue that the omitted factors do not render Steindl's model and insights useless; in fact, his theoretical framework can be used as a basis for incorporating these features. Some work along these directions has already been done, and I will provide a selective survey to provide a flavor of this work.

The nature of Steindl's contribution

What is the main contribution of Steindl's model? Though Steindl's main purpose was the practical one of providing an explanation of stagnation in the US, I submit that his main theoretical contribution was the development of a model of growth and distribution in which a shift towards profits may lead to a lower rate of growth: provided that the relevant condition is met, a rise in m_1, in his model, leads to a fall in g. While this possibility had been recognized by Marx and other underconsumptionists (see Bleaney 1976), and Steindl clearly recognized Marx's and Sweezy's contributions (see Steindl 1952, pp. 243–246), this was the first formal demonstration of the proposition. And being formal, it made clear what assumptions were responsible for the result.

To further assess the precise nature of Steindl's contribution, it may be noted that features of the model responsible for this result are: (1) that the economy has excess capacity; (2) that changes in income distribution brought about by changes in monopoly power change the overall propensity to spend on goods; and (3) that the desired rate of accumulation depends positively on the rate of capacity utilization.[18] Features (1) and (2) were parts of Kalecki's (1971) models. Feature (1) entered Kalecki's model because he assumed that oligopolistic firms responded to a fall in demand by reducing output while maintaining a stable mark-up. Feature (2) was introduced by Kalecki's assumption that workers consumed what they earned while a fraction of profits was saved. These two features of Kalecki's model led him to the conclusion that a shift in income to workers adds to aggregate demand and raises the rate of capacity utilization. Steindl did not, in his 1952 model, focus on the distinction between workers and capitalists within households, his feature (2) coming out of the distinction between firms on one hand, who saved all their income, and households on the other, who saved and consumed. However, in later models, Steindl (1979, 1989) used Kalecki's worker–capitalist distinction rather than his firm–household distinction. Feature (3) was not quite new in Steindl either. It was, for instance, assumed by Hicks (1937) and Kaldor (1940), who made investment depend on income or output, which function, if taken to be linear and divided by the level of capital stock, imply that investment as a ratio of capital stock depends on the rate of capacity utilization. What was new in Steindl, however, was: first, a detailed analysis of why investment depended on the rate of capacity utilization (see Steindl 1952, pp. 12–13, Chap. X) and the assertion that capacity utilization had a separate effect on investment, *independent* of any effect on profits (in contrast with Kaldor's views[19]) and second, and most importantly, an analysis of the implications of bringing the three features together – that a redistribution to low-consuming groups would depress the rate of capacity utilization *and* the rate of growth.[20]

This aspect of Steindl's work has recently inspired a growing literature on the implications of a higher real wage for the rate of growth of the economy. Rowthorn (1981), Dutt (1982, 1984) and Taylor (1983) have developed Steindl-inspired models with different saving propensities for workers and capitalists, and with investment depending on the rate of profit and the rate of capacity utilization, and the models show unambiguously (because of the assumption about the investment function) that a rise in the real wage (or a fall in profit income) increases the rate of growth.[21] Dutt (1990) contrasts a Kalecki–Steindl model with this property with alternative neoclassical, neo-Marxian and neo-Keynesian models. These results have not only been argued to be relevant for advanced mature economies, for which Steindl's work was originally intended, but also for developing semi-industrialized countries (see Dutt 1982, 1984; Taylor, 1983, 1988).

The unambiguous result has been criticized by Bhaduri and Marglin (1990) who use an investment function which makes investment depend on the rate of capacity utilization and the profit share (rather than the rate of profit) to show that the rate of growth can respond positively or negatively to the wage rate. It should be noted that in Steindl's own model a shift away from profits does not unambiguously increase the rate of growth of the economy, because of the presence of internal firm savings as a determinant of investment. Steindl's contribution was not to show that growth *must* rise with a fall in the profit share, but to show that this *may* occur. Bhaduri and Marglin, however, have provided a detailed taxonomy of the different types of responses, shown under what conditions a rise in wages in the Steindlian framework leads to (for instance) wage-led growth or profit-squeeze effects, and thus opened up way for richer variety of outcomes than existed in Steindl-inspired models.

The problem of internal consistency

One central feature of Steindl's model is that in long-run equilibrium the economy can have excess capacity determined by the demand for goods. Several authors (see Auerbach and Skott 1988; Committeri 1986) have recently argued that while this result may be acceptable for the short run, in the long run it is more appropriate to assume that the actual rate of capacity utilization is equal to the level planned or desired by firms, that is, u_0 in Steindl's notation. In Steindl's model, u is not necessarily equal to u_0 in long-run equilibrium. The importance of this should be obvious: since an increase profit margins reduces the long-run rate of growth by reducing the degree of capacity utilization, if the latter is not allowed to fall but held constant at some exogenously given level u_0, the result will not be obtained.[22]

To consider whether this leads to an inconsistency in the Steindlian approach, however, we have to examine what possible mechanisms there are of getting u in line with u_0. Steindl discusses two. The first is that firms, if they find that actual capacity utilization is less than what they plan, will slow down their rate of capacity creation (Steindl 1952, p. 12). This type of adjustment has already been incorporated into Steindl's investment function through the terms α_2. Moreover, if there were any further adjustment along these lines, the lower level of investment would in fact reduce u by reducing aggregate demand, and take u further away from u_0, not closer to it. The result would be the same as that shown in the case of the unstable long-run equilibrium in the model of Figure 4.2, akin to Harrod's knife edge (Steindl 1979, p. 116).

The second mechanism relates to changes in the profit margin, m_1. Excess capacity in firms can lead to price-cutting by them, which, as a result of price competition between firms which drives out firms with higher costs, requires the reduction of the average profit margin (see Steindl 1952, chap. V, pp. 134–135; Steindl 1979, p. 115]). The lower profit margin in the short run, as seen above, will increase the rate of capacity utilization, and push it closer to u_0. While this process may work in theory,[23] Steindl (1952, pp. 135–137) argues that in an oligopolistic environment where the forces of competition are blunted, it will not occur due to the downward inelasticity of profit margins, and it is precisely this that led him to assume a constant m_1 in his model of chapter XIII. He repeated this argument several times later on in Steindl (1979, p. 116; 1985a, pp. 158–159; 1989, p. 173). For instance, in Steindl (1989), he writes that the adjustment through changes in profit margins "to a change in growth does not work in our modern economy and has not worked already for a long time, because cut-throat competition among giant firms is exceedingly dangerous and costly. The elimination of excess capacity by competition does not work."

Moreover, in an oligopolistic environment in situations in which capacity utilization is high and the rate of growth is high as well, existing firms may keep profit margins low to discourage prospective entrants from entering the market because of buoyant conditions.[24] Further determinants of profit margins not discussed by Steindl may also imply that greater excess capacity is associated with *higher* profit margins, not lower, as required in the adjustment mechanism mentioned above. As Kalecki writes, firms might adjust for higher fixed costs by raising their mark-up: since with high excess capacity fixed costs per unit will be greater, this will imply higher mark-ups with lower capacity utilization. Moreover, as Kalecki also discusses, the mark-up will be affected by conditions in the labor market (more of which below). If a higher level of excess capacity is associated with a higher rate of unemployment which makes the position of workers *vis-à-vis* firms weaker, the mark-up may rise as a result of greater excess capacity. Thus, in an oligopolistic environment, even this competitive mechanism will not necessarily lead actual capacity utilization to its planned level in the long run.

The position of the critics is perhaps strengthened by an unwise choice of words: the fact that Steindl calls u_0 the planned rate of capacity utilization, and this name seems to suggest that if actual capacity utilization is not equal to the rate planned by firms, the latter will adjust their behavior, so that we cannot have a long-run equilibrium. If instead we assume that firms simply follow the rule of thumb of reducing investment when, other things constant, greater excess capacity exists, then the problem does not appear to be so great. If we do think in terms of a planned rate of capacity utilization, if we take into account the fact that in an uncertain environment firms do not have a precise level of planned utilization, but a broad band within which they operate, then we can have capacity utilization be endogenously determined by demand conditions as in the model, at least within that band (see Dutt 1990).[25] Thus, there is no necessary inconsistency in the Steindlian framework.

Omissions from Steindl's model

Steindl's model was developed to explain stagnation in the US economy in the 1930s (and latent stagnation earlier) and he incorporated only factors he considered important in that particular context. As Steindl himself has noted, this analysis left out many issues of great current importance; this makes it inappropriate to apply his theory to the more recent phase of stagnation (Steindl 1981, pp. 137–138; 1989, p. 177).

First, Steindl's analysis did not incorporate the labor market. Steindl (1981, pp. 137–138; 1985a, p. 156; 1989, p. 176) has noted the effects of changing conditions in the labor market. A movement towards full employment and the resultant 'wage drift' has counteracted any possible tendency towards a rise in profit margins due to rising industrial concentration.

Second, Steindl did not discuss fiscal issues in detail, only pointing out that a rise in the fiscal deficit has the same effect as a rise in autonomous investment expenditure. He also did not enter into the political economy of the role of the state. His later discussion of post-war events draws a great deal on political-economy aspects, explaining the post-war boom as consequence of state spending on armaments due to superpower conflict and state policy to stabilize the economy due to fears of recession, and holds the state to be largely responsible for recent recessions, due to the reduction in superpower rivalry, and business opposition to full employment policies *à la* Kalecki (Steindl 1979, pp. 118–126). He thus talks of "stagnation policy" rather than "stagnation theory".

Third, he abstracted from open economy issues. Steindl (1981, p. 137; 1989, p. 176) discusses the fact that the tendency to increase the profit function (that is, an increase in m_1) has been offset by foreign competition due to trade liberalization.

Fourth, the model developed earlier abstracted from financial issues, taking the interest rate to be given, and abstracting from issues raised by debt financing by firms. Here Steindl is less guilty than he is for the omissions already noted. His model of Chapter XIII, as mentioned above, assumed that investment depended positively on the share of total capital owned by firms, thereby making investment depend negatively on debt. The model thus could exhibit another kind of instability which was not present in the model discussed above, due to a discrepancy between the gearing ratio desired by firms and the actual gearing ratio. Thus even with investment response to changes in capacity utilization weaker than saving response, the economy could (for instance) descend on a downward spiral with a high level of debt which reduces investment which further increases the relative indebtedness of firms due to the high response of internal saving to lower incomes (see Dutt 1995). Steindl used such financial factors to explain post-war experience: he explained (see Steindl 1989, pp. 174–175) low indebtedness on the part of firms after the war to explain high rates of investment then. But he also went further, explaining (see Steindl 1989, pp. 177–178) the more recent stagnation in terms of a greater interest of large firms with new management structures in financial investments (mergers, takeovers, speculation), thereby weakening the incentives for productive investment, an idea not clearly incorporated in his earlier model.

Fifth, his model abstracted from the role of technological change. The reason, as he makes clear, is that he wanted an *endogenous* theory of stagnation, not one that relied on some exogenous mechanism such as the drying-up of technological progress (see Steindl 1952, pp. 132–133). He thus says that "technological innovations accompany the process of investment like a shadow, they do not act on it as a propelling force" (Steindl 1952, p. 133). Later, especially as a result of his subsequent work on technological progress, he admitted (see Steindl 1976, p. xii; 1979, p. 117) that his model foolishly de-emphasized the role of technological change (though still not admitting the technological wave explanation to be a correct substitute for his explanation). He attributed rapid growth in Western Europe to technological innovation due to technology transfer from the US (Steindl 1979, p. 118). But he also recognized the labor-displacing role of technological change (Steindl 1985b, pp. 231–234) in an economy which could not absorb the increased potential output.

Incorporating omitted issues in Steindl's model

I now turn to how these and other omissions in Steindl's model may and indeed, in some cases, have been rectified. I first consider some general issues, and then comment on the application of Steindl's approach to developing economies. This discussion is not intended to be a complete survey of models in a Steindlian tradition, but rather, to be a selective review to suggest how the Steindlian framework and results can be extended to take account some of the issues which he omitted.[26] Nor is this discussion intended to show how the model explains specific issues of contemporary reality; it merely explores some theoretical issues which are of current relevance.

As Steindl has noted, the profit margin should reflect not only competition among firms, but also the conflict between workers and capitalist firms. One role of this, as already noted above, is to make it difficult for the economy to have a self-correcting mechanism which takes actual capacity utilization to the level planned by firms. Another role is to introduce inflation in the model due to conflicting claims (see Taylor 1983, 1991; Dutt 1990): as argued in Dutt (1990), if firms push up prices when they fail to attain their targeted markup (based on conditions of industrial structure) and wage bargaining pushes up the money wage when workers fail to reach their targeted real wage, we obtain a model in which in equilibrium inflation results due to conflict, and this endogenously determines distribution and the rate of growth. In this framework, greater industrial concentration can not only reduce the growth rate, but also increase inflation (thus causing stagflation), and greater worker strength may increase the rate of inflation and the rate of growth. Dutt (1992a) has built on this framework by endogenizing the targets of workers and firms, making them depend on conditions in the labor and goods markets, respectively, and shown that a Steindlian downward spiral is possible, with worsening income distribution and stagnation, but the economy may also be in a stable zone, experiencing (possibly) cyclical growth.

Fiscal issues have been incorporated into his analysis by Steindl (1979, pp. 113–114; 1985a, pp. 160–161) himself. One important result of this analysis is that even with a balanced budget, greater taxation of profits (which is used to finance either government expenditure or tax-reductions for workers) will lead to a multiplier effect on output, raising aggregate demand by redistributing income from capitalists who save a part of their income, to groups that spend all of it. Thus, the rate of growth of the economy will be increased. This is what Steindl argued to be the case during the expansion of the 1950s and the 1960s. In Steindl (1985a, pp. 159–161]) he also formally examined the implications of introducing a linear government budget surplus equation which makes the surplus depend positively (due to taxes) on Y and negatively on capacity, K, in our notation, in a model like the one discussed above, and showed that the negative effects on u of a rise in m_1 would be mitigated by this modification due to the presence of the tax coefficient. While political-economy aspects relating to the government's behavior and its relation to the capitalist class are difficult to formalize, there is no difficulty in using the model with these amendments to examine the implications of changes in political conditions for fiscal policy, and hence for growth. The model, however, still needs to be modified to consider the effects of changes in the government's debt.[27]

Open economy considerations have been introduced into Steindlian models by several writers.[28] Dutt (1984) argues that a higher degree of monopoly, by raising markups and the price, may make the domestic good less competitive in foreign markets, and thereby accentuate the retarding effects of a rise in monopoly power. In economies in which intermediate imports which enter into prime costs on which firms set markups, however, an increase in the profit margin may in fact have an opposite effect. Blecker (1989) has taken account of the fact that the markup will depend on competitiveness, in line with Steindl's suggestion noted above: the markup is endogenous in the model, depending both on an exogenously-given target markup and competitiveness. With this modification, a fall in the targeted markup, or alternatively, a rise in the money wage may, but need not necessarily, imply an increase in the economy's growth rate. Blecker discusses conditions under which each case is more likely.

Regarding financial issues, as already noted, Steindl himself had a lot to say. However, it is fair to say that he did not adequately distinguish between borrowing *per se* and equity financing in an adequate manner perhaps because, following Kalecki's (1971, pp. 107–109) discussion on the principle of increasing risk, he believed the dilution of earnings with new equity to be as threatening to existing shareholders as the issuance of debt. He also neglected to take into account the effects of endogenous changes in the interest rate (perhaps responding to conditions in bond markets, or to the behavior of banks), and of its effects on spending in an adequate manner (since he did not distinguish between workers and rentiers).[29] However, these issues have begun to be introduced into Steindlian models. Taylor (1991) has modelled asset markets using a Tobin-type portfolio approach, and has shown how the real side of the economy can interact with the financial side to cause financial crises. Dutt (1992c) has distinguished between rentiers, workers, and capitalists, to show how rentier domination (in the sense of a greater rentier share in the economy's capital) can go hand in hand with worsening income distribution and stagnation if rentiers have a higher saving propensity than capitalists, and *a fortiori*, workers.

On technological change, Rowthorn (1981), Dutt (1990) and Lavoie (1992) have considered technological change in Steindlian models. These models have shown that labor-saving technological change can have a variety of effects on the economy, and effects on labor markets, industrial concentration, and aggregate demand have all to be taken into account. Since technological change displaces labor and, given the growth of labor supply, can increase unemployment, it can cause profit margins to increase and possibly reduce the rate of growth along Steindlian lines. Moreover, technological change, if concentrated in larger firms with greater internal resources (as argued by Steindl 1952, Chap. V), may lead to greater concentration and therefore higher profit margins, again possibly reduce the rate of growth. But if technological change increases investment spending (unlike what was argued initially by Steindl, but later acknowledged by him – see Steindl 1981, pp. 135–136), it may, but need not, counter the above effects and raise the rate of growth of the economy. It should also be noted that allowing technological change to play a role in such models does not imply that we are introducing an exogenous determinant of growth (as claimed by Steindl 1952), since technological change can be endogenized (see Dutt 1992b; You 1992) in Steindlian models.

Finally, I turn to developing countries. The application of Steindl's theory to these countries will appear somewhat of a surprise because Steindl's theory is a theory of mature capitalism.[30] However, effective demand considerations have increasingly begun to play a more important role in the discussion of growth constraints in semi-industrialized less developed economies (see Dutt 1982, 1984; Rakshit 1982; Taylor 1983) and this, in principle, provides a role for the Steindlian growth model for these economies. However, less developed countries often have structures very different from those of advanced mature economies, and growth models for these economies have to take into account important issues which are often not very relevant for advanced economies. For instance, many such economies have large agricultural sectors for which it is inappropriate to assume that prices are set in oligopolistic markets, and they are often constrained by the availability of foreign exchange (see Taylor 1983). Consider the case of economies with a large agricultural sector which is flexprice. In such economies a reduction in profit margins due can redistribute income to workers, and raise the demand for agricultural goods (food) sufficiently to raise its price and squeeze the demand for non-agricultural goods, thereby reducing the rate of growth of that sector. However, Steindlian results can also hold if in the long run agricultural growth is determined by government investment in infrastructure which is financed by tax revenues from the industrial sector; not only may reductions in monopoly power in non-agriculture speed up growth, but land reforms changing agricultural income distribution will have the same effect (see Dutt 1991). On the issue of imports and foreign exchange, if capitalists have a higher propensity to import (luxury goods) than do workers, a shift towards workers will not only add to aggregate demand and thus increase growth rates if sufficient foreign exchange is available (or its use can be economized), but may actually make the economy less dependent on imports and thus conserve foreign exchange (see Dutt 1984).

Conclusion

This chapter has argued that in his 1952 book, *Maturity and Stagnation in American Capitalism*, Steindl developed an extremely useful analytical model of growth and distribution in capitalist economies. Though this work has largely been ignored by the profession, it deserves much more attention than it has been given so far.

To make this argument the chapter has first developed a simple model capturing some central aspects of Steindl's theoretical framework. It has then argued that Steindl's main analytical contribution (as opposed to his particular explanation of stagnation in American capitalism) was to develop a growth model in which it is possible for a shift in income distribution towards profits to reduce the rate of growth of the economy in the long run, thus making it possible for greater equity to go hand in hand with faster growth. It has also argued that there such a model is not internally inconsistent. Finally, it has shown that although Steindl's model ignored many features of contemporary reality – a fact noted by Steindl in his subsequent writings – his original model can be extended in various ways to incorporate these missing elements: this is suggested by an examination of some recent work in the Steindlian tradition. Thus, Steindl's work, over fifty years after its publication, provides us with a valuable analytical basis with which to examine the dynamics of capitalist economies, both advanced and less developed.

Acknowledgments

I am grateful to Tracy Mott and an anonymous referee for their useful comments on an earlier draft.

Notes

1 Page references to Steindl (1952) are to those of the 1976 edition. Page references to Steindl's works other than those to Steindl (1952, 1976) are to the pages in Steindl (1990) and not to the pages in their original sources.
2 During the post-war period there was a rapid growth of the subject of development economics which was concerned with the problem of stagnation in less-developed economies. Since the concern here was with stagnation in *backward* economies, and not with the question of stagnation in *mature*, *advanced* economies, Steindl's work at the time (to the best of my knowledge) received no attention from development economists. As we shall see later, this situation has changed in recent years.
3 Kalecki is cited in the book more than any other economist, with the possible exception of Marx. On Kalecki's influence on Steindl, see Steindl (1984, pp. 245–246). Kalecki himself did not, at least until recently, fare a much better fate than Steindl.
4 See, for instance, Baran (1957), Baran and Sweezy (1966).
5 I will later discuss some recent contributions which have been influenced by Steindl's book.

6 This is not to argue that theoretical models and practical policy issues should be separated, but that theoretical work which responds to a policy problem may have relevance in other contexts as well. Steindl (1984, p. 251) has argued very strongly that "we go back to the great tradition of the classics, Kalecki and Keynes, whose work was rooted in the economic policy problems of their time, and derived its relevance from them. They asked what should be done and how. Economic policy is the main inspiration of economic theory."

7 This treatment follows, for instance, Gandolfo (1980) and Jarsulic (1988).

8 For an analysis of a model which incorporates this aspect of Steindl's work, see Dutt (1995).

9 Steindl (1952, pp. 54–55, 66–69, 124–127) has some discussion of two-sector complications in which one sector is oligopolistic and the other is not, to discuss the issue of the maldistribution of savings. He admits that intersectoral issues play no part in his analysis of stagnation due to the growth of oligopolies in a later introduction to the book (see Steindl, 1976, p. xv). Steindl (1989) develops a multisector model, but leaves the sectoral allocations unexplained, the multi-sector complications playing no real role in the analysis. For two-sector models along Steindlian lines, see Dutt (1990, Chap. 6).

10 Steindl's formulation had another term in the investment function, that is, $\alpha_3[(K_f/K)-k_0]$, where $\alpha_3 > 0$ is a parameter, where K_f is the stock of capital internally owned by firms, and where k_0 the neutral reciprocal gearing ratio of firms (that is, the ratio of the stock of own capital to total capital which makes this term involving α_3 disappear). In what follows I abstract from the effects of changes in the ratio K_f/K.

11 Steindl has an extended discussion of the role of stocks and share issue (see Steindl 1952, pp. 142–155), and the relevance of the latter in slowing down the rate of decline of the US economy. However, in the development of the formal model, share issue is formalized essentially as affecting the autonomous part of investment; that is, in increasing α_0 in terms of our notation (see Steindl 1952, p. 211). In this presentation we gloss over the implications of explicitly distinguishing between stocks and bonds, and of introducing share issue into the analysis.

12 The model also does not distinguish amongst households between rentiers who receive interest income and workers who only earn wage income. If the former of these two groups had a higher savings propensity and if the change in the rate of interest changed the distribution of income between them (by reducing the real wage as firms push up their markup rates), the rise in the rate of interest could have a further negative effect on u.

13 The more general case, in which it is likely that $i > a_1$, implies that dg/dt depends also on k. In this case we would need to also consider how k moves over time; we would therefore obtain a two-dimensional system. This would also be the case if desired investment depended on k. Dutt (1995) analyses a two-dimensional dynamic system using phase diagrams.

14 It is assumed that there is enough excess capacity in the economy to prevent it from hitting the full capacity barrier unless it experiences an upward spiral in the unstable case. Given our assumption that $a_1 = i$, it is obvious from (4.13) that u depends only on g and the parameters of the system. Since u rises with g, given the values of the parameters, there will be some value of g_{max}, at which the maximum technologically-possible capacity utilization, u_{max}, which is assumed to be exogenously given, will be reached. We assume that the economy always operates to the left of g_{max} in the stable case of Figure 4.1. In the unstable case, even if $g^* < g_{max}$, if the economy starts from $g > g^*$, the full capacity constraint will. If it hits this full capacity constraint, this model will cease to apply.

15 Another type of instability, relating to a divergence between the firms' desired gearing ratio and the actual gearing ratio (see Steindl 1952, pp. 112–121), cannot be discussed in this model because of our assumption that g^d does not depend on k. But see Dutt (1993).

16 The question would of course have to be settled empirically. For an estimation of these parameters for the US manufacturing sector, see Fazzari and Mott (1986–7).

17 It should be noted that since we assume that $a_1 = i$, the rise in i is accompanied by a rise in a_1, a dividend rule parameter. If a_1 is held constant, less would be redistributed to households, weakening the positive interest effect. See also the comment made above in the text regarding the short-run effect of the change in the rate of interest rate, which applies here as well.

18 All three are required for the result that a rise in m_1 will reduce the rate of growth; only the first two are required for the result that a rise in u_0 will reduce the rate of growth.

19 See Kaldor (1940), footnote 3. Hicks (1937) made the assumption for mathematical completeness (since saving also depended on income).

20 It may be noted that while Kalecki examined the implications of a rise in the markup for the rate of capacity utilization, since his investment equation did not have capacity utilization as a separate variables (he stressed internal savings and changes in profits, among other things), he did not clearly point out the effect on the rate of growth.

21 The models assume away lags in investment spending, in effect assuming that $g = g^d$; the formulation in the present chapter which allows for lags allows a clear analysis of short- and long-run factors at work. The result regarding the relation between growth and distribution is valid as long as excess capacity exists in the economy; when full capacity utilization exists and it is no longer possible for output to increase with a given stock of capital, a higher growth rate requires a lower wage and a higher profit share.

22 See also the discussion of this issue by Lavoie (1992, pp. 327–332).

23 But see Lavoie (1992, pp. 417–421) for an analysis of the difficulties that this process may encounter in a model of conflict inflation in which firms cannot unilaterally fix their profit margins.

24 See Rotemberg and Saloner (1986). Steindl (1952) also recognized that firms would keep profit margins low to discourage entry, as in limit-pricing models.

25 Critics (see Committeri, 1986) have suggested that the constant term in the investment function should be the expected rate of growth in sales and the second term should be a reflection of the gap between planned and actual capacity utilization, and then argue that since in long-run equilibrium actual and expected growth in sales should be equal, planned and actual capacity utilization should also be equal. Aside from the problems already discussed, they overlook the fact that there may be other determinants of investment, such as internal saving and the gearing ratio. Taking these other determinants into account undermines this argument, even if the constant term should be interpreted as the expected growth in sales. Endogenizing the planned capacity utilization rate can also undermine the argument; see Lavoie (1994) and Dutt (1997).

26 In view of the above discussion, a Steindlian model will be taken to be a model which allows for excess capacity to exist in equilibrium, and which, because of differential saving propensities of different income groups, a shift towards profits *may* reduce the economy's rate of growth.

27 You and Dutt (1997) deals with this issue.

28 Steindl himself modified his model (see Steindl 1985a, pp. 159–161) in a simple way to make the trade surplus depend positively on capacity and negatively

(due to imports) on income (using a linear equation) to find that in the short run, a rise in m_1 has a smaller negative effect on u than without this complication, due to the presence of the import coefficient.

29 In joint work with Amit Bhaduri (see Bhaduri and Steindl, 1985), however, he did discuss the role of rentiers and how changes in their political clout could affect the interest rate.

30 It may be noted, though, that Kalecki (1976) did apply some of his ideas of monopoly power and mark-up pricing to the study of the industrial sectors of less-developed economies. Though some versions of his work on financing economic development in these economies did allow for excess capacity in industry and the possibility of quantity adjustments, Kalecki mostly assumed full capacity utilization and market clearing through government fiscal policy parameters.

References

Auerbach, Paul and Skott, Peter (1988) "Concentration, Competition and Distribution: A Critique of Theories of Monopoly capital", *International Review of Applied Economics*, 2, 42–61.

Baran, Paul A. (1957) *The Political Economy of Growth*, New York: Monthly Review Press.

Baran, Paul A. and Sweezy, Paul M. (1966) *Monopoly Capital: An Essay on the American Economic and Social Order*, New York: Monthly Review Press.

Bhaduri, Amit and Marglin, Stephen A. (1990) "Unemployment and the Real Wage: The Economic Basis for Contesting Political Ideologies", *Cambridge Journal of Economics*, 14(4), December, 375–393.

Bhaduri, Amit and Steindl, Josef (1985) "The Rise of Monetarism as a Social Doctrine", in P. Arestis and T. Skouras (eds), *Post Keynesian Economic Theory. A Challenge to Neo Classical Economics*, Armonk, NY: M. E. Sharpe.

Bleaney, M. F. (1976) *Underconsumption Theories: A History and Critical Analysis*, New York: International Publishers.

Blecker, Robert (1989) "International Competition, Income Distribution and Economic Growth", *Cambridge Journal of Economics*, 13(3), September, 395–412.

Committeri, Marco (1986) "Some Comments on Recent Contributions on Capital Accumulation, Income Distribution and Capacity Utilization", *Political Economy*, 2(2), 161–86.

Dutt, Amitava K. (1982) "Essays on Growth and Distribution of an Underdeveloped Economy", unpublished PhD dissertation, MIT.

Dutt, Amitava K. (1984) "Stagnation, Income Distribution and Monopoly Power", *Cambridge Journal of Economics*, 8(1), March, 25–40.

Dutt, Amitava K. (1990) *Growth, Distribution and Uneven Development*, Cambridge: Cambridge University Press.

Dutt, Amitava K. (1991) "Stagnation, Income Distribution and the Agrarian Constraint: A Note", *Cambridge Journal of Economics*, 13(3), September, 343–351.

Dutt, Amitava K. (1992a) "Conflict Inflation, Distribution, Cyclical Accumulation and Crises", *European Journal of Political Economy*, 8, 579–597.

Dutt, Amitava K. (1992b) "On the Dynamic Stability of Capitalist Economies", in A. K. Dutt (ed.), *New Directions in Analytical Political Economy*, Aldershot: Edward Elgar.

Dutt, Amitava K. (1992c) "Rentiers in Post Keynesian Models", in P. Arestis and V. Chick (eds), *Recent Developments in Post-Keynesian Economics*, Aldershot: Edward Elgar.

Dutt, Amitava K. (1995) "Internal Finance and Monopoly Power in Capitalist Economies: A Reformulation of Steindl's Growth Model", *Metroeconomica*, 46(1), 16–34.

Dutt, Amitava K. (1997). "Equilibrium, path dependence and hysteresis in post-Keynesian models," in P. Arestis and M. Sawyer, eds, *Essays in Honour of G. C. Harcourt*, vol. 2, London: Routledge.

Fazzari, Steven M. and Mott, Tracy L. (1986–7) "The Investment Theories of Kalecki and Keynes: An Empirical Study of Firm Data, 1970–1982", *Journal of Post Keynesian Economics*, IX(2), Winter, 171–187.

Gandolfo, Giancarlo (1980) *Economic Dynamics: Methods and Models*, Amsterdam: North-Holland.

Hicks, John R. (1937) "Mr. Keynes and the Classics", *Econometrica*, April, reprinted in J. R. Hicks, *Money, Interest and Wages*, Cambridge, MA: Harvard University Press, 1982.

Jarsulic, Marc (1988) *Effective Demand and Income Distribution*, Cambridge: Polity Press.

Kaldor, Nicholas (1940) "A Model of the Trace Cycle", *Economic Journal*, March, reprinted in Nicholas Kaldor, *Essays on Economic Stability and Growth*, London: Duckworth, 1960.

Kalecki, Michał (1971) *Selected Essays on the Dynamics of the Capitalist Economy*, Cambridge: Cambridge University Press.

Kalecki, Michał (1976) *Essays on Developing Economies*, Brighton: Harvester.

Lavoie, Marc (1992) *Foundations of Post-Keynesian Economic Analysis*, Aldershot: Edward Elgar.

Lavoie, Marc (1995) "The Kaleckian model of growth and distribution and its neo-Ricardian and neo-Marxian critiques," *Cambridge Journal of Economics*, 19(6), 789–818.

Rakshit, Mihir (1982) *The Labour Surplus Economy. A Neo-Keynesian Approach*, Delhi: Macmillan.

Rotemberg, Julio and Saloner, Garth (1986) "A Supergame-Theoretic Model of Price Wars During Booms", *American Economic Review*, 76(3), June, 390–407.

Rowthorn, Robert E. (1981) "Demand, Real Wages and Economic Growth", *Thames Papers in Political Economy*, Autumn.

Steindl, Josef (1952) *Maturity and Stagnation in American Capitalism*, Oxford: Blackwell.

Steindl, Josef (1976) "Introduction", in *Maturity and Stagnation in American Capitalism*, with a new Introduction by the author, New York: Monthly Review Press.

Steindl, Josef (1979) "Stagnation Theory and Stagnation Policy", *Cambridge Journal of Economics*, 3(1), March, reprinted in Steindl (1990).

Steindl, Josef (1981) "Ideas and Concepts of Long Run Growth", *Banca Nazionale del Lavoro Quarterly Review*, no. 136, March, reprinted in J. Steindl (1990).

Steindl, Josef (1984) "Reflections on the Present State of Economics", *Banca Nazionale del Lavoro Quarterly Review*, no. 148, March, reprinted in J. Steindl (1990) *Economic Papers 1941–88*. New York: St. Martin's Press.

Steindl, Josef (1985a) "Distribution and Growth", *Political Economy – Studies in the Surplus Approach*, 1(1), reprinted in J. Steindl (1990) *Economic Papers 1941–88*. New York: St. Martin's Press.

Steindl, Josef (1985b) "Structural Problems in the Crisis", *Banca Nazionale del Lavoro Quarterly Review*, 154, September, reprinted in J. Steindl (1990) *Economic Papers 1941–88*. New York: St. Martin's Press.

Steindl, Josef (1989) "From Stagnation in the 30s to Slow Growth in the 70s", in M. Berg, ed., *Political Economy in the Twentieth Century*, Oxford, reprinted in J. Steindl (1990) *Economic Papers 1941–88*. New York: St. Martin's Press.

Steindl, Josef (1990) *Economic Papers 1941–88*, New York, St. Martin's Press.

Taylor, Lance (1983) *Structuralist Macroeconomics*, New York: Basic Books.

Taylor, Lance (1988) *Varieties of Stabilization Experience: Towards Sensible Macroeconomics in the Third World*, Oxford: Clarendon Press.

Taylor, Lance (1991) *Income Distribution, Inflation, and Growth*, Cambridge, MA: MIT Press.

You, Jong-Il (1992) "Endogenous Technical Change, Accumulation, and Distribution", in A. Dutt (ed.), *New Directions in Analytical Political Economy*, Aldershot: Edward Elgar.

You, Jong-Il and Dutt, Amitava K. (1996) "Government debt, income distribution and growth," *Cambridge Journal of Economics*, 20(3), 335–351.

5 On industry concentration and the transition to monopoly capitalism

A knife-edge model of "Steindlian" dynamics

Marcellus Andrews

Introduction

Steindl's *Maturity and Stagnation in American Capitalism* is a largely forgotten text among academic economists.[1] Yet, despite this neglect, *Maturity and Stagnation* remains an important work that can inspire new thinking about macrodynamics. When one rereads *Maturity and Stagnation*, it is clear that Steindl intended this work to supplant the dominant position of Marx's classically inspired analysis of class conflict, income distribution, and capital accumulation as propounded in Chapter 25 of Volume One of *Capital*. By presenting a macrodynamic theory based on "competition between capitals", Steindl hoped to explain economic stagnation as the consequence of the inevitable concentration of industry associated with capitalist development. This chapter attempts to formalize an aspect of Steindl's theory of capitalist development, namely, the macrodynamic consequences of the transition from a competitive market system to an oligopolistic system. Our goal in doing so is to explore the mechanisms that govern this transition in some detail, thereby gaining a better understanding of the conditions under which industrial concentration may lead to slower growth.

One result of Steindl's analysis of industry dynamics and capital accumulation has been the refinement of the theory of "monopoly capitalism" as an explanation of the internal limits to growth in unregulated market systems. In so doing, Steindl's work exposed the logical links between industrial change and capital accumulation that were implicit but undeveloped in *Capital*, thereby clearing the ground for a theory of growth and development based on the interaction between the functional distribution of income, industrial structure and effective demand. A model of industry dynamics and capital accumulation based on Steindl's work must, at a minimum, examine the relationship between concentration, pricing, the distribution of profits and sales between firms, and the effect of industry dynamics on aggregate capacity utilization and capital accumulation. This difficult set of interconnections plagued Steindl's own attempt to formalize his theory.[2] Nonetheless, a manageable formal model of industrial change and capital accumulation inspired by Steindl's work would be an aid to thinking about macrodynamics.

The model

Any attempt to construct a formal model of the transition from a competitive economy to an oligopolistic system on the basis of Steindl's analysis in *Maturity and Stagnation* is made difficult by the fact that the book contains two very different approaches to industry dynamics. The first approach in the first section of Chapter 5 under the heading "Pattern of Competition Within an Industry: The Case of an Industry with Plenty of Small Producers", presents an overview of competition in an industry characterized by cost differentials between dominant producers and smaller, fringe producers.[3] This section shows how differential growth rates between small and large firms leads to a gradual rise in the degree of industry concentration as larger firms expel less profitable fringe producers. However, the second part of Chapter 5, "The Case of an Industry Where Entry is Difficult", explores the case of an industry that is so highly concentrated that any attempt to engage in price competition among dominant enterprises is likely to be ruinous.[4] Steindl's own formal model is based on the assumption that the market has already reached maturity. Competition in a highly concentrated industry takes place through sales promotion, new product development, and other market expansion devices. In this setting, firm capacity utilization is largely determined by aggregate demand movements rather than by patterns of competition between large and small firms. Once industry concentration has gone beyond a certain point, firm and industry investment behavior responds more to anticipations of movements in aggregate demand (in line with an accelerator model of investment) than to the internal dynamics of competition and concentration within the industry.

By contrast, the model developed below studies the reciprocal interaction of industry dynamics and utilization dynamics at the aggregate level in shaping both macroeconomic evolution and structural change in light of Steindl's analysis of the transition from less to more concentrated industrial structures. In this analysis, firm pricing and investment behavior are driven by the competition for market share and profits within industry as much as by anticipations of market expansion related to the development of aggregate demand.

Industry structure

Firms in the economy produce a single composite good that can be used for either consumption or investment purposes, which implies that the prices of capital goods and consumption goods are identical. The population of firms in this economy is divided into two broad types of producers: a small number of large firms (collectively referred to as the dominant sector) that account for a substantial fraction of total output, and a large number of small firms (called the fringe sector) that supply the remainder of total output. The products of dominant sector and fringe firms are assumed to be very close substitutes, with the consequence that industry demand is divided between these two groups of firms in proportion to each sector's share of production capacity. Given dominant sector capacity (K), fringe sector capacity (x) and aggregate demand (Y), potential output in the economy is $K + x$, aggregate and firm capacity utilization rates are $u = Y/(K + x)$.[5] In addition, $\theta = K/(K + x)$ is the fraction of industry capacity controlled by dominant sector firms. Therefore θY and $(1 - \theta)Y$ are the levels of demand for dominant sector and fringe output, respectively.

Dominant firms jointly determine the price of output (p) on the basis of a markup ($\varphi > 1$) on unit costs (c) which are assumed to be identical across members of the dominant group.[6] Fringe firms are price takers that can produce up to their joint capacity (x) so long as the price of output exceeds fringe sector unit costs (c_x, where $c_x \gg c$). Assuming a common money wage rate (w) for all workers, and that labor is the only variable input in the short run, dominant and fringe firm unit costs of production are $c = w/b$ and $c_x = w(1 + \beta)/b$, respectively, where β ($\beta \gg 0$) is the productivity advantage of dominant sector firms over fringe producers, and b is the level of output per worker among dominant firms. Since dominant firms set the level of prices in the market for output, the level of real profit per

unit of output for dominant and fringe producers is $\left(\dfrac{\varphi - 1}{\varphi} = 1 - \dfrac{1}{\varphi} \right)$ and

$\left(1 - \dfrac{1 + \beta}{\varphi} \right)$, respectively. Further, the rate of profit for dominant and fringe

producers is the product of the level of real profits per unit of output and

the utilization rate for each type of firm i.e. $\rho^D = \left(1 - \dfrac{1}{\varphi} \right) u$ and

$\rho^F = \left(1 - \dfrac{1 + \beta}{\varphi} \right) u$ so that the level of real profits for dominant and fringe

sector producers can be represented by

Dominant firms: $\Pi^D = \rho^D K = \left(1 - \dfrac{1}{\varphi} \right) uK$, and

Fringe firms: $\Pi^F = \rho^F x = \left(1 - \dfrac{1 + \beta}{\varphi} \right) ux$.

Savings, investment and utilization

Savings

Workers are assumed to spend all of their income while capitalists do all saving. For simplicity we assume that the propensity to save out of profits $0 < s < 1$ is common to all firm owners. Given these assumptions, the level of real savings is

$$S = s\left(\Pi^D + \Pi^F\right) = s\left\{\left(1 - \frac{1}{\varphi}\right)uK + \left(1 - \frac{1+\beta}{\varphi}\right)ux\right\}.$$

The expression for aggregate saving can be rewritten as

$$S = s\left\{\left(1 - \frac{1}{\varphi}\right)\theta + \left(1 - \frac{1+\beta}{\varphi}\right)(1-\theta)\right\}u(K+x)$$

$$= \sigma(\theta,u)(K+x)$$

where

$$\left(1 - \frac{1}{\varphi}\right)\theta + \left(1 - \frac{1+\beta}{\varphi}\right)(1-\theta)$$

is the share of profits in national income and $\sigma(\theta, u)$ is a compact expression for the aggregate savings rate. Note that a rise in the fraction of industry capacity controlled by dominant sector firms (θ) raises savings by raising the share of profits in national income. Similarly, a rise in the markup also raises profit share.

Investment

Aggregate investment (I) is simply the sum of dominant sector firm investment (I_D) and fringe investment (I_F). Dominant sector investment is assumed to be positively related to the difference between rate of return on dominant sector capital (ρ^D) and the real rate of interest (r) according to a function of the form,

$$I^D = g^D K = G^D \max(0, \rho^D - r)K$$

where $g^D = G^D \max(0, \rho^D - r)$ is the rate of growth of capacity for dominant firms and $G^D > 0$ represents the sensitivity of dominant sector accumulation to net profit rates. We assume that fringe sector accumulation can be represented by

$$I^F = g^F x = G^F \max(0, \rho^F - r)x$$

with the additional assumption that fringe firm investment is (initially) more sensitive to net profit rates than dominant firm investment i.e. $G^F > G^D$.

Pricing and utilization

Firms in the dominant sector set the value of the mark-up in order to accomplish two distinct and to some extent incompatible purposes: (1) generate substantial net proceeds from the sale of products, including funds to finance future expansion and (2) control the pattern of competition in the industry by using prices to regulate the rate of growth of the fringe sector. The dominant sector is assumed to set the level of the mark-up at $\varphi_{max} > 1 + \beta$ if the rate of profit exceeds the real rate of interest on the assumption that the rate of return on production operations is better than the next best alternative.[7] If $\varphi_{max} > 1 + \beta$ then the dominant sector is permitting the fringe sector to earn positive profits by refraining from exploiting its cost advantage. However, dominant firms are assumed to cut the markup to $\varphi_{min} < 1 + \beta$ if the rate of profit is below the real rate of interest in order to expel a portion of fringe sector capacity, thereby raising the rate of capacity utilization and longer term dominant sector profit rates by pricing below fringe sector production costs. Note that if dominant sector profit rates are above the real rate of interest then

$$\rho^D - r = \left(1 - \frac{1}{\varphi_{max}}\right)u - r > 0 \text{ which implies that the utilization rate } (u)$$

exceeds a critical value $u^D = \dfrac{r\varphi_{max}}{\varphi_{max} - 1}$ with the consequence that we can

rewrite the dominant sector's pricing policy as

$$\varphi = \varphi_{max} \quad \text{if } u \geq u_{min}^D = \frac{r\varphi_{max}}{\varphi_{max} - 1}$$

$$\varphi = \varphi_{min} \quad \text{if } u < u_{min}^D = \frac{r\varphi_{max}}{\varphi_{max} - 1}.$$

In addition, the link between the aggregate capacity utilization rate and rates of dominant and fringe sector growth can be rewritten as

$$g_D = G_D\left[\left(1 - \frac{1}{\varphi_{max}}\right) - r\right]u \quad \text{if } u > u_{min}^D,$$

$$= 0 \quad \text{if } u \leq u_{min}^D$$

$$g_F = G_F\left[\left(1 - \frac{1+\beta}{\varphi_{max}}\right) - r\right]u \quad \text{if } u > u_{min}^F,$$

$$= 0 \quad \text{if } u \leq u_{min}^F$$

where $u_{min}^F = \dfrac{r\varphi_{max}}{\varphi_{max} - \beta - 1}$ is the critical value of the utilization rate for

fringe producers.

Dynamics

We have now assembled all of the building blocks for a two-dimensional model of industry development and medium-term aggregative dynamics. The evolution of the economy is represented by movements in the aggregate utilization rate (u) and the percentage of production capacity controlled by the dominant sector (θ). The movement in aggregate utilization rates is determined by the difference between the rate of growth of

aggregate demand $\left(\dfrac{\dot{Y}}{Y}\right)$ and the rate of growth of capacity

$$\frac{\dot{K} + \dot{x}}{K + x} = \theta g_D + (1-\theta)g_F - \delta$$

i.e.

$$\frac{\dot{u}}{u} = \frac{\dot{Y}}{Y} - \frac{\dot{K} + \dot{x}}{K + x} = \frac{\dot{Y}}{Y} - \theta g_D - (1-\theta)g_F + \delta$$

where $\delta > 0$ is the rate of depreciation of production capacity. Output growth is in turn driven by savings-imbalance (normalized by the level of aggregate production capacity, $K + x$) of a traditional Keynesian variety,[8]

$$\frac{\dot{Y}}{Y} = \lambda_Y \left[\frac{I}{K+x} - \frac{S}{K+x} \right]$$
$$= \lambda_Y [\theta g_D + (1-\theta)g_F - \sigma(\theta, u)]$$

where $0 < \lambda_Y < \infty$ is the speed of output adjustment.

Further, movements in the degree of dominant sector control of production capacity are driven by differences between dominant sector and fringe sector growth rates

$$\frac{\dot{\theta}}{\theta} = (1-\theta)(g_D - g_F).$$

The movement of the aggregate utilization rate and the degree of dominant sector control of capacity in (u, θ) phase space can be subdivided into three distinct regimes that depend on the level of capacity utilization. The structure of phase space in illustrated in Figure 5.1.

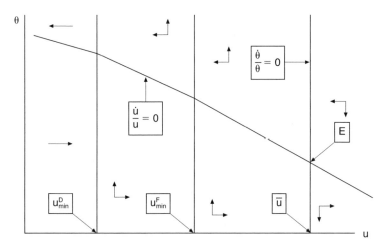

Figure 5.1 The phase space.

Regime I: $\varphi = \varphi_{max}$, $u > u^F_{min}$

The movement of the economy in this region of phase space is represented by the system

$$\frac{\dot{u}}{u} = \lambda_Y[\theta g_D + (1-\theta)g_F - \sigma(\theta, u)] - \theta g_D - (1-\theta)g_F + \delta$$

$$\frac{\dot{\theta}}{\theta} = (1-\theta)(g_D - g_F).$$

If the utilization rate exceeds the critical value u^F_{min} for fringe firms, then both types of enterprises are earning substantial profits. The steady state values of u and θ ($\bar{u}$, $\bar{\theta}$), represented by point E in Figure 5.1 in this region of phase space are defined by the conditions

$$g_D = g_F = g*$$

and

$$g* - \sigma(\bar{\theta}, \bar{u}) - \delta = 0.$$

The Jacobian associated with the steady state in regime I is

$$
J_I = \begin{bmatrix} j_{11}^I & j_{12}^I \\ j_{21}^I & j_{22}^I \end{bmatrix} = \begin{bmatrix} \dfrac{\partial\left(\dfrac{\dot{u}}{u}\right)}{\partial u} & \dfrac{\partial\left(\dfrac{\dot{u}}{u}\right)}{\partial\theta} \\[2em] \dfrac{\partial\left(\dfrac{\dot{\theta}}{\theta}\right)}{\partial u} & \dfrac{\partial\left(\dfrac{\dot{\theta}}{\theta}\right)}{\partial\theta} \end{bmatrix}
$$

which possesses the sign pattern $J_I = \begin{bmatrix} - & - \\ ? & 0 \end{bmatrix}$. (See Appendix for details about the elements of J_I.) The first element of J_I (j_{11}^I) is consistent with the usual structure of Keynesian dynamic models, i.e. where savings is assumed to be more responsive to changes in utilization rates than investment. The second element of J_I (j_{12}^I) says that a rise in the degree of dominant sector control of capacity raises the savings rate because dominant sector firms are more profitable than fringe firms, thereby putting downward pressure on utilization rate. The third element of J_I (j_{21}^I) has an ambiguous sign because of the relative responses of dominant and fringe sector accumulation rates to changes in utilization rates. Since dominant firms are more profitable than fringe firms (due to the technological edge associated with firm size), a rise in utilization rates will put downward pressure on θ if and only if the relationship between dominant and fringe firm responses to changes in net profits satisfies the condition (hereafter called the "fringe condition")

$$
\frac{\partial\left(\dfrac{\dot{\theta}}{\theta}\right)}{\partial u} = j_{21}^I = G_D\left(1 - \frac{1}{\varphi_{max}}\right) - G_F\left(1 - \frac{1+\beta}{\varphi_{max}}\right) > 0
$$

which can never hold so long as $\beta > 0$ and $G_F > G_D$. This means that so long as the accumulation plans of fringe firms are more sensitive to changes in net profit rates than those of dominant enterprises, then the steady state of the system is a saddlepoint. However, if the accumulation rates of dominant sector enterprises are much more responsive to changes in net profits than those of fringe firms (contrary to our initial assumption) then the fringe condition could be satisfied, which would mean that the steady state of the system would be either a stable node or a stable focus.

The dynamic consequences of whether the fringe condition is satisfied are rather important for our understanding of the effect of industry concentration on medium-term economic growth. On the one hand, a situation where the fringe condition is satisfied conveys the image of a highly responsive dominant sector in struggle with more reticent fringe firms, with large firms aggressively moving to grow when utilization rates rise but just as drastically scaling back growth plans when utilization rates fall. By contrast, fringe firms in this situation pursue a more measured approach to growth, responding less rapidly to fluctuations in utilization rates because they are more risk averse or just plain sluggish. The economy would be stabilized by rapid changes in the degree of dominant sector control of productive capacity that offset variations in aggregate capacity utilization, turning the "fringe" sector into the anchor of economic stability.

Yet, sluggishness is more likely to be a characteristic of large enterprises than small ones precisely because large firms with a technological edge have a greater margin of safety in an uncertain world compared to smaller firms that must seize every opportunity to grow and, conversely, be nimble enough to abandon their plans when circumstances are less favorable. Therefore, violation of the fringe condition suggests a world where dominant firms respond more slowly to variations in utilization rates than fringe firms, turning the dominant sector into a follower rather than a leader. In the event the economy experiences a positive shock that pushes the utilization rate above its steady state value in regime I, fringe firms quickly raise their growth rates above those of dominant sector firms, thereby creating a situation of positive investment-savings imbalance and subsequent increases in utilization rates as well as reducing dominant sector control of the economy. This pattern of growth will continue, so long as fringe firms are more responsive to changes in net profit rates (and therefore utilization rates) than dominant sector enterprises until, at the limit, dominant sector control of the economy is completely undermined ($\theta = 0$) and utilization rates are at their maximum ($u = 1$). Conversely, a negative economic shock will push utilization rates down as fringe firms curtail their investment plans, thereby leading to greater degrees of industry concentration. In this case, growing industry concentration shifts the center of gravity of capital accumulation from the responsive to the unresponsive sector with the consequence that slow growth is accompanied by even greater dominant sector control.

Regime II: $\varphi = \varphi_{max}, u^D_{min} < u < u^F_{min}$

The important question in this regime is whether growing dominant sector control of production capacity is associated with rising, falling, or steady utilization rates. The rate of return on fringe sector capital is below the real rate of interest, thereby discouraging fringe sector growth i.e. $g_F = 0$. The movement of the aggregate utilization rate is governed by

$$\frac{\dot{u}}{u} = \lambda_Y(\theta g_D - \sigma(\theta, u)) - \theta g_D + \delta.$$

However, the dominant sector continues to grow (albeit more slowly than in regime I given the lower aggregate utilization rate) so that dominant sector control of production capacity grows over time throughout regime II i.e. $\dfrac{\dot{\theta}}{\theta} = (1-\theta)g_D > 0$. Yet, a rise in dominant sector control has two opposing effects on the degree of investment-savings imbalance. On the one hand, a rise in θ increases the savings rate by redistributing profits away from fringe firms toward dominant producers (hereafter referred to as the savings effect). On the other hand, a rise in θ raises the rate of accumulation by increasing the weight of dominant sector growth in aggregate accumulation (hereafter called the accumulation effect). Note that the slope of the isocline associated with the $\dfrac{\dot{u}}{u} = 0$ locus,

$$\frac{d\theta}{du} = \frac{\partial\left(\dot{u}/u\right)\Big/\partial u}{\partial\left(\dot{u}/u\right)\Big/\partial\theta} = -\frac{\lambda_Y\left(\theta\dfrac{\partial g_D}{\partial u} - \sigma_u\right) - \theta\dfrac{\partial g_D}{\partial u}}{\lambda_Y(g_D - \sigma_\theta) - g_D}$$

is positive if the accumulation effect is stronger than the savings effect (and vice versa). The slope of the $\dfrac{\dot{u}}{u} = 0$ locus in Figure 5.1 in region II assumes that the savings effect is more important than the accumulation effect.

Regime III: $\varphi = \varphi_{min}, u < u^D_{min}$

If the utilization rate falls so low that the aggregate utilization rate is below u^D min, then the aggregate rate of capital accumulation falls to zero, thereby generating a downward spiral in output and productive capacity. The dynamics of capacity utilization are governed by $\dfrac{\dot{u}}{u} = \delta - \lambda_Y\sigma(\theta,u)$, implying that the steady state utilization rate in region III, $\hat{u}$, defined by the condition

$$\frac{\dot{u}}{u} = \delta - \lambda_Y\sigma(\theta,\hat{u}) = 0$$

or

$$\hat{u} = \frac{\delta}{\lambda_Y s\left\{\left(1 - \dfrac{1}{\varphi_{min}}\right)\theta + \left(1 - \dfrac{1+\beta}{\varphi_{min}}\right)(1-\theta)\right\}}$$

is a stable node since $\dfrac{\partial \sigma(\theta, u)}{\partial u} > 0$. Of course, the equilibrium degree of dominant sector control of productive capacity is stable but not unique since neither dominant nor fringe firms are investing in new capacity. This region of phase space is clearly associated with an economic catastrophe generated by the pricing and investment policies of dominant firms.

Figure 5.2 shows the movements of u and θ over time in light of the foregoing analysis. The two paths shown in the diagram illustrate the "knife-edge" quality of growth in the context of this model of industry structure and growth. Paths A and B in Figure 5.2 both begin in Region I of phase space on the assumption that the rate of capacity utilization exceeds $u^D{}_{min}$ so that both dominant and fringe firms are profitable. However, Path A starts at a point above the stable manifold, with the consequences that the rate of growth of the dominant sector exceeds that of the fringe sector by virtue of the higher profit margins earned by large firms. In turn, the increase in the relative size of the dominant sector eventually leads to a situation where the aggregate utilization rate begins to decline (shown by Path A crossing the $\dfrac{\dot{u}}{u} = 0$ locus), which is then followed by a drop in the industry prices in response to growing excess capacity (shown by the fall in u below $u^F{}_{min}$ as the system moves from Region I to Region II). The price war between the dominant and fringe sector further cuts the growth rate of output as a result of the cessation of investment by fringe firms, thereby pushing utilization rates even further down and increasing the degree of dominant sector control. In the long run, the economy will converge to a low level equilibrium (point L in Figure 5.2) that is a technically stable but socially appalling state of affairs.

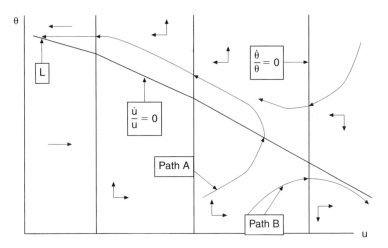

Figure 5.2 The dynamics of u and θ.

Path B differs from Path A in two ways. First, the initial degree of dominant sector control (θ) is much lower. Second, the aggregate utilization rate is high enough to encourage fringe firms to grow more quickly than dominant firms. These two factors mean that the system starts its journey below the stable manifold, so that fringe firms are growing faster than dominant firms. There is a positive feedback effect between the level and rate of change of the aggregate utilization rate along Path B; in this situation, capital accumulation is so rapid that the utilization rate in the system rises over time while the degree of industry concentration falls, thereby gradually pushing the system into a region of explosive growth.

The unlabeled path in the upper right-hand corner of Figure 5.2 is an example of how an economy with high utilization rates and a high degree of industry concentration can fall into a long term slump. Recall that all points to the right of the $\frac{\dot{\theta}}{\theta} = 0$ locus are associated with a decline in the degree of concentration as fringe firms grow faster than dominant firms in response to profit rates. The rapid rise in industry capacity puts downward pressure on utilization rates as well as profit rates, eventually pushing profits down to such an extent that the degree of concentration eventually rises as fringe firms reduce their rates of expansion relative to dominant sector enterprises, thereby nudging the economy on a trajectory like Path A.

Conclusion

The purpose of mathematical formalism in economics should be to explore the logic of complex arguments, using the techniques of analysis and dynamical systems to reveal the nuances in the details of a theory that might be missed by other modes of discourse. Our formal model of Steindlian dynamics could be renamed "On the Importance of Saddle-points in the Theory of Capitalist Development" because of the central role the idea of saddlepoint stability has played the foregoing portrait of growth. Our mathematical treatment of Steindl's theory of development shows the fragility of steady growth in the storm of competition and capital destruction that characterizes a rich view of capitalism.

The approach to growth and development presented here largely ignores the role of distributional struggles between capital and labor in the growth process. Indeed, one virtue of Steindl's approach is to point to the role of struggle between different sectors of capital in shaping the overall pattern of growth. One way of interpreting the foregoing analysis is to say that the victory of large firms in the struggle for the control of markets leads to stagnation, while a vigorous entrepreneurial capitalism holds out the promise for sustained or even accelerating growth. A more complete picture of development must bring labor back into the picture, thereby portraying the process of growth as a struggle between small and large firms for the control of markets on the one hand, and between workers and capitalists over the distribution of income on the other.

Appendix

Stability properties of Regime I

Regime I is represented by

$$\frac{\dot{u}}{u} = \lambda_Y[\theta g_D + (1-\theta)g_F - \sigma(\theta,u)] - \theta g_D - (1-\theta)g_F + \delta$$

$$\frac{\dot{\theta}}{\theta} = (1-\theta)(g_D - g_F)$$

The steady state value of the utilization rate is defined the condition $\frac{\dot{\theta}}{\theta} = 0$ so that $\bar{u} = \dfrac{r}{1 - \dfrac{1}{\varphi} - \dfrac{\beta G_F}{G_F - G_D}}$ while the steady state degree of domin-

ant sector control over production capacity is defined by $\frac{\dot{u}}{u} = 0$ so that $\bar{\theta} = \varphi g * \dfrac{(\lambda_Y - 1)}{s\beta\bar{u}} + \varphi - \beta - 1$. The elements of the Jacobian

$$J_1 = \begin{bmatrix} j_{11}^I & j_{12}^I \\ j_{21}^I & j_{22}^I \end{bmatrix} = \begin{bmatrix} \dfrac{\partial\left(\dfrac{\dot{u}}{u}\right)}{\partial u} & \dfrac{\partial\left(\dfrac{\dot{u}}{u}\right)}{\partial\theta} \\ \dfrac{\partial\left(\dfrac{\dot{\theta}}{\theta}\right)}{\partial u} & \dfrac{\partial\left(\dfrac{\dot{\theta}}{\theta}\right)}{\partial\theta} \end{bmatrix}$$

are

$$j_{11}^I = \frac{\partial\left(\dfrac{\dot{u}}{u}\right)}{\partial u} = \lambda_Y\left(\theta\frac{\partial g_D}{\partial u} + (1-\theta)\frac{\partial g_F}{\partial u} - \sigma_u\right) - \theta\frac{\partial g_D}{\partial u} - (1-\theta)\frac{\partial g_F}{\partial u} < 0$$

$$j_{12}^I = \frac{\partial\left(\dfrac{\dot{u}}{u}\right)}{\partial\theta} = -\lambda_Y\sigma_\theta < 0$$

$$j_{21}^I = \frac{\partial\left(\dfrac{\dot{\theta}}{\theta}\right)}{\partial u} = G_D\left(1 - \frac{1}{\varphi_{max}}\right) - G_F\left(1 - \frac{1+\beta}{\varphi_{max}}\right) = ?$$

$$j_{22}^I = \frac{\partial\left(\dfrac{\dot{\theta}}{\theta}\right)}{\partial\theta} = 0$$

where

$$\sigma_u = s\left[\left(1-\frac{1}{\varphi}\right)\theta + \left(1-\frac{1+\beta}{\varphi}\right)(1-\theta)\right] > 0$$

and $\sigma_\theta = \dfrac{s\beta u}{\varphi} > 0$. The roots of J_1 are

$$R_{1,2} = \frac{-j_{11}^I \pm \sqrt{\left(j_{11}^I\right)^2 - 4j_{21}^I j_{12}^I}}{2}.$$

Note that one root is positive and the other negative since $j_{21}^I < 0$ for reasons discussed in the body of the chapter. Further note that the unstable manifold in (u, θ) space is a downward sloping line passing through the saddlepoint. Finally, the economy's moves from Regime I toward Regime II along a path with rising dominant sector control of the economy and falling utilization rates if the system is perturbed in a manner that pushes u below or θ above their steady state values.

Acknowledgements

This chapter has been immeasurably improved by the patient and insightful advice of Tracy Mott and Nina Shapiro, who were kind in the face of several delays. All remaining errors are the sole responsibility of the author.

Notes

1 Two notable exceptions to economists' neglect of *Maturity and Stagnation* are Taylor (1983, 1985, and 1991) and Dutt (1990). These writers pay special attention to Steindl's analysis of the relationship between capacity utilization and investment spending in their analyses of growth and distribution.
2 See Steindl's comments on the limitations of his own model of growth and stagnation in Steindl (1976, p. 226). Steindl's formal model of growth suffers from the difficulties associated with mixed differential-difference equation system. These types of systems are extremely difficult to use for theoretical analysis, primarily because any study of a mixed system's qualitative properties requires the analyst to solve transcendental equations in order to derive characteristic roots. In general, simpler linear and nonlinear differential equation systems are just as effective in exhibiting many important qualitative properties as mixed differential – difference equation systems without the headaches.
3 Steindl (1976), pp. 40–52.
4 Ibid., pp. 52–55. Steindl's analysis of price competition in a highly concentrated industry is simply a version of the kinked demand curve model of oligopoly. See Reid (1981) for a detailed review of the kinked demand curve approach.

5 This formulation of the model assumes that the capital – capacity ratio is equal to one.
6 Either standard dominant group – competitive fringe models of industry pricing (with a conjectural variation approach to pricing with the dominant group) or a dynamic form of a price leadership model can be used as the basis for the model presented above.
7 This assumption implies that the dominant sector is weighing the short-term profitability of a higher mark-up against the long-term losses associated with the entry of more fringe producers. A high mark-up in a circumstance where utilization rates are also high generates a large profit margin per unit of output in the near term in an environment where dominant sector sales growth is not affected by a growing fringe sector. This pricing strategy implicitly assumes that dominant sector firms expect the growth rate of market demand to exceed their own rates of expansion, thereby leaving room for fringe sector growth. Conversely, dominant sector firms will impose low prices in the industry when their expectations of growth clash with their own expansion plans in ways that require fringe expansion to be curtailed in order to insure adequate levels of utilization and profitability. A full model of growth based on Steindl's analysis of competition in a dominant firm-competitive fringe model of industry structure would therefore include an account of expectation formation as well as an account of the connection between expectations and prices. An explicit model of the process of expectation formation has been left out of this account of Steindl's dynamics in order to permit a two-dimensional representation of growth and industrial change. A fuller, three-dimensional model of Steindlian dynamics developed by the author offers few additional insights into the process of growth at the cost of a considerable rise in analytical and computational complexity. The interested reader should contact the author for the richer model of growth and industry change under conditions of adaptive expectations. A rational expectations approach to Steindlian dynamics, though feasible, so taxes credulity that this phase of the project has been discontinued.
8 See Flaschel *et al.* (1997) for a detailed discussion of Keynesian adjustment dynamics.

References

Beltrami, Edward (1987) *Mathematics for Dynamic Modelling*, Boston: Academic Press.

Dutt, Krishna Amitava (1990) *Growth, Distribution, and Uneven Development*, Cambridge: Cambridge University Press.

Flaschel, Peter, Franke, Reiner and Semmler, Willi (1997) *Dynamics Macroeconomics: Instability, Fluctuations and Growth in Monetary Economics*, Cambridge, MA: MIT Press.

Kaldor, Nicholas (1961) "Capital Accumulation and Economic Growth", in F.A. Lutz and D.C. Hague (eds) *The Theory of Capital Accumulation*, London: Macmillan.

Marx, Karl (1867) *Capital*, Volume One (reprint of 1867 edition by Progress Publishers, Moscow) New York: International Publishers, 1967.

Reid, Gavin (1981) *The Kinked Demand Curve Analysis of Oligopoly*, Edinburgh: Edinburgh University Press.

Steindl, Josef (1976) *Maturity and Stagnation in American Capitalism* (reprint of 1952 edition by Blackwell), New York: Monthly Review Press.

Taylor, Lance (1983) *Structuralist Macroeconomics*, New York: Basic Books.

Taylor, Lance (1985) "A Stagnationist Model of Economic Growth", *Cambridge Journal of Economics*, 9, pp. 383–403.

Taylor, Lance (1991) *Income Distribution, Inflation, and Growth*. Cambridge, MA: MIT Press.

Waterson, Michael (1984) *Economic Theory of the Industry*, Cambridge: Cambridge University Press.

6 Steindl on growth and cycles

Marc Jarsulic

Introduction

Josef Steindl was an economic theorist who always paid close attention to the empirical relevance of his work. When writing about macroeconomic phenomena, he consistently acknowledged the difficult problem of explaining cyclical growth. Over time his approach to this issue changed. In *Maturity and Stagnation in American Capitalism* (1952), he developed a theory of self-sustaining growth that is based on what he termed an endogenous theory of investment. Using this investment theory, he was able to account for growth trends, while being forced to leave the explanation of cycles unresolved. In subsequent work, he modified his position on investment. The idea of endogenously generated investment was replaced by an exogenous theory, where unexplained technical change is seen as the source of growth. Technical change was also used to explain at least part of cyclical behavior, since innovations are characterized as shocks which have a positive bias.

The aim of this chapter is to explore some of the implications of Steindl's account of investment and growth. The evolution of his theoretical ideas will first be outlined. It then will be shown that, with minor modifications, his endogenous investment theory also can provide an explanation of cyclical growth.

An endogenous theory of investment and growth

In *Maturity and Stagnation*, Steindl offers an explanation of investment which seems very contemporary. There he suggests that four factors influence corporate investment: (1) the internal accumulation of funds; (2) the rate of capacity utilization; (3) the debt-capital ratio; and (4) the rate of profit. Of these four explanatory variables, it is internal accumulation which is central to the subsequent modeling effort. And it is this variable for which Steindl (1952, pp. 192–193) provides the most provocative rationale:

> The most important feature of this explanation of the trend is that it is an endogenous theory. It starts from the conviction that in order to

explain the historical phenomenon of growth of capital it is not necessary to have recourse to external influences, such as innovations, population growth, wars, etc. The growth of capital is, on the contrary, viewed as something inherent in the nature of capitalism, and to be explained by much simpler assumptions. The concrete hypothesis which explains growth is this: the mere fact that business concerns accumulate savings is sufficient to induce them (after a certain time) to invest. The internal accumulation, by itself, generates investment, and if there has been growth in the past sufficient to enable entrepreneurs to accumulate funds internally, then this will itself produce a further growth. The growth of capital is in this sense self-perpetuating.

At other points he expands the significance of financial resources, for example using endogenous accumulation to explain technical change (ibid., p. 133):

Innovations, to express this view in its most extreme form, affect only the *form* which net investment takes. Innovations are applied, so runs the present argument, because business has money available, and demand is such to produce a high level of utilisation. The stimulus of these economic factors produces additions to the capital stock, which usually, or very often, embody some innovation, simply because there is usually a stock of innovations and ideas waiting to be applied. Technological innovations accompany the process of investment like a shadow, they do not act on it like a propelling force.

Like Marx, Steindl appears to believe that accumulation is the "Moses and the prophets". Capitalists usually invest in additional capital goods to the limit of their ability to do so. The underlying assumption here appears to be the classical concept of competition: capitalists behave like enemies in a war, struggling for the advantages of size, lower cost, new products all the time. However, Steindl believes that this behavior is tempered by the realities of effective demand and financial constraints. When capacity is insufficiently used, it may make better competitive sense to accumulate financial assets. When utilization rates are high, the limit to expansion is the availability of finance. This financial constraint argument is also developed by Kalecki (1971, pp. 105–109) in his discussion of increasing risk.

It is worth noting that although Steindl did not provide a statistical investigation of his investment theory, the financial effects which he emphasized have been the center of substantial empirical work. The availability of internal finance plays a part in neo-Marxian (Bowles *et al.* 1989), Kaleckian (Fazzari and Mott 1986) and new Keynesian (Fazzari *et al.* 1988) empirical research on investment demand.

A simplified version of Steindl's investment theory forms the basis of the growth model developed in *Maturity and Stagnation*. He begins with an investment function of the form

$$I_{t+1} = \gamma C_t, \ \gamma > 0 \tag{6.1}$$

where I is a moving average of net investment, and C is a moving average of internal financial accumulation. Moving averages are used because of Steindl's belief that the business cycle and growth cannot be adequately treated in a single model. The length and significance of time lags are not explicitly addressed.

To complete the model, a closed economy, a fixed output–capital ratio, and a constant non-corporate savings rate are assumed. Hence, non-corporate savings are

$$S_t = \mu Y_t = \upsilon Z_t, \ \mu, \ \upsilon > 0 \tag{6.2}$$

where Y is a moving average of national income, Z is capital stock, μ is the savings rate, and $\upsilon = (\mu$ multiplied by the output–capital ratio$)$. Under these assumptions, internal accumulation is then

$$C_t = I_t - S_t \tag{6.3}$$

Substituting (6.2) and (6.3) into (6.1) gives

$$I_{t+1} = \gamma I_t - \gamma \upsilon Z_t \tag{6.4}$$

Since $I_t = dZ_t/dt$ (6.4) can be rewritten as

$$dZ_{t+1}/dt = \gamma dZ_t/dt - \gamma \upsilon dZ_t/dt \tag{6.5}$$

which is a differential-delay equation.

The solution of this kind of equation is usually difficult (Gandolfo, 1980, pp. 519–540). Steindl (1952, pp. 200–228), however, does a very neat job of deducing the dynamics inherent in (6.5). He shows that there are two possible outcomes: steady growth of the capital stock, or oscillations in the capital stock, with no growth. Explicitly, the actual outcomes depend on the parameter values γ and υ. Implicitly the outcomes also depend on the one period lag structure, since a different lag structure would affect the characteristic equation of (6.5).[1] If there are oscillations of substantial period, they will represent long swings, since the variable Z is a moving average. These results anticipate those in a famous paper by Pasinetti (1960), which showed that growth and cycles are mutually exclusive outcomes of the linear multiplier-accelerator systems.

A stochastic account of investment and growth

In later work, Steindl (1989, pp. 309–313; 1990, pp. 127–148) significantly modifies the idea that investment demand is endogenously driven. Instead, he suggests that both growth and business cycles have their origin in random technology shocks. What he has in mind (Steindl 1990, pp. 136–137) is a variant on well-established linear-stochastic business cycle theory:

> Let us now start from the idea that investment as such does not have the power to regenerate itself on an extending scale; this is because of the 'incomplete reinvestment' (due to savings outside enterprises and other reasons). Now if additional exogenous investment such as that created by anticipation of innovation profits is added to the incomplete reinvestment, this may complete, and even overcomplete it, and the conditions for a continuing trend are fulfilled...
>
> The role of the above mentioned exogenous factors in the genesis of the trend reminds us inevitably of the role which random shocks play in the cycle which they keep going in spite of its inherent tendency to fade out owing to 'damping.' And indeed, are the new technologies anything but random shocks? The only difference is that they are shocks in one direction mainly – they are mostly stimulating, and therefore impart to the totality of exogenous shocks a bias. This means they will lengthen and accentuate the booms and shorten and weaken the slumps...
>
> ...in my formulation, there will be discontinuously changing initial conditions, exactly like the random shocks which according to R. Frisch and, following him, Kalecki, prevent the cycle from dying down; the only difference being that I assume the shocks have an upward bias which produces the trend.

It is easy to construct a simple macro model which captures the main ideas being advanced here. Suppose that, in a closed economy, income shares are determined by constant mark-ups; aggregate demand consists of investment and consumption; workers do not save; and corporations save all current profit income. Under these conditions equilibrium national income is

$$Y_t = \alpha I_t \tag{6.6}$$

where Y is real national income, I is real net investment, and $\alpha = 1/(1 - \omega)$, where ω is labor's share. Dividing (6.6) by the current real capital stock gives

$$Y_t/K_t = \alpha I_t/K_t = \alpha g_t \tag{6.7}$$

If current investment function is a linear function of last period's retained profits, (6.7) can be rewritten as

$$g_t = \beta g_{t-1} \tag{6.8}$$

where β is the positive constant reflecting the willingness of corporations to invest.

To this difference equation we can add a stochastic term of the form suggested by Steindl. That is, suppose ε_t is a serially uncorrelated random variable with mean $\theta > 0$. Further suppose that ε represents the contributions of technical change to the desired growth rate. Then we substitute for (6.8) the equation

$$g_t = \beta g_{t-1} + \varepsilon_t \tag{6.9}$$

In equilibrium, where $g_t = g_{t-1}$, we then know that

$$g_t = \varepsilon_t/(1 - \beta) \tag{6.10}$$

which obviously requires $1 > \beta > 0$ for this expression to be economically meaningful. Assuming this restriction on β is met, the expected value of g is $\varepsilon/(1 - \beta)$, and it can be said that growth depends on technical change.

By recursive substitution of (6.9) into itself, g_t can be represented as

$$g_t = \Sigma \beta^i \varepsilon_{t-i} + \beta^n g_{t-n} \tag{6.11}$$

Such a moving average of random variables can produce wave-like motion in g_t. Thus technical change would also be responsible for "business cycle" behavior in this economy.

Before accepting such an account of growth and cycles, it might be useful to examine some of the underlying assumptions a bit more closely. First of all, a decision to represent growth theory in a linear difference equation immediately constrains the possible dynamics. At best, one can manipulate a linear difference equation to represent stable growth of a macro variable, as was done in (6.5) and (6.8). However, this may not make tremendous economic sense. Is there really good reason to assume, for example, that $1 > \beta > 0$ in equation (6.8)? Except for a need to rule out explosive long-term growth, which is not observed in capitalist economies, such a restriction on the *local* behavior generated by investment is a requirement of the mathematics. The mathematical format chosen fore-closes, for example, the inclusion of strong *local* multiplier-accelerator effects near the long-run equilibrium.

Moreover, the assumption that technological change is well represented by repeated aggregate shocks is problematic. While it is plausible to think of technical change as a multiplicity of random events hitting the individual firms in the economy, it makes less sense to think of these changes as hitting all firms in the economy simultaneously. The introduction of electrical power, say, will affect every firm at the same time. However, events like the implementation of electrical power happen rarely.

Lots of small shocks, distributed across firms each period, will be unlikely to produce substantial aggregate shocks in any period. Suppose that in every time period the output of each of the N firms in the economy is subject to an additive random technology shock u_i, drawn from a random distribution with mean $\rho > 0$. The weak law of large numbers says that Prob $(\Sigma (u_i/N) - \rho \geq \eta) \to 0$ as $N \to \infty$, for an arbitrarily small positive η. This means that in any one period, the sum of firm-specific aggregate technology shocks will be arbitrarily close to $N\rho$. This will account for trend behavior, but will be unlikely to produce a sequence of aggregate shocks capable of producing an aggregate cycle.[2]

A nonlinear Steindl-like growth cycle model

Steindl's switch to linear-stochastic theory appears to be motivated by a concern to provide an account of both growth and cycles. However, it is possible to show that his original endogenous theory is capable of explaining both phenomena. This can be done by retaining the essential element of the theory – which is the importance of lagged profitability in the determination of investment demand – while recasting its statement in an empirically plausible nonlinear form.

The discrete-time model of (6.6)–(6.8) can be rewritten in continuous form, allowing for time lags in two ways. First, assume that there is an adjustment lag between desired and actual rates of investment, caused by implementation lags. Then investment will be determined by the differential equation

$$dg/dt = \beta(g^d - g), \beta > 0 \tag{6.12}$$

where g is the actual rate of capital stock growth and g^d is the desired rate of growth.

Second, assume that (6.6) and (6.8) can be replaced with continuous-time analogues

$$Y/K = \alpha g \tag{6.13}$$

where $\alpha = 1/s$, $1 > s > 0$, and s is the marginal propensity to save; and

$$g^d = f(\pi(t-\theta)) \tag{6.14}$$

where π is the profit rate, and θ is the time lag between profit receipt and investment decision. It will also be assumed that $f(\pi(t-\theta))$ has positive upper and lower bounds. The upper bound can be attributed to finance constraints on investment, and the lower bound to steady animal spirits. Within these bounds $df/d\pi(t-\theta) > 0$.

Finally, let the profit rate be determined by

$$\pi(t) = h(Y/K) = h(g) \tag{6.15}$$

where h is a nonlinear function for which

$$dh/dg = \begin{cases} > 0 \text{ if } g < g\sim \\ 0 \text{ if } g = g\sim, \\ < 0 \text{ if } g > g\sim \end{cases} \tag{6.16}$$

where $g\sim > 0$.

The replacement of the proportional relationship between utilization and profitablity in (6.16) is empirically motivated. The work of several business cycle researchers (Boddy and Crotty 1975; Weisskopf 1979; Hahnel and Sherman 1982; Bowles *et al.* 1989) has shown that profitability falls before business cycle peaks. This relationship is approximated by taking Y/K as an index of general cyclical position.

Equations (6.12)–(6.16) reduce to

$$dg/dt = \beta(H(g(t-\theta)) - g) = F(g, g(t-\theta)) \tag{6.17}$$

where $H(g(t-\theta)) = f(h(g(t-\theta)))$, and $dH/dg(t-\theta) < 0$. This is a continuous-time, nonlinear analogue to Steindl's equation (6.5). Given the restrictions on $f(\pi(t-\theta))$, (6.17) will have positive upper and lower bounds. It also will be assumed that (6.17) has a unique, non-zero equilibrium value g^*.

To determine the local behavior of (6.17) the classic results of Hayes (1950) can be used. First, (6.17) can be linearized to give

$$y = Ay + By(t-\theta) \tag{6.18}$$

where $y = g - g^*$, $A\ \partial F/\partial g \mid g = g^*$, and $B = \partial F/\partial g(t-\theta) \mid g = g^*$. Then the eigenvalue λ of (6.18) is found by solving $\lambda = A\theta + B\theta e^\lambda$. As Burger (1956) shows, the Hayes results can be summarized compactly. The real part of λ will be negative, and the equilibrium value g^* stable, if and only if one of the following holds:

(a) $-1 \leqslant B\theta$ and $A < -B$
(b) $B\theta < -1$ and $A < B$
(c) $B \leqslant A < -B$ and $[\text{arcos}(-A/B)/(B^2 - A^2)^{1/2}] > \theta$.

From (6.17) we know that $A = -\beta$ and $B = \beta dH/dg(t-\theta)$. It can be seen that many plausible combinations of β, $dH/dg(t-\theta)$ and θ can violate conditions (a)–(c). Therefore g^* could easily be locally unstable.

With local instability will come non-convergent dynamical behavior for g. Since g cannot converge to g^* if displaced from it, $dg/dt \neq 0$ near g^*. However, since g has upper and lower bounds, and since the sign of dg/dt changes with the value of g, g will neither collapse to zero nor explode to infinity. Hence (6.17) will exhibit some sort of oscillatory behavior. That is, the dynamical system produces growth and cycles. Hence, it seems reasonable to claim that there is significant unexploited explanatory power in Steindl's endogenous theory of investment.

Conclusion

Steindl's views on cyclical growth underwent significant change over time. In *Maturity and Stagnation* he advanced the view that, with the appropriate qualifications for utilization and other matters, the availability of internal funds would provide sufficient reason for capitalist firms to invest. This idea, embedded in a linear differential-delay framework was used to provide an account of long-term growth. The question of business cycles was put aside.

In later work, Steindl sought to explain cyclical growth, still using investment behavior as the basis of dynamics. However, investment behavior was represented as being driven by exogenous, stochastic technical change. When joined to a linear difference equation framework, such a model does provide an explanation of growth and cycles. Yet it is an explanation with inherent difficulties.

With minor alteration, however, Steindl's theoretical framework can explain cyclical growth without invoking technology shocks. The inclusion of mild nonlinearity, consistent with the behavior of profits and investment demand over the business cycle, will do the trick. Hence it appears that Steindl, unlike some academics, was unduly modest about the richness of his work.

Notes

1   Suppose $Z_t + \theta = er^{(t+\theta)}$. Then (6.5) can be written as $rer^{(t+\theta)} = \gamma re^{rt} - \gamma v e^{rt}$. This gives the characteristic equation $rer^\theta - \gamma r + \gamma v = 0$. This makes θ a determinant of the solution values of r.
2   This criticism also applies to the so-called "real business cycle" theory, currently in vogue, and has been developed elsewhere (Mankiw 1989).

References

Boddy, J. and Crotty, R. (1975) "Class Conflict and Macro Policy: The Political Business Cycle", *Review of Radical Political Economics*, Spring, 7(1), 1–19.
Bowles, S., Gordon, D. and Weisskopf, T. (1989) "Business Ascendancy and Economic Impasse", *Journal of Economic Perspectives*, 3, 107–134.
Burger, E. (1956) "On the Stability of Certain Economic Systems", *Econometrica*, 24, 488–493.

Fazzari, S., Hubbard, R. and Petersen, B. (1988) *Financing Constraints and Corporate Investment*, Brookings Papers on Economic Activity, 1, 141–206.

Fazzari, S. and Mott, T. (1986) "The Investment Theories of Kalecki and Keynes: An Empirical Study of Firm Data, 1970–82", *Journal of Post Keynesian Economics*, 9, 171–187.

Gandolfo, G. (1980) *Economic Dynamics: Methods and Models*, New York: Elsevier.

Hahnel, R. and Sherman, H. (1982) "The Rate of Profit over the Business Cycle", *Cambridge Journal of Economics*, June, 6, 185–194.

Hayes, N. (1950) "Roots of the Transcendental Equation Associated with a Certain Difference-Differential Equation", *Journal of the London Mathematical Society*, 25, 226–232.

Kalecki, M. (1971) *Selected Essays on the Dynamics of the Capitalist Economy*, Cambridge: Cambridge University Press.

Mankiw, N. (1989) "Real Business Cycles: A New Keynesian Perspective", *Journal of Economic Perspectives*, 7, 79–90.

Pasinetti, L. (1960) "Cyclical Fluctuations and Economic Growth", *Oxford Economic Papers*, 12, 215–241.

Steindl, J. (1952) *Maturity and Stagnation in American Capitalism*, New York: Monthly Review Press.

Steindl, J. (1989) "Reflections on Kalecki's Dynamics", in M. Sebastiani (ed.), *Kalecki's Relevance Today*, New York: St. Martin's Press, pp. 309–313.

Steindl, J. (1990) *Economic Papers 1941–88*, New York: St. Martin's Press.

Weisskopf, T. (1979) "Marxian Crisis Theory and the Rate of Profit in the Post-War U.S. Economy", *Cambridge Journal of Economics*, December, 3, 340–377.

Part III
Maturity and stagnation

7 Methodology and industrial maturity in Steindl's capitalism

Jan Toporowski

As an economist, I am the product of England and Kalecki.

(Steindl 1989, p. 98)

Monopoly appears to be deeply rooted in the nature of the capitalist system: Free competition, as an assumption, may be useful in the first stages of certain investigations, but as a description of the normal state of the capitalist economy it is merely a myth.

(Kalecki *Collected Works*, henceforth *CW*, 1990, vol. I, p. 252)

Methodology

At the beginning of his classic study of industrial statistics, *Random Processes and the Growth of Firms* (Steindl 1965), Joseph Steindl quoted Kalecki's mordant observation that "Economics consists of theoretical laws which nobody has verified, and of empirical laws which nobody can explain." Despite its seeming addiction to conventional economic wisdom from early parts of the century, there can be little doubt that the economics profession at the end of the twentieth century is more empirically informed than it was when Kalecki made his comment. Unfortunately much of its "realism" falls too readily into "abstracted empiricism" (Mills 1970, Chap. 3), which sacrifices logic and consistency in the process of specious methodological refinement, and gives results that cast little light on the "central problems" of our time (Kalecki 1971).

This fault cannot be found in the work of Josef Steindl, which is among the best of post-war empirical economic analysis, and remains a model of applied endeavour for economists. The excellence of Steindl's empirical and theoretical work may in large measure be attributed to its adherence to two methodological principles which distinguish it from that of virtually all his contemporaries among economists. [The signal exception among them is "the most important colleague of his life", Michał Kalecki (Shapiro 1990).] There is a classic and seamless breadth about his analysis. His economy is an organic one, in which the general is found in the particular, and the particular constitutes the general by more than just summation (Whitehead 1938, Chap. X). Like Ricardo, Marx and Kalecki, Steindl moves freely between the micro-economics of the individual firm, and the macro-economics of the economy, both of which are treated as different aspects of the same processes, in which the same principles are at work. In contrast to this, neo-classical economics, and contemporary versions of it, tend to reduce the macro-economic to micro-economic principles and activities. In reaction to that, Keynes and his followers sought to investigate macro-economic processes *per se*, and seek micro-economic insights from them.

The second methodological principle for which Steindl stands out among economists is his mathematical empiricism. Like Kalecki, Steindl was a first-class mathematician. But Steindl advances his mathematical analyses twice over: once as mathematical functions, and again as prose to show how the conclusion, which he has reached by mathematical reasoning, is arrived at by an actual process of economic activity in the real world. This kind of dual reasoning is also found in Kalecki, and it explains why the analyses of the two former colleagues are able so effectively to negotiate the passage between the Scylla of unreal abstraction and the Charybdis of "abstracted empiricism" (cf. Mills 1970). Next to their work, the fictional rationales of more conventional mathematical economics from Walras onwards, with their auctioneers and implicit contracts, have an air of implausibility about them.

Steindl's empirical analysis does not just set out the variables which can be combined to reproduce the capitalist economy in all its richness and variety. This would be an impossible task in which even a genius with a Napoleonic attention to detail would eventually lose direction. Nor is Steindl concerned with reproducing the "main features" of a capitalist economy. There is too little in his work about, for example, money, consumption or the workings of the labour market. Rather, Steindl, like Kalecki, may be regarded as identifying and explaining the crucial problems of his time (Kalecki 1971; Toporowski 1991).

The remainder of this chapter focuses on the central problem that Steindl investigated in his most famous work, *Maturity and Stagnation in American Capitalism* (henceforth *MSAC*) (1976), namely, why American capitalism, which had proved to be so dynamic in the nineteenth century, declined repeatedly into stagnation between the 1890s and the Second World War. A proper re-evaluation to Steindl's own high standards (see above) would require a study that was at least as thorough as the one he undertook of this subject. This is precluded by the austerity of academic life in mature British capitalism. This chapter therefore concentrates on two issues: the logic of Steindl's analysis, and its capacity to elucidate the "central problems" of our time.

The role of competition

According to Steindl, the dynamic period of capitalism is one in which firms compete with each other in two ways. First of all, they compete in the classic Marxian/Schumpeterian way to get the best return on their capital, imitating each other's profitable innovations and making capitalism "progressive" in this way. Steindl rightly pointed out that this never actually leads to any equalisation of the rate of profit (*MSAC*, p. 67). Steindl subsumed this as cost-based competition between firms in their markets. Firms do this by engaging in "sales efforts". In the case of small firms, this strategy entails reducing prices and profit margins in order to achieve their planned capacity utilisation. For larger firms, "sales efforts" involve advertising campaigns, product differentiation, or innovating with new products and processes. Unlike conventional economists, whose explanation of competition reduces it to a rather vague principle of profit-maximisation and price flexibility, which is supposed to be the most fundamental instinct of entrepreneurs, Steindl had a simple and far more realistic economic rationale for competition: Firms engage in "sales efforts" because their productive capacity is under-utilised.

This has two interesting implications. The first concerns the nature of competition. It suggests that competition depends on "sales effort", rather than the presence of a number of firms in a market. A monopoly engaged in a "sales effort", because of its excess capacity, may therefore be more competitive than a large number of firms operating at or near full capacity, and therefore content merely to continue selling what they are currently selling.

The second concerns the nature of the firm. The clear reason for seeking to utilise capacity is in order to obtain a cash flow out of which to defray the costs of that capital. This suggests a notion of the capitalist firm as one engaged in securing a return on its capital, as a specific form of the more general, and more vague, profit-maximising imperative. Securing some adequate return on specific capital assets is *the* real problem faced by companies precisely because profit-maximisation may require capital which the company does not possess, a problem faced by many small businesses and businesses in developing countries. While conventional economics sees no problem with borrowing or leasing such capital, Steindl adhered to Kalecki's Principle of Increasing Risk, according to which the amount of capital which a firm may obtain with minimal risk of default is in direct proportion to its existing shareholders' funds (equity plus accumulated reserves) (*MSAC*, Chapter IX; Steindl 1945, Chapter IV; Kalecki *CW*, vol. II, pp. 277–281).

The effect of "sales effort" competition is to drive the smaller ("marginal") firms out of business. The remaining firms eventually reach their target capacity utilisation, but with a narrower profit margin. In the longer term, as the market share of the largest firms increases, they also engage in monopolistic combinations, until the stage of monopoly capitalism is reached. At this stage, excess capacity is less of a financial burden on oligopolistic firms. Their market domination allows them to secure a larger profit margin on the capacity that is in use. This larger profit margin helps to defray the costs of the unused capacity. Nevertheless, excess capacity discourages investment to expand productive capacity. Lack of investment therefore causes monopoly capitalism to stagnate.

Years later, in his Preface to the 1976 edition of *MSAC*, Steindl admitted that technological innovation can nevertheless generate an expansionary trend, a comment which he expanded upon in Steindl (1981). This complicates his argument in the following way: if indeed corporations are unwilling to expand their capacity, then in what ways are they innovating? If they are only renewing existing capacity (being discouraged by its excess from expanding it), then an expansionary trend would require replacement of existing capacity with more capital-intensive techniques.

Alternatively, the technological innovation may be occurring in the remaining competitive enclave of the economy. In this case, stagnation would imply a declining competitive sector. This would be consistent with Steindl's argument that the oligopolistic sector can manipulate prices so as to secure higher rates of profit and internal accumulation of funds for firms in that sector, as opposed to firms in the competitive sector (*MSAC*, pp. 124–126). With excess capacity discouraging entry by new firms into the oligopolistic sector, it is nevertheless possible for technological innovation to be confined to the competitive sector. There it may spread by the classical Marxian mechanism of a higher rate of profit for innovators, which rate is then reduced as competitors take up the innovation. But to support the notion of general stagnation, it is necessary to argue that the competitive sector itself is insignificant, or else that it is not expanding in the long term.

This latter analysis is certainly very consistent with some aspects of the economic stagnation experienced in the United States and Britain during the 1980s, especially the low economic growth combined with under-funding and under-investment in innovative competitive industries (with the possible exception of fashionable information communications technology). However, this under-funding is certainly not because of higher rates of profit in traditional "smoke-stack" industries, which have not experienced higher than average internal financial accumulation. On the contrary, older industries have experienced severe profit crises and cash outflows. This is mentioned in passing here as a particular problem in the application of Steindl's analysis to capitalism at the end of the twentieth century. A simpler explanation of this seeming inconsistency is advanced later in the chapter.

The question of technological innovation also deserves only passing mention here, because it is peripheral to Steindl's analysis in *MSAC*. Indeed, he specifically excluded it with the formulation that "Innovations

... affect only the *form* which net investment takes" (*MSAC*, p. 133). Much more central to his argument than production was the analysis of how competitive and oligopolistic firms operate in the markets which they supply. Here Steindl adopted a partial equilibrium approach. This consists of determining a particular equilibrium, and showing the forces that move firms from that to a subsequent equilibrium, what Hicks called the "Traverse" (Hicks 1965, Chapter XVI).

At the end of the twentieth century this may appear a somewhat dated procedure for an economist who was radical enough to conclude his work with a chapter in which he argued that his theory is in accord with Marx's essential insights. Half a century ago, it was accepted as valid and innovative among the radical economists of the time. One has only to think of Paul Sweezy's "kinked" demand curve, and Joan Robinson's *Theory of Imperfect Competition* to realise that a large part of the radical economists' agenda at that time consisted of translating more traditional (Marxian) economics into the technical analysis of conventional economics. Joan Robinson, for example, described her *Essay on Marxian Economics* as 'an outline of Marx's argument, looked at from the point of view of a modern academic economist' (Robinson 1957, p. 5). In spite of his Austrian roots, Steindl began his *Small and Big Business* with a critical examination of "Marshall and the Representative Firm".

Almost inevitably, this endeavour led the concepts and methodology of conventional academic analysis to be introduced into their more radical economics. Such cross-fertilisation is the very essence of theoretical progress in academic economics (Toporowski 1991). But it is questionable whether the notion of equilibrium belongs in the analysis of the dynamics of real economies. Traditional partial and general equilibrium shows how an economic situation is determined by a metaphysical reality that is *immanent* in that situation. Economic dynamics shows how an economic situation is determined by its *antecedents*. By the time *MSAC* came out, Joan Robinson had abandoned *Imperfect Competition* as a "cul de sac" and had come round to Kalecki's view that economic growth was the "central problem" of economic theory. The more Marshallian post-Keynesian Hicks tried to have it both ways by creating an economic dynamics based on successive immanent equlibria. Apart from his early works, the more radical Kalecki did not use equilibrium in his analysis of economic dynamics.

In *MSAC* Steindl used partial equilibrium to explain the economic consequences of competition and oligopoly. This equilibrium is static in the usual sense that it shows the situation to which a particular change would give rise, i.e., the position after the consequences of that change have been exhausted. But it is also static in the sense that the factor which he chooses to hold constant in determining the effects of company tactics is demand. The fixing of demand (or, more strictly, the non-price determinants of demand) in order to examine the effects of changes in other factors recurs, often as an implicit assumption, throughout *MSAC* (e.g., pp. 42 ff., 54, 122, 124, 238, 245–246).

Steindl used this kind of equilibrium as an expository device, (for example on pp. 46–47 a different concept of equilibrium is advanced "in the sense that there is no concentration going on"), and no claims are made for its realism. Nevertheless, it plays a key role as the context in which the effects of competition and oligopoly are analysed.

It is necessary here to distinguish the demand faced by an individual firm, and the demand faced by the industry overall. In examining the consequences of competitive tactics and strategy within an industry, Steindl held constant the demand faced by the industry, so that changes in the sales of individual firms could be attributed to their competitive behaviour. In a stagnant or stabilised economy, changes in sales reflect competitive position. However, when an economy is affected by business cycles and instability, changes in individual firms' sales are the outcome of economy-wide changes, as well their tactics of competition. Only in retrospect, when all the firms in the business know what total demand was, can they identify changes in market share. Moreover, economy-wide changes also affect firms' need and wish to be competitive. In a boom, firms are likely to experience rising profit margins even as new firms are entering the market. A recession may reduce the profit margins of even effective cartels such as the European steel industry in the early 1980s. Accordingly, in a boom, when virtually all firms experience rising sales, few firms are likely to have to resort to "sales efforts" with the aim of taking customers away from other firms in their business. In a recession, even an effective monopoly may be forced to cut costs, eliminate capacity and innovate in order to hold its cash outflow in line with its sales revenue[1].

The key question therefore is not what firms do, or what they are forced to do, competing with each other in a state of relatively constant overall market demand, but what firms do in response to changes in their demand, or sales of their respective output. If demand changes, firms can choose to change either their prices, or the volume of their output, or some combination of both. The balance of their choice is a crucial factor in economic growth, stagnation and inflation, especially in the modern capitalist economy. Far from being "a state of business democracy where anybody endowed with entrepreneurial ability can obtain capital for starting a business venture", the modern capitalist economy demands a large entry fee from new firms. When "The most important prerequisite for becoming an entrepreneur is the *ownership* of capital" (Kalecki *CW*, vol. II, p. 280), a situation which Steindl analysed with characteristic thoroughness in Steindl (1945), the response of existing firms in an industry is far more important than the response of potential new entrants.

In an unpublished paper, written as this author was trying to make sense of firms' actual pricing and output decisions [Toporowski 1990], it is argued that firms tend to respond to changes in demand according to the price-elasticity of demand for their output, relative to the slope of their average cost curve. The argument follows Kalecki in assuming constant marginal costs up to the point of full capacity utilisation (Kalecki *CW*, vol. II, pp. 120–121), so that, with overhead costs included, the average cost curve will be downward-sloping. The slope of the demand curve depends on such factors as the degree of standardisation of output in the industry, as well as degree of competition. Standardisation tends to be higher in capital-intensive industries, because of the need to secure mass markets for their output. Such industries will therefore tend to face demand curves which are flatter than their average cost curves. Firms in capital-intensive industries tend to raise output more than their prices when demand increases, in order to spread their higher overheads over a larger output. For the same reason, they tend to lower prices more than output when market demand falls. We call these Category I firms (see Table 7.1).

For firms engaged in less capital-intensive activities, product differentiation is more feasible and these firms will have, by definition, smaller overhead costs. Their average cost curves therefore tend to be flatter than the demand curve that each firm faces. These firms are therefore more inclined to raise prices (rather than output) if market demand increases, and to reduce output (rather than prices) if market demand falls. These we call Category II firms.

There may of course be some firms whose cost structure and market demand make them fall exactly on the boundary in between these two

Table 7.1 Characteristics of Category I and Category II firms

	Category I	*Category II*
Response to an increase in market demand	tend to raise output more than prices	tend to raise prices more than output
Response to a decrease in market demand	tend to cut prices more than output	tend to cut output more than prices
Capital-intensity of production	high	low
Price-elasticity of demand	high	low
Industrial activity	primary, heavy manufacturing, large-scale construction	light manufacturing and and services
Economic sector	investment, some wage goods, small share of luxury goods	luxury goods, some wage goods, small share of investment goods

categories. This group of firms is likely to be indifferent between price and output adjustments to changes in demand. However, the condition for such indifference is that profits should be the same at all levels of output, for all prices at the new level of demand. This is likely to arise rarely, if at all, since it would imply that any change in sales revenue is exactly equal to the change in costs, which would mean that the change in price would have to equal the variable cost per unit.[2] In general, most companies will fall into one or other of the two categories.

Another way of looking at this system of responses to changes in demand is to examine what causes firms to change prices. In general, firms prefer to expand output, rather than raise prices, until they get to the point at which their capital equipment is fully utilised after which, if demand carries on rising, they will raise prices, in the short term. Because of business cycles, most capital-intensive firms operate for most of the time at less than full capacity utilisation. Less capital-intensive firms can adjust their capacity more easily to demand. Therefore, when demand rises, capital-intensive firms are more likely to take the opportunity to raise their levels of production. Less capital-intensive firms, which are more likely already to be operating at full capacity, are therefore more likely to raise their prices when demand continues rising. Later on, of course, these firms will consider investing in additional capacity to expand their now higher profit-margin business.

When demand is falling, capital-intensive firms have a greater need to maintain high levels of production, and they are therefore more likely to cut their prices. Less capital-intensive firms, with a smaller need to maintain high levels of production, are more likely to reduce output in order to maintain their profit margins. Thus, firms using a lot of capital equipment rarely raise their prices because their level of production infrequently reaches the full potential of the firm. Firms using relatively little capital equipment are more likely to raise prices more often because they operate more at full capacity. Conversely, large capital-using concerns lower their prices more often because they have a greater need to keep up their capacity utilisation, while firms using less capital equipment are less likely to cut their prices precisely because it is easier for them to cut their output. What causes firms to change output is the need to take into production unused capacity (in the case of capital-intensive companies), or the need to reduce less profitable business (in the case of companies with smaller capital overheads).

It follows that an economy in which the more capital-intensive Category I activities predominate tends to experience expansive booms, broken by sharp periods of mainly price deflation. By contrast, an economy in which the less capital-intensive, Category II, activities prevail will tend to experience price-inflationary booms, broken by output-deflationary recessions. It was precisely the transition from the first type of economy in nineteenth-century America, to the second kind in the twentieth century that Steindl set out to investigate in *Maturity and Stagnation in American Capitalism*.

What makes capitalism transform itself from a dynamic, expansive system of production and distribution, into a stagnant, inflation-prone economic system? In this analysis the answer is relatively simple: firms engaged in capital-intensive activities suffer more from problems of excess capacity in a recession than firms in Category II, which have comparatively lower overheads. In a recession, Category I firms experience large losses, while losses among Category II firms will be more modest. While costs may be cut substantially in less capital-intensive industries by laying off the workforce, the same tactic is proportionately less effective in capital-intensive industries. Moreover, apart from their lower overhead costs, Category II activities use capital equipment, such as that employed in offices or retailing, that is more easily transferred to other activities. A shop may be converted into a cafeteria, but there is only a limited range of buyers for a steel-smelter. Accordingly, Category II equipment tends to have a higher resale value, and Category I firms therefore suffer more from the devaluation of their capital in a recession.

These factors make for more stable profit margins in Category II activities, such as light manufacturing and services, while Category I activities experience more extreme swings between profits and losses. This difference may not matter in the early decades of capitalism, when entrepreneurs control their own enterprises and imbue it with their own "productionist" ethos. But, as the joint stock system comes to prevail over private companies, the general accumulation of capital gives way to securing a positive return on capital assets (to provide a steady return to rentiers) as the central goal of the capitalist enterprise. Instead of being a steel baron, or engineering king, the successful modern entrepreneur is more likely to be a merchant banker or retailer.

However, as we noted, Category II firms tend to raise their prices more than their output in a boom, and reduce output more than prices in a recession. Accordingly, the Category II economy is notable for precisely that combination of stagnation and inflation that characterised the American and the British economies in the 1980s. A feature of that inflation is that the prices of Category I products have tended to stagnate or fall, while those of Category II have tended to be stable or rise.

How does Steindl's analysis fit into this somewhat summary analysis of transition from dynamic growth to stagnation? Essentially, both analyses share the same component elements. The key difference lies in the role accorded to competition and market power. Steindl's partial equilibrium is Marshallian, and accords the moment of competition in markets the critical role. Steindl is non-Marshallian in allowing that this competition may be cost-based with innovating firms obtaining higher rates of return on capital.[3] In the analysis presented here, competition is merely a feature of market activity and itself is determined by the technical characteristics of production, its economic function and the business cycle. If competitive pressures change, it is because of the trade cycle and the changing composition of activities in an economy. In *MSAC* competition causes firms to cut prices when demand falls in a recession. The elimination of competition leads to stagnation precisely because the excess capacity that characterises oligopoly causes firms to cut investment rather than prices in a recession. In the analysis presented above, stagnation is brought on by the decline of heavy industry, with its apparatus of market control in monopolies and cartels, and the rise of the light industrial and service economy, with its apparatus of market control by advertising and product differentiation.

How luxury destroys wealth

The second pivotal step in Steindl's analysis is the moment of aggregation. Steindl does this by adding up companies and industries to obtain the economy as a whole (*MSAC*, p. 107). There are therefore two effective levels in his analysis: companies grouped according to industry at the micro-economic level, and all companies and firms summed up together regardless of economic function.

This kind of aggregation inevitably places greater emphasis on the role of competition (or its absence) in markets, and correspondingly diminishes the function of the intermediate structure of industry, i.e., the composition of industrial activities. Indeed, as was noted above, when Steindl does divide the economy into sectors, it is into competitive and oligopolistic sectors, which are distinguished by the structure of their product markets, rather than by their economic function.

From this relatively undifferentiated aggregation, Steindl and his followers derive the fundamental economic problem of monopoly capitalism, the realisation of surplus. This inevitably follows from such an analysis: if total incomes are divided into wages and profits, and demand from wages and profits is held constant (*that* partial equilibrium again!), then an increase in profit margins must require some increase in expenditure from outside the household and corporate sectors for that profits increase to be "realised". This could be deficit spending by the government or by the foreign sector (a foreign trade surplus) (Kalecki 'On Foreign Trade and Domestic Exports' *CW*, vol. I).

Accordingly, Baran and Sweezy (1968) emphasize militarism, imperialism, wasteful expenditure, conspicuous consumption and advertising, as means of "realising surplus", and they analyse structural change in the American economy as the resolution of this "problem". Steindl himself explains the long post-war boom as due to the absorption of this surplus, principally by "the stream of commercially exploitable innovations, arising as a by-product of the development of military technology and research since the last War" (which presumably overcame the inhibition of oligopolies' existing excess capacity), and "vastly increased public expenditure . . . in large part financed by taxation of profits" (*MSAC*, Introduction to 1976 edition).

This kind of analysis presupposes that the activities in the industrial core of the economy have not fundamentally changed since the early years of capitalism, except for technological innovation and more monopolistic methods of selling their output. Profit margins in this oligopolistic sector should have risen with the elimination of competition, to result in stagnation during the inter-war period, followed by a boom in the 1950s and the 1960s, as governments following Keynesian policies assisted in the realisation of monopoly profits.

Arguably, profit margins in the traditional oligopolistic industries have not been secure. In large measure this has been due to the rise of competition from the newly-industrialised countries, documented in Auerbach (1988) and Wells (1989). Furthermore, since the Second World War, new, "competitive", services and light manufacturing have flourished, in part because with smaller overhead, investments in them have secured profits relatively more rapidly, while the more traditional heavy industries have suffered periodically from severe losses[4].

Moreover, from the 1970s onwards it has become clear that the older capitalist countries have been gradually abandoning the more heavy industrial activities whose expansion was a signal feature of their industrialisation. Some of those industries, such as ship-building in the UK had started their decline as long ago as the 1920s.

This structural change cannot be explained in the categories of Steindl's analysis, and it can only be partially explained by Baran and Sweezy's surplus absorption theory. In order to examine in greater social and economic detail the dynamism of early capitalism, and the stagnation of its maturity, it is helpful to use an intermediate three-sector stage of aggregation, following Kalecki. This divides up total production into wage goods and investment and luxury goods, according to whether they are purchased out of wages or profits. Such a distinction provides a more detailed and specific way of linking up this analysis with distributional changes.

Broadly speaking, wage goods may be said to fall approximately equally into the two categories, with consumer durables clearly belonging to Category I, and consumer services clearly in Category II. Investment goods are generally Category I goods, produced using more capital-intensive techniques (notwithstanding the size of machine tool manufacturing firms and shifts, for example, in the steel industry, towards smaller production units). Luxury goods, in large measure, financial and personal services, seem to fall mostly in Category II. A notable feature of the few luxury goods that are Category I goods is that, because of the tendency of Category I commodity prices to fall relative to the prices of other goods, such articles (e.g., cars and airline travel) eventually become wage goods.

Moreover, as originally luxury services such as banking or department stores become mechanised, and therefore more dependent on a high volume of sales to cover absolutely if not relatively higher overheads, they also tend to become wage goods.

Dynamic capitalist economies are broadly characterised by a predominance in them of wage goods and investment activity. This kind of an economy is precisely the type that responds most vigorously to Keynesian fiscal and redistributive policies: Expanding demand genuinely does give rise to expanding output in a relatively non-inflationary way right up to the point of full employment. If Keynesianism could abolish the trade cycle, then it would be possible to speculate about how long such a policy could keep such an economy in a state of dynamic, non-inflationary full employment.

But business cycles bear most heavily on those capital-intensive activities that are the basis of such a wage goods and investment economy. As Category II activities come to take up a greater share of the economy, Keynesian fiscal and redistributive measures become less effective and more inflationary. As Category I activities contract, the wage and investment goods that they supplied must now be purchased from abroad, so that eventually Keynesian demand expansion leads to balance of payments deficits and inflation. This explains the ineffectiveness of the Keynesian fiscal expansion of the UK economy by the Labour government in the 1970s, and of the French economy by the socialist government in the early 1980s. These failures can be contrasted with the effectiveness of such an expansion in the more primitive capitalist economy of Japan at that time.

The Category I economy is also characterised by a relatively more equal distribution of income. The smaller corporate legal, advertising and financial sectors of capitalism in its prime reflect the larger share of profits devoted to investment, and the less conspicuous consumption of capitalists still wedded to the "Protestant ethic" of hard work, simple living, and the reinvestment of profits.

The situation is substantially different in the Category II economy, in which a larger share of profits goes on corporate management, legal and financial services, entertainment, accountancy, and advertising. The mature capitalist economy is serviced by an army of professional servants and advisers, who constitute a correspondingly larger and wealthier middle class than before. This should not be taken to mean that in capitalist countries such a class of what Malthus called non-productive consumers did not exist before capitalism matured. It did, but it serviced a pre-industrial ruling class. Burke's nostalgic remark that "the age of chivalry is dead. That of sophisters, economists, and calculators has succeeded; and the glory of Europe is extinguished for ever" may be interpreted as an elegy for the service class of the old order, to which he belonged, and a regret for the de-mystified, unromantic service class of the new order. In America, where the new capitalist society was implanted in a more primitive social and economic environment, the old order was a colonial phenomenon that was obviously weakened by the American Revolution and withered after the Civil War destroyed its last redoubt in the slave economies of the Confederacy.

But luxury consumption does not itself create wealth. As Steindl pointed out (*MSAC*, pp. 166–168), for all its glitter the "New Era" of the 1920s was a period of economic stagnation in which capital expansion virtually ceased. In one fundamental respect the pro-business policies of Calvin Coolidge are similar to the 'supply-side' economics of his eventual successor, Ronald Reagan, and of Britain's Prime Minister throughout the 1980s, Margaret Thatcher. All three promoted policies to redistribute income from wages to profits, in the belief that this would make business invest more, and hence make the economy as a whole more dynamic and prosperous. In this way, and because capitalism was maturing, all three stoked up booms of luxury consumption: Scott Fitzgerald's "Jazz Age" had its counterpart in the "wine bars and Porsche cars" boom of the 1980s. Both were celebrated as a "sound" return to capitalist prosperity, before they collapsed into deep recession precisely because the luxury goods sector is the most inflationary of all.

In between the two luxury booms was the long post-Second World War boom. It may be that this lasted so long because it allowed surplus to be realised more easily than before, as Baran and Sweezy suggest, and certainly the innovations and the fiscal expansion of that period contributed to its vigour, as Steindl argues. But in terms of the analysis here, it was a success because post-war reconstruction, the consumer durables boom, and the arms race concentrated demand in exactly those industries which were likely to expand production and demand in a relatively non-inflationary way (Kalecki, in "The Economic Situation in the U.S.A.", *CW*, vol. II, mentions specifically the key role of "heavy industry" in the boom).

The decline of heavy industry in the United States and Britain made it more difficult to repeat this operation. It did not work for President Carter in the United States, or for the Labour Government in Britain during the 1970s. Since Keynesianism seems not to work any more, perhaps the stagnation of capitalism in Britain and the United States or, more specifically, a succession of luxury booms and slumps, may be now irreversible. The balance of payments problems of both countries, and the progressive abandonment of technologies in the investment goods sectors of the two economies, would seem to indicate that both are on the way to becoming developing countries again. As their respective investment sectors shrink, both countries lose indigenous technologies and become dependent on their foreign trade for investment goods and technology (cf. Lim 1991).

Statistical evidence

The statistics of aggregate production unfortunately do not allow us to divide it up into Category I and Category II commodities, or into wage goods, luxuries and investment goods. Many items, such as steel, may enter into all categories and expenditure types. But certain implications of this reconstruction of Steindl's and Kalecki's analysis may still be illustrated statistically.

Table 7.1 shows the proportion of employment in manufacturing, industry and services, in total employment in the civilian economies of the United States and the United Kingdom since 1960. Category I activities, in which output tends to rise in a boom rather than prices, and prices tend to fall rather than output in a recession, are more capital-intensive and tend to be concentrated in industry, and manufacturing in particular. Table 7.2 shows how the share of employment in these activities has fallen in the United States since the late 1960s, and in the UK since the end of the 1950s. In the United States in 1968, 35.4 per cent of civilian employment was in industry. By 1990, this had fallen to 26.2 per cent. In the UK, the share of industrial employment fell from 47.7 per cent in 1960 to 29.0 per cent in 1990. Similar trends have affected manufacturing employment.

By contrast, employment in services, that are Category II activities (prices tend to rise proportionately more than output in a boom, and output tends to fall proportionately more than prices in a recession) has increased in both countries over the three decades, from 58.2 per cent in the United States and 47.6 per cent in the United Kingdom, in 1960, to 70.9 per cent and 68.9 per cent respectively in 1990. It is therefore possible to infer a shift in employment from Category I to category II activities.

To some degree, this shift in employment is due to the more rapid pace of labour productivity in manufacturing industry. However, comparable data on the share of services in output is more difficult to obtain and is complicated by the way in which the output of the services sector is meas-

Table 7.2 Employment in industry and services as a proportion of total civilian employment

% of employment in	1960	1968	1974	1978	1982	1986	1990
USA							
Manufacturing	26.4	27.5	24.2	22.7	20.4	19.1	18.0
Industry	35.3	35.4	32.5	31.1	28.4	27.7	26.2
Services	58.2	59.4	63.4	65.2	68.0	69.3	70.9
UK							
Manufacturing	38.4	36.4	34.6	32.0	27.3	24.2	22.5
Industry	47.7	45.2	42.0	39.1	34.6	30.8	29.0
Services	47.6	51.3	55.1	58.2	62.7	66.7	68.9

Source: OECD (1995).

ured by employment in that sector. A consistent set of output data would therefore show a more modest rise in the share of services in output, but still a rise, and a correspondingly lesser fall in the share of industrial and manufacturing output. Moreover, within the services sector, certain services (such as retailing and banking) have experienced concentration into large corporate units dependent on sales volume to cover high overheads. It is an open question whether this concentration has made them more capital-intensive (relative to labour or sales).

It was argued above that an implication of such a shift is that economic booms would tend to become weaker and more inflationary. Tables 7.3 and 7.4 show economic growth and rates of inflation (measured by the GDP deflator) in the USA and the UK between 1957 and 1991. The period is divided up into intervals of boom and recession according to the rate of change of real GNP (GDP in the UK). A recession was defined, as when the change in real GNP/GDP between two years was less than one

Table 7.3 US growth and inflation

	Mean annual % change in	
	Real GNP	*GDP deflator*
1957–1958	–1.15	2.50
1958–1969	5.65	2.56
1969–1970	–0.48	5.43
1970–1973	4.95	5.24
1973–1975	–1.32	10.01
1975–1979	4.77	7.50
1979–1982	–0.13	8.40
1982–1989	4.13	3.13
1989–1991	–0.20	4.04

Source: OECD and IMF data, with author's calculations.

Table 7.4 UK growth and inflation

	Mean annual % change in	
	Real GDP	*GDP deflator*
1957–1958	–0.24	1.69
1958–1961	4.23	2.29
1961–1962	0.91	3.26
1962–1973	4.00	6.96
1973–1975	–1.10	24.52
1975–1980	3.05	14.15
1980–1981	–1.75	11.40
1981–1989	3.30	5.07
1989–1991	–0.20	6.84

Source: OECD and IMF data, with author's calculations.

percentage point. This definition is somewhat arbitrary but not unreasonable: the only ambiguity concerns the recession of 1961–1962 in Britain.

The tables confirm that economic booms have indeed become weaker and more inflationary in both the UK and the USA. In the United States the mean annual percentage growth rate in real Gross National Product has fallen from 5.65 per cent during the 1958–1969 boom to 4.13 per cent during the 1982–1989 boom. During the first of these booms, the United States suffered a mean annual percentage rise in prices throughout the economy of 2.56 per cent. During the 1982–1989 boom, prices rose on average by 3.13 per cent.

In Britain similar changes took place. During the boom of 1958–1961, real output rose on average by 4.23 per cent, but only by an average of 3.3 per cent between 1982 and 1989. Prices during the first boom rose by an average of 2.29 per cent. During the last boom they rose on average by 5.07 per cent.

It should also be pointed out that the data is also consistent with a long-term trend towards monopoly, of the kind put forward by Steindl about the period from the 1880s to the 1930s. Under monopoly or oligopoly firms faced with recession raise their prices to recover the cost of their excess capacity. But that excess capacity also discourages them from investing. A consequence of such a long-term trend towards monopoly would be longer (because of more sustained excess capacity) and more price-inflationary recessions. Tables 7.3 and 7.4 show recessions in the USA and UK getting longer and more inflationary, although the most inflationary recessions were those of the 1970s and early 1980s, as too were the most inflationary booms.

Table 7.5 shows price changes during the year up to June 1992 for a cross-section of commodities, divided up into manufactured goods and services. It is apparent that the prices of services (Category II commodities) rose faster than the prices of manufactured goods (Category I commodities). This is also consistent with Steindl's hypothesis: manufactured goods are internationally traded and it can be argued that there is therefore more competition among suppliers of these goods than among suppliers of services, and hence a lower rate of inflation.

Further evidence of different rates of inflation in different sectors of the economy is provided in the OECD's *Economic Outlook* for 1995. This shows that in the decade from 1980 to 1989, UK business investment as a percentage of GDP was roughly the same in real terms (i.e., excluding changes in the price of investment goods) as it was in nominal terms throughout the decade. After the onset of recession in 1990, investment in nominal terms fell more rapidly than it did in real terms (OECD 1995). These relative changes indicate that the prices of investment goods rose at the same rate as general price inflation over the period 1980 to 1989, including the boom years of 1981–1989. However, after recession set in, in 1989, general price inflation exceeded that in the investment goods sector.

Table 7.5 Price changes of manufactured goods and services in the USA and the UK

% change in price in year up to June 1992	United States	United Kingdom
Goods		
Audio-visual equipment	−1.5	5.0
Electrical appliances	−1.1	−0.6
Women's clothing	3.3	−1.7
Sports goods	2.2	2.1*
Furniture	2.6	2.5
Services		
Hair cut	nil	7.4
Car insurance	7.6	30.0
Theatre (best seat)	12.0	12.0
Sports club (annual fee)	nil	11.2
Health care	7.5	n.a.
Postage	nil	10.3

Source: "Why services are different", *The Economist*, 18 July 1992.

Note
* includes toys and photographic equipment.

Thus, over the period of the cycle as a whole, capital goods prices were rising more slowly than prices of wage and investment goods. Relative to GDP at least, prices in the investment goods sector fell more than output in the recession, even if their relative movements were less clear in the boom. However, allowing for the greater productivity of successive vintages of investment goods would suggest, that in the boom, output of capital goods rose more, or their prices fell more, than is indicated by these figures, while in the recession, output fell less, and prices fell more. This would be consistent with the view that capital goods producers are largely Category 1 firms.

Conclusion

Steindl's analysis of capitalist maturity and stagnation was a pioneering attempt to think systematically through the longer-term history and, by implication, the future of capitalism. The key point of his analysis is competition and the tendency in capitalist markets for competition to be eliminated. From this tendency, Steindl derived his thesis that capitalism tends towards stagnation, because the price of monopoly profits is excess capacity and a reduced willingness to invest. This chapter suggests that competition may not in practice play such a leading role in determining the characteristics of capitalist development. Those characteristics can be derived from firms' responses to changes in demand, which in turn are largely determined by the technical characteristics of output and production. Capital-intensive industries firms tend to increase output more than prices when demand increases, and decrease prices more than output if demand falls. Conversely, less capital-intensive firms tend to raise prices more than output if demand rises, and cut production more than prices if demand falls. The latter are concentrated in the luxury goods sector. It is the expansion of this sector, and the continuing decline of heavy industry, that account for the increasing ineffectiveness of Keynesian policies of fiscal expansion, and the stagnation and mass unemployment that are such a feature of the most "advanced" capitalist countries. The statistical data seems to support this view but it is also consistent with Steindl's greater emphasis on the role of competition.

In a very real sense, the points of controversy raised in this chapter are mere details, advancing Steindl's own conclusions. In Steindl (1989) he noted the contribution to the economic stagnation of the 1980s of the decline of heavy industry, the rise of the rentier firm, and the impoverishment of the welfare state. Although he emphasised the importance of competition during the long Keynesian boom, the intensity of that competition may even have increased during the 1980s (Auerbach 1988). Steindl's pioneering examination of capitalism has the ingredients for its extension into an age of post-industrialism and the decay of Keynesianism. But the proportions need to be adjusted. The distribution of income and the structure of industry, rather than competition, are the key policy issues of capitalism in our time.

Acknowledgements

I am grateful to Nina Shapiro, Tracy Mott, Geoff Harcourt and Victoria Chick for very helpful comments on an earlier draft of this chapter. The faults left in this chapter remain the author's responsibility. In particular, it does not consider developments after the early 1990s, when capitalism came much more strongly under the influence of the financial markets, whose inflation shifted demand even more towards luxury consumption than previously. This is examined in Mair, Laramie and Toporowski (2000). However, while Steindl did reflect in his later papers on some of these changes, he could not have anticipated them at the time when he developed his pioneering analysis of capitalist industry.

Notes

1 Steindl discusses the effects of excess capacity in a recession in Chapter 10 of *MSAC*.
2 Let the cost function be written as $\pi = P.Q - F - V.Q$ where π is gross profit, P is the price of output, Q is output, F is the fixed or overhead cost, V is the variable cost per unit. As a difference equation, this becomes $\Delta\pi = \Delta P.\Delta Q - V.\Delta Q$. A firm will be indifferent between price and quantity changes if none of them make any difference to profits. Setting $\Delta\pi$ equal to zero and rearranging gives $\Delta P.\Delta Q = V.\Delta Q$ or $\Delta P = V$.

3 Shapiro (1986) expands this line of argument.
4 This comparison is not altogether a fair one, since Steindl uses a gross profit margin concept that includes interest on bonds, while the argument in this chapter uses a gross profit margin *after* payment of interest. This would obviously understate the surplus, or operating profit, of highly geared heavy industries. Operating profit may be a more appropriate concept, but it is not given for a representative range of industries. However, interest charges are not the only costs of maintaining capital assets, and it seems reasonable to suppose that those other costs, principally depreciation, are incurred in proportion to the capital stock. Logic would therefore suggest that a more capital-using firm would have higher costs overhead costs at a given level of production than a less capital-intensive concern.

References

Auerbach, P. (1988) *Competition: The Economics of Industrial Change*, Oxford: Basil Blackwell.

Baran, P. A. and Sweezy, P. M. (1968) *Monopoly Capital: An Essay on the American Economic and Social Order*, Harmondsworth, Penguin Books.

Hicks, J. (1965) *Capital and Growth*, Oxford: Oxford University Press.

Kalecki, M. (1971) "Theories of Growth in Different Social Systems", *Monthly Review*, 5, pp. 72–79.

Kalecki, M. (1990, 1991) *Collected Works*, edited by J. Osiatyński, Oxford: Clarendon Press, vol. I, 1990; vol. II, 1991.

Lim, J. Y. (1991) "A Kaleckian Three-Sector Model for Third World Countries", *Journal of Contemporary Asia*, 21, 1, pp. 3–12.

Mair, D., Laramie, A.J. and Toporowski, J. (2000) 'Weintraub's Consumption Coefficient: Some Economic Implications and Evidence for the U.K.', *Cambridge Journal of Economics*, 24, 2, March, pp. 225–236.

Mills, C. Wright (1970) *The Sociological Imagination*, Harmondsworth: Penguin Books.

OECD (1995) *Economic Outlook*, Paris: Organisation for Economic Co-operation and Development, May.

Robinson, J. (1957) *An Essay on Marxian Economics*, London: Macmillan.

Shapiro, N. (1986) "New Industries and New Firms", *Eastern Economic Journal*, Vol. 12, No. 1, Jan./Mar. pp. 27–43.

Shapiro, N. (1990) "Josef Steindl", in P. Arestis, and M. Sawyer, (eds) *A Biographical Dictionary of Dissenting Economists*, Aldershot: Edward Elgar.

Steindl, J. (1945) *Small and Big Business*, Oxford: Basil Blackwell.

Steindl, J. (1965) *Random Processes and the Growth of Firms*, London: Charles Griffin and Co.

Steindl, J. (1976) *Maturity and Stagnation in American Capitalism*, New York: Monthly Review Press.

Steindl, J. (1981) "Some Comments on the Three Versions of Kalecki's Theory of the Trade Cycle", in N. Assorodobraj-Kula *et al.* (eds) *Studies in Economic Theory and Practice: Essays in Honour of Edward Lipinski*, Amsterdam: North Holland.

Steindl, J. (1989) "From Stagnation in the 1930s to Slow Growth in the 1970s", in Maxine Berg (ed.) *Political Economy in the Twentieth Century*, Oxford: Philip Allan.

Toporowski, J. (1990) "Profits, Wages and Industrial Structure", draft chapters, unpublished typescript.

Toporowski, J. (1991) "Two Enigmas in Kalecki's Methodology", *History of Economics Review*, No. 16, Summer, pp. 90–96.

Wells, J. (1989) "Uneven Development and De-industrialisation in the UK since 1979", in F. Green (ed.) *The Restructuring of the U.K. Economy*, Hemel Hempstead: Harvester Wheatsheaf.

Whitehead, A. N. (1938) *Science and the Modern World*, Harmondsworth: Penguin Books.

8 Market-limited growth and twentieth-century economic history

Rethinking economic stagnation in the American case

Michael A. Bernstein

> Almost all merchants and manufacturers save ... much more rapidly than it would be possible for the national capital to increase, so as to keep up the value of the produce. But if this be true of them as a body, taken one with another, it is quite obvious that, with their actual habits, they could not afford an adequate market to each other by exchanging their several products.[1]

The stagnation thesis

While concern with the problem of economic instability has punctuated the history of economic thought for several centuries, it is hardly surprising that the Great Depression of the twentieth century inspired a vast literature on the issue of investment failure and the maladjustment of investment plans.[2] In particular, the persistence of the depression and the over a decade-long weakening of economic performance that it caused prompted several investigators to formulate a "stagnation thesis" concerning mature capitalist economies. It was within this theoretical tradition that Josef Steindl made his remarkable contribution, *Maturity and Stagnation in American Capitalism*, in 1952.[3] Many empirical and theoretical inadequacies in other long-run arguments concerning the depression had spurred efforts to develop a more coherent and verifiable approach to the study of secular mechanisms in the inter-war period. Steindl's research, in this regard, attempted to resolve these weaknesses directly.

The literature that had focused on long-run factors in the American depression was distinctive in holding that the New York Stock Market crash of 1929 was less important than certain developments in the economy that had deleterious impacts throughout the inter-war period. Some authors — for example, Seymour Harris and Paul Sweezy — argued that during the 1920s the distribution of national income became increasingly skewed, lowering the economy's aggregate average propensity to consume. Others, such as Charles Kindleberger, W. Arthur Lewis, and

Vladimir Timoshenko, focused on a secular shift in the terms of trade between primary products and manufactured goods, due to the uneven development of the agricultural and industrial nations. This change in the terms of trade, they argued, created a credit crisis in world markets when bad crop yields occurred in 1929 and 1930. At the same time that agricultural economies were losing revenue because of poor crops and declining world demand, the developed economies were contracting credit for the developing nations and imposing massive trade restrictions such as America's Hawley-Smoot Tariff of 1930. As the agricultural nations went into a slump, the industrialized countries (most notably the United States) lost a major market for their output. Hence, the downturn of 1929 became more and more severe.[4]

Industrial organization economists, Adolf Berle and Gardiner Means most prominent among them, sought an explanation of the depression in the increasing extent of imperfect competition in the American economy of the early twentieth century.[5] Downward inflexibility of prices after the crash of 1929, caused by the concentrated structure of American industry and the impact of labor unions, intensified the effective demand problem and prevented the price system from reaching a new equilibrium at full employment. On the one side, "sticky prices" further limited the already constrained purchasing power of consumers. On the other, to the extent that noncompetitive pricing predominated in the capital goods sector, producers were less willing to buy new plant and equipment. Excessive real wages, held up by union pressure and New Deal policy, further contributed to persistent disequilibrium in labor markets. Price inflexibility thus inhibited the recovery of both final product demand and investment demand.[6]

There were several weaknesses in all these theories. Those authors who focused on an increasingly unequal distribution of income or on administered pricing did not marshal unambiguous evidence to make their case, nor did they specify precisely how such factors came to life in the inter-war economy. While Berle and Means claimed to have demonstrated a relative price inflexibility in concentrated economic sectors during the 1930s, their critics were unconvinced. Insofar as the aggregate price-level fell by one-third in the early 1930s, they argued, how inflexible could the general price system have been? The sticky prices thesis also relied on an assumption of perfect competition in all markets other than those where the imperfections existed. If this assumption were relaxed, the thesis did not hold. As Michał Kalecki pointed out, if "sticky wages" were responsible for the length of the depression, it followed that a reduction in wages would have eliminated the persistent disequilibrium. If, however, there were imperfections in product markets as well, a reduction in nominal wages would have lowered real wages, thereby exacerbating the effective demand crisis. Only if price adjustments were general and followed *instantaneously* by increased investment would the sticky prices thesis concerning the 1930s hold.[7]

The terms of trade argument similarly had a major flaw. The major weaknesses in the American economy of the inter-war period were domestic, and the collapse of demand on the part of primary product-exporting nations was not highly relevant. America's dependence on foreign markets was not significant in the inter-war years. During the 1920s, exports as a share of the nation's gross national product had annually averaged only a bit over 5 percent. A fall in export demand then could not have played a major role in worsening or prolonging the Great Depression.[8]

Continued research on secular mechanisms in the Great Depression necessarily relied upon the work of Joseph Schumpeter on cyclical processes in modern economies. Schumpeter held that the inter-war period was an era in which three major cycles of economic activity in the United States (and Europe) coincidentally reached their nadir.[9] These cycles were (1) the Kondratieff, a wave of fifty or more years associated with the introduction and dispersion of major inventions; (2) the Juglar, a wave of approximately ten years' duration that appeared to be linked with population movements; and (3) the Kitchin, a wave of about forty months' length that had the appearance of a typical inventory cycle.

Schumpeter's efforts were paralleled by those of Simon Kuznets and, more recently, Moses Abramovitz and Richard Easterlin. Kuznets was successful in documenting the existence of waves of some fifteen to twenty years in length. These periodic swings, according to Abramovitz, demonstrated that in the United States and other industrialized countries "development during the nineteenth and early twentieth centuries took the form of a series of surges in the growth of output and in capital and labor resources followed by periods of retarded growth." Significantly,

> each period of retardation in the rate of growth of output ... culminated in a protracted depression or in a period of stagnation in which business cycle recoveries were disappointing, failing to lift the economy to a condition of full employment or doing so only transiently.[10]

Most, if not all, of the "Kuznets Cycle" literature was concerned with the explicit dating of the long swings that appeared in the data. It seemed clear that these swings involved changes in resource endowments (including the size of population) and alterations in the intensity of resource utilization.[11] The specific behavioral mechanisms that could account for the Kuznets phenomenon (and its precise manifestation in the United States in the 1930s) were necessarily the focus of continued debate. It is in this context that one can understand the large literature on "secular stagnation" upon which Steindl had such a striking impact.

Broadly speaking, the so-called stagnation theorists of this century grouped into those who evinced a "Schumpeterian pessimism" about the declining incidence of innovations and new technologies, and those who shared a "Keynes–Hansen pessimism" concerning the shrinkage of investment outlets owing to a decline in the rate of population growth.[12] Both groups agreed that stagnation or, as it was sometimes called, economic maturity involved

> [a] decrease of the rate of growth of heavy industries and of building activity ... [and] the slowing down of the rate of growth of the total quantity of production, of employment, and usually of population. It [also involved] the rising relative importance of consumer goods.

They also believed that "the appearance of industrial maturity raise[d] profound questions concerning the ability of an enterprise system to produce a progressive evolution of the economy".[13]

The "Keynes–Hansen" pessimism held that as population growth fell off, and as major markets in housing, clothing, food, and services consequently contracted, outlets for new investment were quickly limited to those created by the introduction of new technology or new products. To the extent that recovery from a depression required investment outlays above and beyond the level of depreciation allowances, an upturn would be dependent on the availability, in an adequate volume, of opportunities in new industries and processes. If these were not forthcoming, as some stagnation theorists believed was true of the 1930s, the only avenue out of the slump would be deficit spending to augment consumer purchasing power. But political barriers to such government action in the 1930s left many economies mired in an environment of excess capacity and inadequate demand.[14]

There was a serious inadequacy in the arguments concerning economic maturity and population growth. The theory conflated population with effective demand. As one critic put it:

> It is sometimes maintained that the increase in population encourages investment because the entrepreneurs anticipate a broadening market. What is important, however, in this context is not the increase in population but in purchasing power. The increase in the number of paupers does not broaden the market. For instance, increased population does not mean necessarily a higher demand for houses: without an increase in the purchasing power the result may well be crowding of more people into the existing dwelling space.[15]

A more systematic theory had to argue that, for secular reasons, the purchasing power of the population, rather than the size of the population itself, fell in advanced capitalist systems.

Much like the population theory, the variant of the stagnation theory that focused on the decline of innovation and technical change, as a factor in the distress of the 1930s, embodied many inconsistencies and question-able assertions. The lower rate of technical change, and the decline in the number of major innovations, that were posited as a primary cause of the inability of the economy to recover in the course of the Great Depression, were deemed to be exogenous factors derived from the state of technical knowledge at the time.[16] Little justification of this position was offered. Furthermore, meager attention was given to a seeming contradiction in the argument. If during the 1930s little technical change took place, why did not the eventual reduction in the amount of capital equipment avail-able (owing to firm exits and the periodic obsolescence of plant) result in a revival of capital goods output?[17]

There was one further objection to the technology argument that was apparent to some of the stagnation theorists themselves. There was an implicit assumption made that new innovations were always of the capital-using type; thus, had innovation occurred in the 1930s, net investment demand would have absorbed large capital outlays thereby generating a robust upturn. But if innovations were capital-saving, this argument foundered. Heavy investment in earlier stages of economic growth (in, for example, railroads, motor cars, and housing) may have given way (in later periods) to newer forms of investment in managerial technique and information processing. These latter innovations may not have absorbed very large amounts of investment expenditure at all. While they may have therefore improved the organization and efficiency of production, their impact on aggregate spending would not have been adequate to the task of systematic recovery.[18]

The contribution of Josef Steindl

Josef Steindl provided the most sophisticated version of the economy, maturity idea. Not surprisingly, he did so in part by explicitly situating the Great Depression in the United States within a long-term development framework. His work linked economic stagnation directly with the behav-ior of capitalist enterprise, thereby avoiding the mechanistic qualities of many of the stagnation arguments as well as their frequent appeals to exogenous factors. Steindl's version of the maturity thesis was that long-run tendencies toward capital concentration, inherent in capitalist devel-opment over time, led to a lethargic attitude towards competition and investment.[19] Specifically, the emergence of concentrated markets made difficult, and in some cases impossible, that expulsion of excess capacity required for revival after a trough.

Steindl argued that in any given industry, there existed a hierarchy of firms based upon the relative level of prime production costs. Such a hier-archy would exist because firms would have grown at different rates, entered the industry at varying times, and therefore installed equipment of assorted degrees of cost-effectiveness given their past profit performance (and their differential access to outside funds). The gross margin, *Ei*, for the *i*th firm, therefore, could be expressed as:

$$E_i = P_i Y_i / (wL_i + M_i)$$

where P_i was the firm's output price, Y_i the level of output, and where w, L_i, and M_i were respectively the wage-rate, the size of the hired labor force, and the level of materials costs facing the firm. (Steindl assumed, at least initially, that the wage-rate was not employer specific.) This gross margin, Steindl held, was the fundamental competitive resource of the firm. It provided internal funds for investment and the securing of outside loans. For Steindl, it was obvious that the extent of a firm's internal funds was often directly proportional to its ability to secure credit from the public by means of bonds, equity issues, or bank loans. This was primarily due, in his view, to the "good will" that was commonly associated with firm size. Larger firms clearly had access to funds (both internal and external) far in excess of those for smaller firms.

In addition, a larger gross margin would enable a firm to initiate sales and advertising efforts and quality campaigns (product differentiation) that could possibly allow it to appropriate other (less powerful) firms' markets. Most important, the gross margin could provide the means with which a firm might innovate and apply technically superior methods to production. The resultant savings in costs would be the basis of price cuts to drive competitors out of the market. Smaller firms that could not introduce these superior techniques would thereby experience a shrinkage in profit margins resulting from the price war. The inability of these firms to employ new techniques might simply be due to the fact that they could not pay the price to install them. In fact, to the extent that patent laws existed, they might not have the funds for research and development efforts to deploy new methods themselves.

Figure 8.1 allows for the graphical depiction of the competitive process of which Steindl conceived. The ray VR expresses the cost hierarchy of the industry with the most inefficient firms at the higher point of the ordinate — their output is lower in keeping with the notion of their minimal share of the market. Assuming that a standard mark-up pricing rule is used in the industry, VW describes a gradient of prices that expresses the differences in costs incurred by the various firms. Triangle RVW is thus the gross margin of the total industry. The hierarchy of profit margins becomes immediately apparent. The firms with the larger margins (owing to lower costs) have larger shares of the market by assumption. Assume that demand increases in the industry, with the leading firms expanding output to S′ from S. Their large margins allow for the introduction of cost-cutting techniques at R′. Should the resulting increase in profit margins cause the leading firms to accumulate such that their rate of expansion rises above the market rate, a price cut ensues in the struggle for a greater

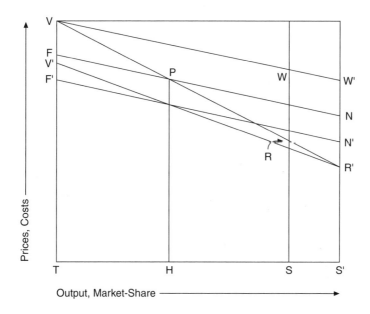

Figure 8.1 Schematic representation of the competitive structure of an industry (source: Steindl (1976, p. 44), Figure 3).

share of the market. At the new (lower) price level FN, the least efficient
firms are forced out due to the excess of their production costs over the
market price. Producers TH are thus eliminated.

Consider a situation where the market in question is more concentrated
than in the foregoing case. Presumably, the cost differentials among firms
are less severe insofar as, over time, a small number of firms have become
dominant by means of similar technology, sales efforts, and so on. Thus,
the spectrum of costs structures is now V′R′, not VR′. This being the case,
the expulsion of a certain number of firms from the industry, by a
competitive drive for market share, requires a larger price reduction than
in the first case. The price level FN, sufficient to expel producers TH
before, now threatens the economic existence of no one. To expel firms
TH, at this point, would require a further cut in the price level to F′N′. The
unwillingness to engage in more severe price cutting of this kind stems
from the fact that large reductions in price can invite retaliation that may
generate a downward spiral of the price structure in general.[20]

Price inflexibility in concentrated industries is intensified during depressions and this has an important impact on the response of firms to economic fluctuations. The net revenue of firms tends to be so jeopardized in
a slump that strategies of price reduction are viewed as unfeasible. There
may even be incentives to raise prices in order to compensate for the
reduction in the volume of sales. For a given industry, therefore, the

impact of a decline in the rate of growth (i.e., the aggregate rate of capital accumulation) will depend on the extent to which the industry is concentrated. In a sector where the squeezing out of competitors is relatively easy, large declines in demand will result in the reduction of profit margins (for each firm) as prices are cut. By contrast, in a concentrated market, profit margins will tend to be inelastic in the face of reductions in demand.

At the macroeconomic level the implications of inelastic profit margins for cyclical performance are most profound. Insofar as price reductions do not obtain in the event of a decline in the rate of growth, the necessary adjustment of sectoral rates of expansion to the aggregate rate will require reductions in the rate of capacity utilization. When viewed in terms of the sector as a whole, if prices are fixed, output must fall to bring gross margins down. If industrial structure were more competitive, excess capacity would not result from a decline in the accumulation-rate; rather, prices would fall.

Reductions in capacity utilization imply not only declines in national income but also increases in unemployment. In the presence of underutilized capacity, firms will be increasingly disinclined to undertake any net investment. A cumulative process is thereby established wherein a decline in the rate of growth, by generating reductions in the rate of capacity utilization, will lead to a further decline in the rate of expansion as net investment is reduced. Individual firms, by believing (in ways comparable to Malthus' "merchants and manufacturers" of old who "save … much more rapidly than it would be possible for the national capital to increase") that decreases in their own investment will alleviate their own burden of excess capacity, merely intensify the problem economy-wide. The greater the proportion of the nation's industry that is highly concentrated, the greater the tendency for a cyclical downturn to develop into a progressive (and seemingly endless) decline.

A further consequence of the existence of highly concentrated sectors in the national economy is the impact it has on effective demand. The higher profit margins secured by large firms are indicative of an increasingly skewed distribution of output that, when combined with the reluctance of firms to invest (or otherwise spend) their revenues, generates a rising aggregate marginal propensity to save. Declining effective demand is combined with rising excess capacity when a slump occurs. The potential for recovery, barring the intervention of exogenous shocks, government spending, or the penetration of foreign markets, is therefore greatly lessened.

What is central to Steindl's thesis, and what endows it with much of its appeal, is the conception of long-term alterations in industrial structure that make the economy as a whole more incapable both of recovering from cyclical instability and of generating continued growth. The emergence of oligopolistic market structure is taken to be inherent in the process of capitalist development insofar as that process is coterminous with the development of large-scale manufacturing techniques. Economic maturity and the threat of stagnation result because the growing incidence of "[o]ligopoly brings about a maldistribution of funds by shifting profits to those industries which are reluctant to use them".[21] In order to escape stagnation, capital must be redistributed either to more competitive sectors or new industries, although such shifts can only proceed (given the difficulties of obtaining technical knowledge and good-will in new product lines) with considerable time lags.

Rethinking economic stagnation

Interestingly enough, there exists no clear relationship between stagnation and concentration in American manufacturing during the Great Depression. By applying a static conception of market structure, investigators have tended to focus on the number of firms in an industry as the primary determinant of a sector's competitiveness. The difficulty lies in the fact that cross-section data on firm numbers provide no information concerning those differentials in costs that are the basis of pricing strategies. Given large disparities in techniques and costs, it is possible that a small number of enterprises may, over time, engage in large amounts of competitition. Conversely, a sector with a large number of identical firms may prove to be quite lethargic, given the absence of cost differentials that can be competitively exploited. Not surprisingly, therefore, the historical record of the 1930s seemingly does not give Steindl's argument unqualified support. Some highly concentrated industries were relatively vibrant during the decade, while others less so, appeared virtually moribund.[22] In addition, the data on sectoral shares of wages in the value-added, that Steindl cited as indices of competitiveness, were similarly misleading.[23] A rising (falling) turn in the wage-share may not necessarily indicate a competitive decline (non-competitive rise) in the industry's gross margin, but rather may demonstrate changes in the labor-intensity of that sector's technology over time. Clearly, the evidence concerning market structure was a frail reed upon which Steindl attempted to base his theory. Whether a given industry is dynamic or not involves several issues that are not directly linked with numbers of firms or the extent of capital concentration — issues having to do with the industry's position in the economy's input–output matrix; the durability of its output; and the relative maturity of the industry with respect to the shifting composition of the economy as a whole.

The weakeness in Steindl's analysis do not, of course, obscure the importance of his contribution to an understanding of the Great Depression in particular, and of maturity in capitalist economies in general. That importance derives from the fact that Steindl attempted to situate the decade of the 1930s within a larger historical framework. In this context, he could view the Great Depression as the outcome of an interaction between cyclical forces dating from 1929, and tendencies of long-run development spanning a half-century or more.

Steindl's conception of long-term capitalist development was obviously embedded within a theoretical tradition that began with Marx. That tradition posited the concentration of capital as the major expression of secular growth. To attempt to grasp capitalist development in terms of the increasing concentration of capital, as Marx and Steindl did, it was necessary to locate the primary determinants of growth in the production process itself, i.e., in the firm. Changes in the role of markets, markets being defined as both loci of purchasing power and as collections of needs for specific kinds of goods, had no place in the theory.[24]

Conceptually, capitalist economies may avoid (and, in the latter half of this century, have avoided) tendencies toward stagnation through exogenous stimuli such as war, territorial expansion, or international monetary networks that privilege some industrial systems relative to others, and of course through product innovation and technical change. Indeed, it is this last potential avenue for expansion that has been both common in fact, and most germane to the extension of the neoKeynesian and neoMarxian theoretical frameworks. Even so, such compositional transformations in modern economies occasion a great deal of instability and unpredictability in performance.

Secular changes in the growth performance and potential of various industries must offset declines in certain groups with rises in others. The chance that such changes in sectoral performance will proceed smoothly is small — and economic history provides ample testimony to this fact.[25] While the possibility of terminal stagnation has not been realized in advanced capitalist states, nevertheless economic performance in those economies, throughout the past four decades of this century has been at times erratic and often premised more on external developments than internal mechanisms of recovery and expansion.

Secular transitions in development involve the decline of old and the rise of new industries. These alterations in the composition of national output tend to be discontinuous and disruptive not because of imperfections in markets but rather because of forces inherent in the accumulation of capital over time. First, the ongoing expansion of the capitalist economy is coterminous with the advance of scientific and technical knowledge that transforms production techniques, cost structures, and the availability of raw materials, and that creates entirely new inputs and outputs. Consider, for example, the emergence of fossil fuels, the replacement of natural fibers with synthetics, and the rise of internal combustion as a means of locomotion. Entire industries are made obsolete or virtually so, while new ones are created. Second, the structural milieu in which product and technical changes take place is itself a product of economic growth.

Concentration of capital may lead to unequal access to investment funds, which obstructs further the possibility of easy transitions in industrial activity. Because of their past record of profitability, large enterprises have higher credit ratings and easier access to credit facilities, and they are able to put up larger collateral for a loan. Equity issues by such firms are more readily financed and sold, and such firms can avoid takeovers more easily than small firms. Large firms, too, may have commonalities of interest with financial institutions through interlocking directorates. All these factors may impede the flow of capital out of old and into new sectors, thereby making shortfalls in aggregate economic performance much worse.

Compositional and structural change in economies may also precipitate serious unemployment problems that interfere with the achievement of full capacity output. New industries may have differing capital intensities and skill requirements, relative to older sectors, that complicate (or possibly even prevent) the absorption of unemployed workers. The problem may be twofold: newer industries may not grow fast enough to provide employment opportunities for those laid off in older sectors; but even if higher growth rates are achieved, the newer industries may require different amounts and altogether different kinds of labor for their production. Structural unemployment may be the troubling and persistent consequence.

Finally, changes in the relationship of a national economy to the world economic system may also be responsible for wide fluctuations in macroeconomic behavior. A resurgence of competition from other national systems previously excluded from or inadequately prepared for international commerce may seriously affect the fortunes of domestic industries grown used to protected or exclusive markets. Transformations in international currency systems, whereby a nation's monetary unit that had previously served as *numeraire* and means of international clearance is rapidly integrated into a general floating currency system, will also profoundly change the performance characteristics of that economy. Inflationary pressures at home now may translate into an export boom as a currency is devalued; while deflationary patterns may yield an upswing in imports to the detriment of domestic producers. Policy flexibility and independence may also be constrained as a nation's economy becomes more open to economies elsewhere. Domestic changes in fiscal and monetary policy will now have international trade consequences as well. Modulations of interest rates, for example, will affect the flow of capital across national borders as investors compare rates of return in various nations.[26]

National economic performance may also, in a mature setting, require increasing involvement of the state itself. Maintaining sufficient outlets for net investment expenditure might possibly involve deficit spending to bolster effective demand; direct government purchases of goods and services (particularly of public goods such as infrastructure and military and law-enforcement equipment); and government oversight of the penetration of foreign markets. These efforts might conceivably be paralleled by rising outlays by private firms on sales efforts, distribution mechanisms, and various means to enhance consumer credit.[27] While for most neoclassical economic theorists, fiscal and monetary mechanisms stand as instruments of periodic countercyclical policy, for neoKeynesian and neoMarxian economists governmental involvement in mature economies may be a permanent (and ever increasing) feature of modern industrial states.

The American case

Steindl had, of course, focused his work on the inter-war economic crisis of the 1930s. His central theses regarding maturity and stagnation in advanced capitalist economies seemed particularly compelling when viewed in terms of the historical experience of the Great Depression. Yet both the post-war record, at least in the case of the United States, and some of the theoretical lacunae in his earlier claims, led Steindl to modify some of the arguments of his 1952 book. With the 1976 republication of *Maturity and Stagnation in American Capitalism*, he allowed that technical innovation, product development, public spending, and research and development initiatives might provide the means to escape from investment inertia. Even so, he was extremely concerned that most accumulation strategies, in mature capitalist nations, would be focused on military-industrial activity and war itself. Using both public and private investment funds for other purposes, while obviously desirable, would be "exceedingly hard" given "the workings of [U.S.] political institutions".[28]

The wisdom (not to mention the prescience) of Steindl's 1976 observations is made apparent so soon as one surveys the more recent evolution of American capitalism. American accumulation in the latter half of this century has, on the one side, confirmed many of Steindl's suppositions regarding expansion in advanced industrial states. On the other, it has demonstrated both the unique and abiding flexibility of capitalism in the face of contradictory tendencies toward underutilization, and the importance (even at times the possible centrality) of political and social forces often understood by economists to be exogenous. In all these respects, contemporary history portrays the conceptual power and importance of what Steindl had to say when he first examined the crisis of the 1930s. But it also reminds us of the unyielding impacts of contingency and human agency in economic performance over time.

World War II had achieved in the United States, of course, what the New Deal could not — economic recovery. With the start of war in Europe, the unemployment rate had already begun to fall so that by the time of the Japanese offensive at Pearl Harbor, only 7 percent of the labor force remained idle. American entry into the war brought almost instantaneous resolution of the persistent economic difficulties of the inter-war years. Between 1939 and 1944 the national product, measured in current dollars, increased by almost 125 percent, ultimately rising to $212 billion by 1945.

Yet as World War II came to a close many economists and business people worried about the possibility of a drop in the level of prosperity and employment to one far below that of the war. But these apprehensions proved to be unwarranted.[29] By 1946, gross national product fell less than the post-war reduction in government spending; unemployment did not even reach 4 percent; consumer spending did not fall at all, and eventually rose dramatically. Although recessions occurred between 1945 and the mid-1970s, most of them lasted only about a year or less, and none of them remotely approached the severity of the Great Depression of the 1930s. During these three decades American manufacturing output steadily increased with only minor setbacks. According to the Federal Reserve Board's index, manufacturing production doubled between 1945 and 1965, and tripled between 1945 and 1976.

Such robust economic performance is hardly surprising in wartime — especially when conflict is global and, with a few exceptions, kept outside of national boundaries. What is most striking about the American economic experience linked with World War II was the enduring growth and prosperity of the *post-war* years. Consumption and investment behavior played a major part in this great prosperity of the late 1940s and 1950s. As soon as Germany and Japan had surrendered, private and foreign investment in the United States rose quickly. On the domestic side, reconversion was itself an investment stimulus. Modernization and deferred replacement projects required renewed and large deployments of funds. Profound scarcities of consumer goods, the production of which had been long postponed by wartime mobilization needs, necessitated major retooling and expansion efforts. Even fear of potentially high inflation, emerging in the wake of the dismantling of the price and wage controls of the war years, prompted many firms to move forward the date of ambitious and long-term investment projects. On the foreign side, both individuals and governments were eager to find a refuge for capital that had been in virtual hiding during the war itself. Along with a jump in domestic investment, therefore, a large capital inflow began in late 1945 and early 1946.

Domestic consumption was the second major component of post-war growth. Bridled demand and high household savings due to wartime shortages, rationing, and controls, coupled with the generous wage rates of the high-capacity war economy all contributed to a dramatic growth in consumer spending at war's end. The jump in disposable income was bolstered by the rapid reduction in wartime surtaxes and excises. And the baby boom of the wartime generation expressed itself economically in high levels of demand for significant items like appliances, automobiles, and housing. G.I. Bill benefits additionally served to increase the demand for housing and such things as educational services with associated impacts on construction and other industrial sectors.

Foreign demand for American exports grew rapidly in the immediate post-war years. In part, the needs of devastated areas could only be met by the one industrial base that had been nearly untouched by war-related destruction. Explicit policy commitments to the rebuilding of allied and occupied territories, such as the Marshall Plan in Europe, also served to increase the foreign market for the output of American industry. Even so, one of the most significant contexts within which the impressive post-war growth of the American economy took place was the unique and special set of arrangements developed for international trade at the Bretton Woods Conference in 1944.

When the allied nations' financial ministers gathered at Bretton Woods in New Hampshire, just before the war's end, they were concerned to reconfigure world trade and financial flows so that the disputes so characteristic of the inter-war years 1919–1939 could be avoided and stability maintained. Along with the creation of an International Bank for Reconstruction and Development, and of an International Monetary Fund, the conference decided to establish fixed exchanged rates between the US dollar and all other internationally traded currencies. The value of the dollar itself was set in terms of gold at $35 per ounce. This installed a benchmark against which the value of all other currencies was measured. As the American economy was, by far, the most powerful at the time, it seemed prudent and indeed necessary that its currency play such a central international role.

American post-war prosperity and the benefits of world economic leadership continued throughout most of the 1950s. The added fiscal stimulus of the Korean War also played a role in maintaining the high levels of growth and employment characteristic of the decade. Republican President Dwight Eisenhower, carrying on in the tradition of his Democratic predecessor Harry Truman, repeatedly committed his administration to the practice of compensatory demand management. But the prosperity of the 1950s, while robust and impressive, nevertheless weakened by 1957. This set the stage for the arrival of a new brand of economics in Washington, imbued with the doctrines of Keynesianism.

From the "New Frontier" policies of John Kennedy, to the "Great Society" agenda of his successor Lyndon Johnson, through the declaration of a "New Federalism" by Richard Nixon, there ensued an era of sustained central government intervention in the nation's economic life. The self-assurance of many, but not all of the "new" economists of the early 1960s, that the goal of achieving simultaneously acceptable levels of unemployment and inflation could be realized, has more recently been shattered. But throughout the 1960s and much of the 1970s, and for some even during the 1980s, the perceived obligation of government to secure overall economic stability was not seriously questioned and remained one of the more important changes of twentieth-century American economic history.

Economic stagnation: past and present

Historical specificity notwithstanding, American economic performance in the latter half of [the twentieth] century appears to conform in many major respects with the general analytical propositions of Steindl's inter-war analysis. The ability to forestall and/or overcome tendencies toward economic stagnation has depended upon a varied and uncommon set of circumstances both global and domestic in their genesis and impact. But a continuation of such a charmed existence is apparently no longer possible. Steindl himself noted, in 1976, that "the cheerful extroverted era of [post-war] growth has apparently come to an end". He held that the reasons for this were "the reduction of tension between the superpowers ... the increase in tension within the capitalist countries ... and ... the emergence of environment, raw material, and energy problems".[30]

In the midst of a return to the weak and intermittent growth of earlier decades of [the twentieth] century, there has also obtained an altogether reactionary (re)orientation of fiscal and monetary policy. A resurgence of general equilibrium approaches to cyclical phenomena has prompted the formulation of a "new classical macroeconomics" and the rise of a "rational expectations school".[31] These intellectual developments, linked with political events having to do with the backlash against the progressive politics of the New Frontier and the Great Society, eliminated Keynesian thinking from the formulation of responses to contemporary economic problems. Thus, we have the more recent attempts to balance fiscal expenditures (and, until recently, tighten monetary variables) in the face of unemployment and shortfalls in national product.

There is, of course, a major difference between past decades and today, in this regard, at least in the United States. Timid countercyclical policy in the inter-war period was to some extent the result of ignorance and misplaced confidence in old remedies. Today, slow-growth policies are derived from the politics of reaction and resentment. To put it in the words of Josef Steindl once again, contemporary "arguments against full employment have got the upper hand in the councils of the powers, and thus we witness stagnation not as an incomprehensible fate, as in the 1930s, but stagnation as a policy".[32]

Acknowledgments

For comments on a previous draft, I am very grateful to Tracy Mott and Nina Shapiro.

Notes

1 From Malthus (1976 pp. 423–424).
2 I have surveyed much of this literature (published in English and as it applied to the US experience) in Bernstein (1985).
3 See Steindl (1976).
4 See Harris (1948); Sweezy (1968); Lewis (1950, pp. 55–56); Kindleberger (1973, pp. 292–293); and Timoshenko (1933, pp. 541–543).
5 See, for example, Means (1935) and Means and Berle (1968).
6 See Reynolds (1939); and Thorp and Growder (1941). Interestingly enough, Backman (1939) challenged the empirical relevance of the administered prices theory and argued (on p. 486) that in order to understand the low levels of output that prevailed during the thirties, one had to examine the "character of the market; durability of the product; capital goods versus consumers' goods; joint demand; stage of development of an industry; [and] necessaries versus luxury products".
7 See Kalecki (1969, pp. 40–59).
8 See U.S. Department of Commerce (1975), part 2, series U201–206, p. 887.
9 See Schumpeter (1939), vol. 2, pp. 905–1050.
10 See Kuznets (1958) , Abramovitz (1961), and Easterlin (1968).
11 See Abramovitz (1961, p. 241).
12 As suggested by William Fellner (1954). It should be pointed out that Fellner had earlier rejected all arguments concerning stagnation on the grounds that none of their propositions could be formulated in behavioral terms. See Fellner (1941).
13 The quotations are taken from McLauglin and Watkins (1939).
14 See Hansen (1939) and Keynes (1937). A complete, if rather polemical exposition of the stagnation thesis may be found in Terborgh (1945).
15 From Kalecki (1943). Also see Sweezy (1940). As Terborgh (1945) argued on p. 181: "There is no rigid physical relation ... between the number of families in the country and the amount and value of the housing they will pay to occupy. Demand depends not only on their number, but on their incomes."
16 See Hansen (1941, pp. 279ff.), and Kalecki (1962). Kalecki did concede, on pp. 134 and 147, that innovations might not be wholly exogenous and might, in fact, be influenced (with appreciable lags) by changes in profit-rates, output, and the size of the capital stock. Even so, he also argued, elsewhere, that the exogeneity of technical change indicated that "long-run development [was] not inherent in the capitalist economy". See Kalecki (1968, p. 161).
17 As admitted by Kalecki (1971, p. 30).
18 See Kalecki (1968, p. 159), and Hansen (1941, pp. 310, 315). Reflecting on the differences in innovation that may obtain in an economy over time, Hansen noted (on p. 314): "The transformation of a rural economy into a capitalistic one is something distinctly different from the further evolution of a society which has already reached the status of a fully-developed machine technique."
19 The following exposition, both textual and graphic, is derived from Steindl (1976), Chs II–V, IX, XIII; and Steindl (1945, pp. 48–54, 63–66). The idea that large concentrated firms eschew major investment opportunities, owing to a desire to maintain their dominant market position, also played a role in the conception of economic stagnation developed by Michał Kalecki. See Kalecki (1943, p. 92); and Kalecki (1968, p. 159).
20 This particular assertion obviously ties in with the kinked demand curve theory of oligopoly. See, for example, Sweezy (1939).
21 From Steindl (1976, p. xv).

22 Explicit documentation for these claims may be found in Bernstein (1982), Chs III–IV.
23 See Steindl (1976), Ch. VIII.
24 This is not say that both theorists did not address the problem of effective demand, but rather that their conception of the role of markets was fairly limited in scope. Steindl, in particular, did not fully consider the effect of investment strategies geared toward product diversification and sales efforts.
25 See, for example, Aldcroft (1977), Bernstein (1987), Dahmen (1970), and Svennilson (1954).
26 Interestingly enough, Keynes suggested to Roy Harrod in 1942 that "the whole management of the domestic economy depends upon being free to have the appropriate rate of interest without reference to the rates prevailing elsewhere in the world. Capital control is a corollary to this". See Crotty (1983, pp. 59–65) and Keynes (1980, pp. 148–149). Also see Keynes (1933) and Williamson (1985).
27 Steindl, at one point, noted that expanded systems of consumer credit were a means by which investment opportunities could be maintained in mature economies. See Steindl (1966).
28 See Steindl (1976, pp. xii–xiii).
29 In fact, it was this dramatic post-war economic performance, one that seemingly belied the stagnation theories of the inter-war years, that in part prompted Steindl to open the new introduction to the 1976 edition of *Maturity and Stagnation* with the observation that "[t]he first (1952) edition of this book appeared at a time which could not have been less propitious for its success." See Steindl (1976, p. ix).
30 From Steindl (1976, p. xvi). Steindl also remarked here, on pp. xvi–xvii, in words that today seem as apposite as they did over sixteen years ago that

> the political and psychological basis of the postwar boom has been sapped by such developments as these: public spending ... [has] decreased ... the competition in technology ... and education unleashed by Sputnik has flagged; the development in these fields has been dominated instead by [an] internal reaction against intellectuals and youth ... the cooperation between the capitalist powers has broken down ... [and] the internal stresses of groups contending for shares in the national income have shown themselves as inflationary.

31 See, for a significant and influential example, Lucas, (1975, 1977). Also see Steindl (1984).
22 From Steindl (1976, p. xvii). On the political constraints within which counter-cyclical policy is often formulated, see the pathbreaking essay of Kalecki (1972). Also of interest, in this regard, are Nordhaus (1975) and Fair (1978).

References

Abramovitz, Moses (1961) "The Nature and Significance of Kuznets Cycles", *Economic Development and Cultural Change*, 9, 225–248.

Aldcroft, Derek H. (1977) *From Versailles To Wall Street: 1919–1929*, London: Allen Lane.

Backman, Jules (1939) "Price Inflexibility and Changes in Production", *American Economic Review*, 29, 480–486.

Bernstein, Michael A. (1980) "Problems in the Theory of Production and Exchange: An Essay in Classical and Marxian Themes", *Australian Economic Papers*, 19, 248–263.

Bernstein, Michael A. (1982) "Long-Term Economic Growth and the Problem of Recovery in American Manufacturing: A Study of the Great Depression in the United States, 1929–1939," unpublished Ph.D. dissertation, Yale University.

Bernstein, Michael A. (1987) *The Great Depression: Delayed Recovery and Economic Change in America, 1929–1939*, Cambridge: Cambridge University Press.

Bernstein, Michael A. (1985) "Explaining America's Greatest Depression: A Reconsideration of an Older Literature", *Rivista di Storia Economica*, 2 (second series), 155–174.

Crotty, J.R. (1983) "On Keynes and Capital Flight", *Journal of Economic Literature*, 21, 59–65.

Dahmen, Erik (1970) *Entrepreneurial Activity and the Development of Swedish Industry: 1919–1939*, [trans., A. Leijonhufvud], New York, Irwin.

Easterlin, Richard A. (1968) *Population, Labor Force, and Long Swings in Economic Growth: The American Experience*, Cambridge. MA: National Bureau of Economic Research.

Fair, Ray (1978) "The Effect of Economic Events on Votes for President", *Review of Economics and Statistics*, 60, 158–173.

Fellner, William (1941) "The Technological Argument of the Stagnation Thesis", *Quarterly Journal of Economics*, 55, 638–651.

Fellner, William (1954) "Full Use or Underutilization: Appraisal of Long-Run Factors other than Defense", *American Economic Review*, 44, 423–433.

Hansen, Alvin H. (1939) "Economic Progress and Declining Population Growth", *American Economic Review*, 29, 1–15.

Hansen, Alvin H. (1941) *Full Recovery or Stagnation?*, New York: Norton.

Harris, Seymour (1948) *Saving American Capitalism: A Liberal Economic Program*, New York: Knopf.

Kalecki, Michał (1943) *Studies in Economic Dynamics*, London: George Allen and Unwin.

Kalecki, Michał (1962) "Observations on the Theory of Growth", *Economic Journal*, 72, 134–153.

Kalecki, Michał (1968) *Theory of Economic Dynamics: An Essay on Cyclical and Long-Run Changes in Capitalist Economy*, New York: Monthly Review Press.

Kalecki, Michał (1969) *Studies in the Theory of Business Cycles, 1933–39*, New York: Augustus M. Kelley.

Kalecki, Michał (1971) *Selected Essays on the Dynamics of the Capitalist Economy, 1933–1970*, Cambridge: Cambridge University Press.

Kalecki, Michał (1972) "Political Aspects of Full Employment", in M. Kalecki, *The Last Phase in the Transformation of Capitalism*, New York: Monthly Review Press. pp. 75–83.

Keynes, John Maynard (1933) "National Self-Sufficiency", *Yale Review*, 22, 755–769.

Keynes, John Maynard (1937) "Some Economic Consequences of a Declining Population", *Eugenics Review*, 29, 13–17.

Keynes, John Maynard (1964) *The General Theory of Employment, Interest and Money*, New York: Harcourt, Brace & World.

Keynes, John Maynard (1980) *Activities 1940–1944: Shaping the Post-War World; The Clearing Union*, in D. Moggridge, (ed.) *The Collected Writings of John Maynard Keynes*, vol. 25, Basingstoke: Macmillan.

Kindleberger, Charles P. (1973) *The World in Depression: 1929–1939*, Berkeley, CA: University of California Press.

Kuznets, Simon (1958) "Long Swings in the Growth of Population and in Related Economic Variables", *Proceedings of the American Philosophical Society*, 102, 25–52.

Lewis, W. Arthur (1950) *Economic Survey, 1919–1939*, New York: Blakiston.

Lucas, Robert E. (1975) "An Equilibrium Model of the Business Cycle", *Journal of Political Economy*, 83, 1113–1144.

Lucas, Robert E. (1977) "Understanding Business Cycles", in K. Brunner and A.H. Meltzer (eds), *Stabilization of the Domestic and International Economy*, Amsterdam: North-Holland, pp. 7–29.

Malthus, The Reverend Thomas R. (1976) *Principles of Political Economy Considered With a View to Their Practical Application*, in P. Sraffa with M.H. Dobb (eds), *The Works and Correspondence of David Ricardo*, Cambridge: Cambridge University Press, 1976, vol. II.

McLaughlin, G.E. and Watkins, R.J. (1939) "The Problem of Industrial Growth in a Mature Economy", *American Economic Review*, 29, 1–14.

Means, Gardiner C. (1935) "Price Inflexibility and the Requirements of a Stabilizing Monetary Policy", *Journal of the American Statistical Association*, 30, 401–413.

Means, Gardiner C. and Berle, Adolf A. (1968) *The Modern Corporation and Private Property*, New York: Harcourt, Brace and World.

Nordhaus, William (1975) "The Political Business Cycle", *Review of Economic Studies*, 42, 169–190.

Reynolds, Lloyd G. (1939) "Producers' Goods Prices in Expansion and Decline", *Journal of the American Statistical Association*, 34, 32–40.

Schumpeter, Joseph A. (1939) *Business Cycles: A Theoretical, Historical, and Statistical Analysis of the Capitalist Process*, New York: McGraw-Hill.

Steindl, Josef (1945) *Small and Big Business: Economic Problems of the Size of Firms*, Oxford: Basil Blackwell.

Steindl, Josef (1966) "On Maturity in Capitalist Economies", in *Problems of Economic Dynamics and Planning: Essays in Honour of Michal Kalecki*, Oxford: Pergamon, pp. 423–432.

Steindl, Josef (1976) *Maturity and Stagnation in American Capitalism*, New York: Monthly Review Press.

Steindl, Josef (1984) "Reflections on the Present State of Economics", *Banca Nazionale del Lavoro Quarterly Review*, 148, 3–14.

Svennilson, Ingvar (1954) *Growth and Stagnation in the European Economy*, United Nations Economic Commission for Europe.

Sweezy, A.R. (1940) "Population Growth and Investment Opportunity", *Quarterly Journal of Economics*, 55, 64–79.

Sweezy, P.M. (1939) "Demand Under Conditions of Oligopoly", *Journal of Political Economy*, 47, 568–573.

Sweezy, P.M. (1968) *The Theory of Capitalist Development*, New York: Monthly Review Press.

Terborgh, G. (1945) *The Bogey of Economic Maturity*, Machinery and Allied Products Institute.

Thorp, W. L. and Crowder, W. F. (1941) "Concentration and Product Characteristics as Factors in Price-Quantity Behavior", *American Economic Review*, 30, 390–408.

Timoshenko, Valdimir P. (1933) *World Agriculture and the Depression*, Ann Arbor, MI: Michigan Business Studies 5, University of Michigan Press.

United States Department of Commerce (1975) *Historical Statistics of the United States: Colonial Times to 1970*, Washington, DC: United States Government Printing Office.

Williamson, J. (1985) "On the System in Bretton Woods", *American Economic Review*, 75, 74–79.

9 Monopoly capitalism and stagnation

Keith Cowling

In Maxine Berg's recent book, Josef Steindl has argued that his explanation of the stagnationist tendency of the first one-third of the twentieth century could not be straightforwardly applied to that of the last one-third because of the rise in the power of labour and the growth of international competition (Steindl 1990). He also argued that "The development and persistence of oligopolistic market structures over a long time cannot have been without effect on the internal structure, organisation and management of firms", which had in turn led to a greater emphasis on market control and a weakening of the incentive to invest. I shall below examine some aspects of the dynamic interactions between these features of the system. I shall conclude that the rise to dominance of the transnational organisation of production within the modern giant firm over the past twenty to thirty years has at one and the same time created an intense international competition for jobs and eroded the disciplines of international competition in the product market by internalising the processes and impact of international trade. Josef Steindl is being too modest: his explanation of the stagnationist tendency of the first third of the twentieth century remains highly applicable today, because firms have reorganised in the face of the dual threat that he described. In the light of this conclusion I shall outline an appropriate policy response.

The basic monopoly capitalism argument

The argument advanced in monopoly capitalism theory is that monopolising tendencies within the older industrialised countries of the world would lead eventually to a stagnation tendency due to a deficiency of aggregate demand within that part of the world economic system and this in turn would lead to a more general stagnation.[1] Rising concentration leads to rising gross profit margins which implies a potential for the share of profits to rise, but whether or not this is realised depends on the impact of the process on aggregate demand. The immediate impact would be a downward revision in planned investment in line with the planned reduction in the rate of output within those sectors where the degree of monopoly has increased. The reduction in aggregate investment, in the absence of compensating adjustments elsewhere, would lead to a reduction in the level of profits in the whole system, which would lead to further outbacks in investment and thus generate a cumulative process of decline. Compensating, upward adjustments in investment elsewhere may of course take place, for example, via a process of diversification, but such adjustments are likely to involve considerable lags.

Any deficiency in investment could be made up by an increase in consumption out of the increased potential flow of profits, but this is unlikely to happen fast enough nor to the required extent. Managerialism, reflected in rising intra-corporate consumption out of non-reported, potential profits, and here I refer to all those expenditures *within* the corporation which contribute directly to managerial utility but which represent a deduction from profits, many, or perhaps most, of the trappings of office, could provide at least a partial antidote to such a deficiency in demand, but it contains its own contradictions. Although in *aggregate* by tending to maintain demand, managerialism serves to maintain profits, it will be seen as something to be minimised by those interested in the flow of *reported* profits. Thus, although the growth of giant firms operating in oligopolistic markets gives rise to a substantial growth in managerial discretion arising as a result of their increasing isolation from the sanctions of both capital and product markets, with all the associated expenditures that is likely to entail, such discretion will inevitably lead to measures to curtail it. The innovation of efficient internal control systems, like the multi-divisional organisational form which decentralises operational responsibility to production divisions whilst centralising control of capital flows, thus creating an efficient and well-informed internal capital market, will impose very real limits on the ability of managerial capitalism to overcome a latent tendency to stagnation.

Other adjustments are possible. Aggregate demand could be maintained via a growing net export surplus, but there is little reason to suppose that this is likely to follow a rise in the degree of monopoly within a particular economy, indeed just the reverse could happen, see Koo and Martin (1984), for an interindustry analysis of the United States.[2] If the rise in the degree of monopoly is a general trend within the world industrial system as a whole, as indeed appears to be the case, see, for example, Amin and Dietrich (1991) for the case of the EC, then it is even less likely that a growing export surplus could be maintained over an extended period, since it would raise the issue of how the rest of the world's growing trade deficit was to be financed. The present international debt crisis could be seen as a consequence of a rising degree of monopoly in the industrial and energy sectors of the world economy, and the imposed, deflationary response has further deepened the world slump.

Aggregate demand could also be maintained by reducing the aggregate propensity to save via advertising and product innovation, and we can rely on the system of monopoly capitalism to generate such a response. But this sort of investment would seem incapable of properly fulfilling this role given its essentially procyclical character. Whilst we are concerned with a long-term tendency this is not separable from the process of cyclical fluctuation: the long-term tendency is embedded in the short-term cycle and cannot be isolated from it. Advertising and product innovation tend to mimic the behaviour of investment in general and so seem ill-equipped to fill the role of replacing investment within the structure of aggregate demand.

Of course, if all else fails, governments could step in to manage aggregate demand in order to secure the full employment of resources. But clearly we cannot simply assume this sort of response. We have seen over recent history how Monetarism has replaced Keynesianism generally within the national governments and supra-national institutions of the world's advanced industrial countries. The apparently Keynesian policies of the United States during the 1980s seem to have arisen largely fortuitously out of the supply-side economics and military expansion of the Reagan administration. What is most remarkable about the US case is that despite the continuing substantial, and indeed increasing, budget deficit the economy shows no sustained propensity to generate full employment.

It may be concluded that although mechanisms are available to mitigate any stagnationist tendency, precipitated by a tendency for the degree of monopoly to increase, none is automatic. It would therefore appear that a stagnationist tendency could be seen as an inevitable consequence of the maturing of the monopoly capitalist system. Some will nevertheless argue that a slump in demand will induce a price cutting response and thus remove the initial cause of the slump. Indeed, it may be conjectured that the impact of a substantial fall in demand may cause an oligopoly group to fly apart. Each member of the group observes that its own sales have dropped and assumes that its rivals have been engaged in price-cutting, or similar market share augmenting strategies. It therefore responds with similar strategies, However, if the explanation for the original observation is in fact a general slump in demand, this will gradually become more obvious to the group. Faced with such mutual adversity we may anticipate that the group will tend to come together to solve its mutual problems. Thus, the *initial* impact of the turn-down in demand may well be a reduction in price-cost margins, but if the slump persists, we can expect to see a recovery in margins as the degree of collusion within the oligopoly group increases. Evidence is now available to support this conjecture for the UK, Cowling (1983), Conyon (1989); Norway, Berg (1986); and the US, Bils (1987). Thus it would seem that stagnationist tendencies will not be alleviated by a reversion to more competitive behaviour with the onset of slump.

Transnationalism and demand-side explanations[3]

The present system of monopoly capitalism has, in the latter half of the twentieth century, become increasingly dominated by giant economic organisations with a transnational base: the transnational corporations. I shall argue that the stagnation of demand has become a more pressing issue within such a world not only because it has become more likely, but also because it has become more unmanageable.

First, transnationalism is one of the *mechanisms* whereby the monopolisation tendency evolves. Transnationalisation has introduced, an added dimension of control over the market – it brings control by giant firms to the pattern and dimensions of trade and therefore undermines the possible impact of trade in restraining, monopoly or oligopoly pricing behaviour within national markets as well as promoting collusion within such markets via the development of multi-market contacts, see Cowling and Sugden (1987), Chapter 3. In the process of establishing such control, these giant firms may engage in various forms of economic warfare, the outcome of which in the transitional period may be a reduction in price, although even this outcome is less likely than advertising and product rivalry which will tend to enhance rather than undermine the degree of monopoly.[4]

Second, transnationalism results in a greater imbalance of power between capital and labour and therefore tends to hold down wage costs which may have implications for the distribution of income and thus for aggregate demand. Such developments will tend to reinforce the direct effects of monopolisation on distribution.

Third, the existence of a transnational production base itself contributes to the tendency for prices to be held in periods of recession: a recession in one country can lead to plant closure in that country, with the market being sourced from foreign plants. The growth of transnational firms allows for the more flexible adjustment of production to falling demand and thereby serves to hold price levels when otherwise they may have fallen.

Fourth, the evolution of transnational production orchestrated exclusively, at least for much of the formative period of the process, by the giant corporations of the advanced industrial countries, will almost inevitably lead to the extension of the forces of monopoly capitalism into countries and indeed continents where it initially had a less than secure footing. Increased infiltration of the institutions, mechanisms and ideas of monopoly capitalism will inevitably transform the nature of the economies of the newly industrialising countries. At such a point the intrusion may be seen as a dynamic and progressive force, and yet the seeds of stagnation are carried through into new territory and will ultimately grow and tend to dominate the progressive forces in the same way as in the older established industrial countries.

Thus, in the long term, we can expect that, as a result of the evolution of dominant transnationals and their spread across the world economy, the general degree of monopoly in product markets will tend to rise, this rise will be spread across a greater fraction of the world economy, and as a result the underlying stagnationist tendency of monopoly capitalism will be enhanced.

Transnationalism also has a role in serving to sustain the tendency for the propensity to save to increase as the socialisation of capital proceeds (Pitelis 1986). The growth of pension funds, coupled with the growth in corporate retained earnings, appears to have had a major impact in raising the ratio of aggregate savings to private disposable income (Marchanté 1987).[5] Given that such an increasing propensity to save is likely eventually to raise the issue of the realisation of profits in a world of monopoly capitalism, it may be argued that the whole process is likely to falter as profitable investment opportunities tend to dry up. This predicament, as Pitelis has argued, may be avoided by going transnational. Funds which might otherwise have been invested in the domestic economy, or not saved, will now be able to flow smoothly to foreign locations, whilst still serving the direct interests of those controlling the corporations involved. Thus the initial aim of gathering the savings of a broader spectrum of the population in order to allow corporate empires to grow can be sustained by extending the firm internationally as opportunities to invest domestically contract as a direct result of the effect of the whole process on domestic aggregate demand. Transnational flexibility serves to sustain a second stagnationist tendency.

The impact of the two general tendencies to stagnation identified above will be accentuated by the associated political developments arising in a world where the power of the transnationals is growing. By acting generally to curtail the power of labour and the nation–state, the transnationals are acting to contain forces which may otherwise tend to redistribute income away from profits. The consequence is that whereas a stagnationist tendency could be averted by appropriate redistributions via the political process, this will be rendered increasing unlikely as a result of the increased political power provided by the transnational organisation of production.

But the political process is also affected in another way. The existence of transnational corporations serves to reduce the effectiveness of the policies of the nation–state aimed at securing full employment. Keynesian demand management will prove less effective because of the greater leakage via imports induced by the transnational organisation of production. Thus the incentive to adopt Keynesian policies will be weakened, whilst at the same time pressures to impose classical supply-side responses would increase (see later). The system effect would be that the stagnationist tendency of the world economy would be augmented by general pressures to move away from Keynesian demand management and substitute policies requiring general wage-cutting.

Supply-side explanations

We have examined two, complementary, demand-side explanations of stagnation, in both of which transnationalism has a role. We now seek to establish that the emergence of such a stagnationist tendency within a specific country at a particular point in history may have a supply-side explanation. The first supply-side explanation relates to the interaction between transnational capital and organised labour and the second to the expansion of unproductive activity within a certain type of advanced capitalism.

Associated with the evolution of the monopoly capitalist system, with its growth of ever more dominant giant firms, was the related increase in the power and militancy of organised labour. This in turn led to an accelerating wage–price spiral coupled with political developments that culminated in the growth of the social wage – social expenditures biased in favour of workers and their families. Capital flight to other locations more conducive to capital accumulation tended to follow wherever conditions facilitated it. The present era, where production and markets are controlled by giant corporations with a transnational base and where national and international controls over trade and capital flows have been progressively reduced, with certain exceptions like the continuing tension over Japan, provide those conditions. The combination of unified international markets and giant international firms bestriding them provided a ready mechanism for the processes of deindustrialisation to develop wherever the conditions for capitalist accumulation were weakened.

Corporate structures have evolved in ways that facilitate this process. Increasingly the major corporations are becoming coordinating agencies for large numbers of production units scattered round the globe, each supplying services to the dominant organisation at competitive rates and paying competitive wages. This represents an extension of the notion of the multi-divisional corporation with its centralisation of strategic, capital-allocation decisions, coupled with the decentralisation of operational production decisions. Now strategic marketing and production decisions are being added to the headquarters function, with smaller business in satellite relation with the dominant corporation. The dominant corporations' basic role is then to secure an allocation of production internally *or externally*, consistent with cost minimisation, whilst maintaining or enhancing market control.

The generally observed tendency is either towards subcontracting to other, usually smaller, capitalist organisations (or even to individual households) at home or abroad, thus circumventing some of the difficulties giant organisations inevitably generate as a result of the growth in power of organised labour, or the switching of production and investment to new sites where labour is unorganised, has no history of large-scale organisation or has been cowed by a repressive regime. Such tendencies are manifest *within* as well as *between* countries – between the North-East and the South within the United States, as well as between the United States and Mexico or Hungary. The central feature is an increasing geographical flexibility of capitalist production which allows capital to escape the clutches of organised labour and must ultimately weaken the position of labour in the areas of production which remain.

It is often argued that deindustrialisation within the USA and Europe has been induced by the rising dominance of Japanese capital – that is a new international division of labour may have come about, but it has not been managed or controlled by the giant corporations of the old order; rather a new order prevails. When analysing the relative performance of national economies this may appear to be so; but if we measure changes in world sales classified by the nationality of the parent company the advance of European industrial capital since 1967 has exceeded that of Japanese industrial capital, being achieved by a relatively rapid expansion of foreign production (Dowrick 1983). Our conclusion must be that the deindustrialisation the West as a whole experienced in the 1970s and early 1980s cannot be ascribed to Japanese expansionism. The high relative growth rate of Japanese industrial capital in the 1960s took place in a period of relative buoyancy in economic activity in the West. It seems clear that the forces of deindustrialisation which have been most obvious in Europe have been most active during a period when European industrial capital was increasing its share of the world economy.

What of the global consequences of these processes? I would argue they are socially inefficient. Capital has become increasingly mobile leaving a trail of social disruption in its wake and imposing huge growth costs on the industrialising nations. Whilst it may be profitable for each transnational corporation to adopt such an existence, although in a longer-term perspective this must be dubious, it means that an international transmission mechanism for production, investment and jobs will have been largely adopted for income distributional reasons. Whenever workers act to raise wages, or control the intensity and duration of work, they will lose their jobs to other groups of less well-organised and less militant workers in other countries. Thus deindustrialisation is a consequence of the struggle between labour and capital in such a world. The process is basically inefficient because it is motivated by issues of control and distribution – the control of the work process by those who hire labour, and distribution in favour of those who control the location of production. The allocation of production and investment is not guided primarily by questions of efficiency – that is, getting more output from given resources. Two points arise: the *direction of move*ment is not determined by questions of social efficiency and the *frequency of movement* will generally exceed the social optimum. Misdirection is possible because of distributional considerations – excessive frequency arises because transnationals are not faced with the full social costs of their locational decisions.

The second supply-side explanation relates to the growth of unproductive activities within certain types of advanced capitalism. Such activities can be defined as those serving to maintain and reproduce an existing set of entitlements to the social product (Wolff 1987). This incorporates ruling, warfare, religion and controlling circulation. Wolff's estimates for the United States reveals that all the increase in employment over the period 1947/67 was in unproductive activity. He also found a strong inverse relation between unproductive activity and net capital formation. He defines unproductive activity as socially irrational output which implies a diversion from capital accumulation. The stagnation of American capitalism in the 1970s and 1980s he sees as related to its growth – to an historical decision taken by US capital to divert major resources to marketing rather than to advance by technological growth as in the case of West Germany and Japan. Of course in static Keynesian terms unproductive expenditures are simply an ingredient in aggregate demand and thus would appear socially rational. It is only in a dynamic perspective that they appear socially irrational, and even from this perspective it remains unclear. If it were possible that American capitalism, given its historical circumstances, could have followed the West German/Japanese route, and if this route had yielded a superior level of economic welfare then one may so conclude. But this seems almost to be denying history. Simply holding back on these unproductive activities, like advertising, the law and war does not in itself guarantee a more dynamic economy. It would appear that Wolff is addressing the symptoms of a deeper malaise whose cure has yet to be identified.

A system without democratic planning

I now turn to those characteristics of the system of transnational production which feed in *directly* to the process of global stagnation. They turn on the limitations of the international planning of the allocation of production by the transnationals on a sector-by-sector basis within the world economy as a whole.

First, the additional flexibility offered by transnational production implies greater instability due to more frequent relocation and therefore income and expenditure loss in a world with considerable frictions; the problem being created by a relatively smooth process of adjustment taking place within a private system of planning which itself is not confronted with the wider social costs. For countries (and regions) where production and investment are moving out, unemployment will inevitably rise and purchasing power will be lost, leading to a downward spiral in economic activity in general. The new nomadism will contribute to the quantitative significance of this effect, but also the frictions within such a system are partly endogenous to the process.

Clearly, there are many *external* frictions involved in any process of deindustrialisation or reindustrialisation such that labour, plant and equipment will not immediately be taken up by new firms, even in a situation where there is potential demand for such capacity. However, new production will often be averse to moving into areas where old production has moved out because of the characteristics of the labour force. This may in part be that the skills of such a labour force are inappropriate to the new production. But this is unlikely to be the whole explanation. For the same reason that production left, production will not be brought back: capital is seeking a malleable, unorganised, easily controlled group of workers and therefore prefers new, unorganised industrial workers in new areas, or perhaps women and young people, being often new entrants to the labour market and therefore typically unorganised, in the older areas. Glyn and Rowthorn (1988) offer some relevant empirical observations on the decomposition of unemployment in Western Europe.[6]

This sort of response usually means that workers have to move to the jobs rather than jobs being moved to the workers and thus *accentuates* all the rigidities imposed by the social infrastructure. Forcing the migration of individual workers contributes to the aims of the employer, but at great social cost: the speeding-up of the process of regional decline plus all the adjustment costs imposed on the families involved. And yet the removal of the initial forces of stagnation becomes conditional on such disintegration: a dynamically inefficient social process has been inaugurated. Of course, as a consequence, other areas are being industrialised so that the net loss in income is determined by the output of workers in the industrialising areas prior to the switch in production, assuming the output of the product they are moving to remains unchanged.

The second characteristic I want to focus on which feeds in directly to the processes of global stagnation is the form of integration of the international economy. The growth of international firms means that stagnationist tendencies generated in any one country, by any one or combination of the processes previously analysed, will be immediately transmitted across many countries, eventually leading to feedbacks on the originating country. The development of transnational production patterns will tend to speed up and amplify an international stagnationist tendency. Thus an *integrated* world economy is produced without an *overall* planning mechanism and yet with an international system of planning operating within each of its major constituent parts, the transnationals themselves. Thus rather than having the stability which could result from international integration within a supra-national planning authority operating at the macroeconomic level across national economies, we have the growing

instability of international integration organised by individual transnational corporations.

Perhaps the most vivid example of the integration of the world
economy within the capitalist system resulting in a heightened degree of
instability is the world financial system. Over recent history, with increasing liberalisation and the diffusion of advanced information technology,
the system has become almost completely and immediately integrated.
The outcome has been enormous instability induced by international currency speculation. The resulting huge short-term gyrations in exchange
rates in the 1980s undermined the ability of industrial capitalism to plan its
investment and production policies and make informed locational
decisions. Sharp cutbacks in investment in tradeable goods because of the
substantial increase in the degree of uncertainty surrounding such
decisions appear to have been the consequence and continue to be so. The
central point is that the very flexibility of unregulated financial capital has
impaired the efficiency of industrial capital. But clearly this is not a matter
simply of flexibility, but one of unregulated flexibility: government have
little control over the process. The phenomenal growth of the Eurocur-
rency market decisively altered the balance of power, with international
commercial banks emerging as a main focus of financial power, largely
independent of the control of national monetary authorities, see Bhaduri
and Steindl (1983, p. 7).

To conclude, I have advanced the view that the growth of the dominance of transnational corporations may have accentuated stagnationist
tendencies already endemic within monopoly capitalism. But have I over-
stated the case? Is it not true that some of the characteristics of these giant
organisations militate against such tendencies? Surely the additional flexibility is a good not a bad, in terms of allowing the rapid adaptation of the
world economy to new conditions? And surely also, these giants act to
innovate and diffuse new products and processes more rapidly through the
world economic system?

On the first point it is clear that a certain amount of flexibility is going
to be a good thing. Steindl (1966), for example, suggests that the existence
of diversified giant corporations allows for the ready diversion of
funds from monopolising to competitive sectors of the economy, thus
tending to sustain the rate of investment. But the significance of this
process depends on the bounds of the system in terms of democratic
control. Economics normally relates to nation–states in which case a
sharp distinction has to be drawn between flexibility between monopolising and competitive sectors *within* the nation–state compared with that
same flexibility *between* nation–states. This raises the issue of the transnational and its flexibility which appears *qualitatively* different from that of
the purely domestic firm. But this has arisen because we have chosen to
focus on the nation–state. Similar issues arise for communities within
nation–states; for villages, towns, cities, regions, the optimality of the flexi-

bility of giant firms takes on a very different meaning. Diversification of production within a community is likely to be desirable, but the diversification of production within a typical transnational usually offers little in this regard.

Turning to the innovatory activity of the transnationals, it can readily be accepted that major innovations can serve to nullify stagnationist tendencies, either by reducing costs or stimulating demand. Two questions arise: has the development of such innovations been enhanced by the growing dominance of the transnationals, and what is the nature of these innovations in a monopoly capitalist world? On the first point the available evidence indicates that technological progressiveness will not normally be promoted by the monopolisation of the system of production, see Scherer and Ross (1990) for a recent survey of the evidence. Despite controlling most of the recorded research and development, the giant corporations have not provided the origins of the major technological innovations. For example, a recent investigation of innovations in the UK over the period 1945–1983 gives strong support to the view that innovatory activity has been retarded by high levels of concentration and restrictions on entry (Geroski and Stewart 1991). However the transnational organisation of production does mean that once innovation takes place, then international diffusion should rapidly follow. But we must keep clear the purposes and consequences of such diffusion. The innovation of new products by these firms is an attempt to secure and enhance their market positions and hence will contribute to the general tendency for the degree of monopoly to increase over time. While in the short term such innovations may give a boost to investment, in the longer term they constitute a force contributing to the stagnationist trend.[7] Similarly with process innovations. Although those who control the transnationals will be motivated by the search for efficient techniques, this will include the "efficiency" provided by control over the workforce. New technology will tend to reflect the search for control, which will inevitably have distributional implications. In addition, there will be a bias embedded in the new technology favouring a system of production and control suited to the transnational giant. Both effects will tend to sustain a stagnationist tendency; to reverse it requires an accelerating rate of innovation which seems unlikely.

Democratic planning and the transnationals

I have argued that left to its own devices the monopoly capitalist system will tend to secular stagnation. Democratic intervention within the macroeconomy has become more important as the economic system has become more concentrated and therefore more prone to stagnation. But such intervention has been undermined in two ways: by the political power of big business in pushing governments away from full employment policies at certain conjunctures and by the reduction in the efficiency of Keynesian-type interventionist policies resulting from the transnational evolution of the organisation of production. As a result, the balance of forces has dramatically shifted against the democratic demand for full employment policies.[8] Although there will inevitably be shifts back to programmes offering a greater commitment to the reduction in employment, as we have seen in the USA and France and more recently in Britain, these are likely to be less dramatic than was true during the Long Boom so long as the countries involved fail to take decisive action to raise significantly the degree of their own economic autonomy.[9] Without such action, Keynesian reflation will be restricted by the immediate and dramatic consequences for the balance of payments.

Given the degree to which democracy throughout the world is limited by the lack of economic democracy and the growing concentration of economic power, a democratic programme has to offer an alternative system of economic planning containing mutually reinforcing demand- and supply-side strategies. The market would remain as a potentially efficient allocational device, when set within the appropriate democratically determined framework.

Demand-side policies aimed at restoring full employment are to be seen as a response to the *symptoms* of crisis induced by the system of monopoly capitalism, not the underlying causes. Given that the system is operating well below capacity, there is no reason to suppose that a substantial increase in output could not be achieved at prevailing price and wage levels. It seems reasonable to expect a strong output, response to any expansion of demand which is seen to be more than transient, and *incremental* employment could be subsidised within such an expansionary policy in order to secure a rapid turn-around. So what's the catch? Perhaps two – the balance of payments and inflation. Analysis at this point requires specific investigations of the peculiarities of particular economies, but a few general points arise from our analysis:

1   The possible disadvantage of exchange rate depreciation as a response to balance of payments problems are minimised in a world of transnational corporations operating in oligopolistic markets – there can be no presumption that prices will either fall with an appreciating currency or rise with a depreciating one, see Cowling and Sugden (1989). The transnational responds to variation in exchange rates by adjusting the location of production and the balance of trade flows: prices will be determined by local (oligopolistic) market conditions.

2   There is a strong general case for imposing controls over trade and capital flows in a world dominated by transnational corporations – free trade increases the leverage of capital over both workers and governments; conversely, a willingness to intervene will contain such leverage.

3   The stronger the commitment to sustained expansion, the lower will tend to be the rate of inflation *within* the period of transition to full employment. If demand increases, but there is great uncertainty about whether or not it will persist, then firms will not respond with an increase in output; but they will be induced to increase prices.

4   Whilst inflationary problems may not be expected to be significant in the short run, it is still desirable to institute mechanisms for inflation control. A permanent system of price controls should be introduced as the basic structure of control over inflationary tendencies in a monopoly capitalist system. Such controls would also negate any stagnationist tendencies arising from the growth of more concentrated structures, and would indeed remove one of the incentives for such growth. Wage and salary controls are also warranted.

Demand-side policy is crucial in the short run, but the fundamental economic issue lies on the supply side: the erosion of national and regional economic autonomy by the dominant transnationals. The dominance of the regulatory function of government (although *in itself* of declining significance), has to be displaced by its developmental function – that is its direct involvement in the birth, growth and death of industries. But in neither strategic planning of the future, nor allocative procedures of the present, should the system be a pure one. Industrial policy will partially supplant the market system, but the market will continue through the interstices of such strategic planning – the democratic strategy would incorporate the market. Industrial policy appears as an attempt by national, regional and local communities to regain control of their economic futures. Industries, both old and new, which appear viable and indeed strategically important in a long-run perspective, but which are vulnerable in the short or medium term without significant intervention, have to be identified and nurtured, However, it is clear that such intervention is a difficult and dangerous project: it is difficult to identify certain areas of economic activity on which resources should be concentrated and dangerous to remove certain areas from the discipline of international competition. I believe we can learn much from Japan. We shall need something like MITI, plus a variety of broadly-based participative structures aimed at generating an overall consensus in favour of such intervention. Because no broad consensus for economic planning exists (indeed, after 1989, there is an almost total absence of discussion about it – except to reveal an almost total prejudice against it), it can only begin to filter back on to the democratic agenda by starting with cases where such consensus exists (perhaps transport and energy) and then allowing people to gain experience by being involved in the process. Participation is thus essential and a piecemeal/step-by-step approach is required to allow people to get used to it. Even in the present political climate, it is glaringly obvious to a broad spectrum of people in Britain that strategies for coal, oil, electricity and gas need to be coordinated for any sensible pattern of energy production and use to emerge; similarly with road and rail transport. The spillover from the successful planning of these sectors would be a growing willingness to accept that economic planning has a crucial role within a market economy.

The attempt to create relatively autonomous national economies may appear, at first sight, a paradoxical response to the imperialism of the transnationals. A more conventional response is to accept the existing order and then, in some cases, to recognise national Keynesianism as increasingly anachronistic in such a world. The logic of this position, for Keynesians, demands a coordinated response across nations to secure a break-out from world stagnation. However, whilst recognising that coordinated reflation is a crucial component of a policy response I am arguing that it should be seen as the culmination of a process in which a network of relatively autonomous national communities is created, rather than simply representing the injection of a higher level of demand into a world economic system which otherwise remains fundamentally unchanged, together with all its inevitable contradictions. Nevertheless we are awash in a sea of comment which unreservedly recommends the free play of market forces at the international level; protectionism is bad, opening up markets is good. To my mind, economic arguments which once had substantial validity, and which of course retain some, are being pushed far too far by otherwise reasonable people, to the exclusion of other far more fundamental matters. Keynes himself advocated a substantial degree of self-sufficiency and economic isolation because "we all need to be as free as possible of interference from economic changes elsewhere, in order to make our own favourite experiments towards the ideal social republic of the future", see Keynes (1982, p. 241).

Of course, many will see any attempt to cut off the nation–state from some of the forces of the international economy as beggar-my-neighbour policies. In a world stagnating under such forces, this would seem wide of the mark. The aim of such a strategy is not to induce a stagnation of demand for the output of the rest of the system, but to establish the conditions whereby a particular society can thrive and prosper. I have argued that to achieve this at the present time requires that individual nations sever at least some of the international connections which have been established by transnational capital. Dynamic, fully employed economies are not a threat to each other, but they cannot be established without some degree of isolation from world capitalist forces.

Acknowledgements

The original version was presented at a conference in Honour of Josef Steindl, Vienna, May 22 1992. This chapter was originally published in

Review of Political Economy, vol. 7, no. 4, October 1995. This journal's website can be found at http://www.tandf.co.uk.

Notes

1 See for example Steindl (1952), Baran and Sweezy (1966) and Cowling (1982).
2 It is interesting to reflect on the current balance of payments positions of the United States and Japanese economies. The United States has demonstrated a strong *concentrating* tendency over the 1980s, Attaran and Saghafi (1988), coupled with the growth of a substantial trade *deficit*, whereas the Japanese economy has revealed a *deconcentrating* trend, Adams and Brock (1988), coupled with the emergence of a substantial trade *surplus*.
3 A fuller analysis of the underlying relationships is developed in Cowling and Sugden (1987).
4 Recent evidence suggests that within the European car market exchange rate fluctuations have *not* been seen as opportunities to engage in price competition, see Cowling and Sugden (1989).
5 Of course there has been much discussion about the *falling* propensity to save in the 1980s. No doubt this has been linked to the freeing-up and indeed huge promotion of the credit-supplying industry. This is likely to have had a one-off impact, rather than some continuing major effect on the underlying tendencies. The latest evidence points to a rising propensity to save as people try to recover sustainable credit–income ratios.
6 Now of course this process is subject to various constraints: social and physical infrastructure clearly matter. It is also the case that the characteristics of the labour force will change as a consequence of the experience and duration of unemployment: recently General Motors described as "the most flexible union arrangements in Europe" (*Financial Times*, April 6th 1990) its agreement about a new engine plant with unions in Merseyside, an area previously notorious for union militancy and presently notorious for long-term unemployment.
7 A fundamental distinction has to be drawn between product rivalry among the many and among the few. A rivalry that maintains deconcentrated structures has very different macroeconomic implications.
8 In the face of their present domestic crises it was interesting to see the USA and France trying to push unemployment to the top of the OECD agenda early in 1992 (*Financial Times*, May 11th 1992), while Britain, from a less compelling political position, was adopting a "low key approach" which is now in the process of revision in the turmoil of policy reappraisal following departure from the ERM. This is in the context of an increase of five million in OECD unemployment since 1990 which has reversed most of the reduction in unemployment levels which had been achieved since the mid-1980s. The February OECD level was estimated at 7.2 per cent and that for the EC at 9.2 per cent.
9 It will be argued that international policy coordination offers a way out. Certainly international reflation will pose fewer problems than Keynesianism in one country, but the technical solution of international policy coordination by no means guarantees those policies to be full employment ones, witness the recent EC Finance Ministers discussions in Oporto (*Financial Times*, May 11th 1992) where coordination to boost growth was agreed, but fiscal/monetary reflation was rejected, in favour of lower budget deficits, wage moderation and promotion of flexibility in the labour market. Deeper political and economic changes will be required to bring reflationary policies back onto the agenda.

References

Adams, W. and Brock, J. (1988) "The Bigness Mystique and the Merger Policy Debate: An International Perspective", *Northwestern Journal of International Law and Business*, 9, 1–48.

Amin, A. and Dietrich, M. (1991) *Towards a New Europe? Structural Change in the European Economy*, Cheltenham: Edward Elgar.

Attaran, M. and Saghafi, M. (1988) "Concentration trends and profitability in the US manufacturing sector 1970–84", *Applied Economics*, 20, 1497–1510.

Baran, P. and Sweezy, P. (1966) *Monopoly Capital*, New York: Monthly Review Press.

Berg, A. (1986) "Excess Capacity and the Degree of Collusion: Some Estimates for the Norwegian Manufacturing Sector", *International Journal of Industrial Organization*, March, 99–108.

Bhaduri, A. and Steindl, J. (1983) *The Rise of Monetarism as a Social Doctrine*, Thames Papers in Political Economy.

Bils, M. (1987) "The Cyclical Behaviour of Marginal Cost and Price", *American Economic Review*, December, 838–855.

Conyon, M. (1991) "Monopoly Capitalism, Profits, Income Distribution and Unionism", PhD thesis, University of Warwick.

Cowling, K. (1982) *Monopoly Capitalism*, London: Macmillan.

Cowling, K. (1983) "Excess Capacity and the Degree of Collusion: Oligopoly Behaviour in the Slump", *Manchester School*, December, 341–359.

Cowling, K. and Sugden, R. (1987) *Transnational Monopoly Capitalism*, Brighton: Wheatsheaf.

Cowling, K. and Sugden, R. (1989) "Exchange Rate Adjustment and Oligopoly Pricing Behaviour", *Cambridge Journal of Economics*, 13, 373–393.

Dowrick, S. (1983) *Notes on Transnationals*, Mimeo, Department of Economics, University of Warwick.

Geroski, P. and Stewart, G. (1991) "Competitive Rivalry and the Response of Markets to Innovative Opportunities", in S. Arndt and G.W. McKenzie (eds) *The Competitiveness of the UK Economy*, London: Macmillan.

Glyn, A. and Rowthorn, R. (1988) "West European Unemployment: Corporatism and Structural Change", *American Economic Review*, 78, 194–199.

Keynes, J. (1982) "National self-sufficiency", *New Statesman and Nation 1933*, reprinted in D. Moggridge (ed.) *The Collected Writings of John Maynard Keynes*, Vol. XXI, London: Macmillan.

Marchanté, A. (1987) "An Analysis of the Relationship between Corporate and Personal Savings, Pooling Cross-Section and Time Series Data of 13 OECD Countries, 1964–1980", MA dissertation, University of Warwick.

Pitelis, C. (1986) *Corporate Capital: Control, Ownership Saving and Prices*. Cambridge: Cambridge University Press.

Scherer, F. and Ross, D. (1990) *Industrial Market Structure and Economic Performance*, 3rd edn. Boston: Houghton-Mifflin.

Steindl, J. (1952) *Maturity and Stagnation in American Capitalism*, Oxford: Oxford University Press.

Steindl, J. (1966) "On Maturity in Capitalist Economies", In *Problems of Economic Dynamics and Planning: Essays in Honour of Michał Kalecki*, Oxford: Pergamon Press, pp. 423–434.

Steindl, J. (1990) "From Stagnation in the 1930s to Slow Growth in the 1970s", in M. Berg (ed.) *Political Economy in the Twentieth Century*, London: Phillip Allen.

Wolff, E. (1987) *Growth, Accumulation and Unproductive Activity: An Analysis of the Post-War US Economy*, New York: Cambridge University Press.

10 Trend and cycle

Josef Steindl

The long-term development

Instead of referring to the trend I could equally well refer to long-term development or long-term growth but I do not intend to deal with it in the manner of the usual growth theory which is the method of comparative steady states. I should rather prefer to deal with it in the same way as with the trade cycle which is usually represented by a difference or other functional equation which together with given initial conditions will trace out the process. The initial conditions are important because it is through them that exogenous factors are introduced into the process. These exogenous factors take account of the fact that our models cannot embrace the whole world or the whole of history and must therefore start from facts which are given from outside. The method of comparative steady states tends to bypass this problem of exogenous influences and that is only too natural since they involve great difficulties. It may be thought, however, that by avoiding these difficulties we may miss the right understanding of the actual process and expose ourselves to the risk of great misunderstandings.

Anybody who writes on long-term growth is in danger of taking a larger bite than he can chew. I want at least to reduce the risk by limiting myself to the demand aspects of the problem. This is the question which occupied Rosa Luxemburg: How can capitalism, bent on high accumulation rates as it is, find markets for its products? At times the question seems pointless, at other times it becomes so urgent that people wonder whether there is any future in producing more goods.

The basis from which I start is Kalecki's view (1943, 1954, 1968) on long-run growth, on what he calls the trend. He was exceedingly brief on this subject, but I think that the following two statements contain the essence of what he wrote:

a   A positive trend will only be generated by a continuing exogenous influence, that is, if we exclude the influence of public spending and of export surpluses, by continuing technological change which promises extra profits to the innovator.

b   The exogenous influence is combined with endogenous elements and it is the two in their combined and mutual interaction which produces the trend. Kalecki in this connection speaks of a "semi-autonomous trend". The endogenous element corresponds to a long-term memory, that is to the evolution of the economy in the recent past (where recent is to be understood as a series of years, perhaps embodying a whole trade cycle).

This requires a few comments: the term endogenous must be specified by reference to a theoretical system, which embodies all the relations (the feedbacks or couplings) between the elements of the system. In the present case the system is the macroeconomic model of the main elements of the social accounting system such as investment, income, profits, wages and employment, etc. More specifically it is the framework of Kalecki's theory of the trade cycle.

The essence of Kalecki's position is that he denies the possibility of explaining the trend by reference to endogenous factors alone (see his polemic against Harrod (Kalecki 1962)) but equally also refuses to regard it as a purely exogenous phenomenon. The present chapter is concerned with a discussion of the two sets of factors and the role which the one or the other may play in the generation of the trend. It is thus basically no more than an attempt to elucidate and elaborate the broad hints which Kalecki has given on the subject.

Trend and cycle

Trend and cycle are concepts which arise in the statistical analysis of time series. They are distinguished and separated *ex post*. Is there an economic meaning in these concepts which relates them to economic behaviour? Some such meaning is certainly presupposed in the theories of several authors: Kalecki's pure business cycle, Harrod's analysis of long-term growth and cycle. The underlying economic idea seems to be this.

The trend is a slow movement, non-reversible, and the underlying type of behaviour is based on long-run perspectives ("long-run expectations") and perhaps also on long-run memory.

The cycle is a relatively quick movement, reversible, based on short-run memory (current or rather recent experience) and, it seems implied, short-run perspectives. (Short run in this context refers to events within the course of a single business cycle, while long run goes beyond the experience of a cycle.)

Once these intuitive interpretations are accepted, it becomes rather puzzling that many authors from Aftalion to Frisch and Kalecki have regarded the trade cycle as essentially produced by fluctuations in fixed capital investment. But we are inclined, with Keynes, to think of fixed investment as based on a long-run perspective and not merely on the spur of the current boom. And it seems rather irrational to base it on short-run memory, which is on the current or very recent market data.

One could imagine a variety of possible conclusions from this dilemma. The most radical conclusion would be that the business cycle is not a matter of fluctuations in fixed capital investment but rather a matter of inventory accumulation. In this way the contradiction would be cleanly eliminated. This is the path chosen by Goodwin in his paper 'The problem of trend and cycle' (Goodwin 1982 p. 116) where he appeals to the empirical work of Abramovitz which demonstrates the large extent and impact of fluctuations in inventory accumulation in the course of the cycle. Naturally Goodwin recognises that there are large fluctuations in fixed investment in the cycle as well but he regards these as induced by the inventory accumulation.

Goodwin's paper has led me to the following idea: it is reasonable to think that much of fixed investment is planned, projected and prepared with a long-run perspective and quite independently of the cyclical conditions. This is especially true where the investment is motivated by technical considerations. It is only the timing of the ultimate realisation of the project which very often (but not necessarily) is synchronised with the cycle. The investment projects in question are not necessarily planned with a view to immediate execution but may be kept in store for some time. The time when they are taken out and executed is often the beginning of a recovery when an atmosphere of optimism infects the planner and overcomes his hesitations. A rational motive will be that at this juncture finance usually is cheapest and easiest to obtain. It may be noted that by this last explanation we also bypass an old contentious question: whether or how far the rate of interest has an effect on investment. Even if it has none in the sense in which the question was always understood, it would with high plausibility affect the timing of the investment. Even modest differences in the cost of borrowing in different periods of time might have a strong influence on the choice of time for execution of a big investment project.

The idea of distinguishing two things: whether or how to invest, and when to invest enables us to understand the double role of investment, as an irreversible trend component embodying new techniques, and as the dominant motor of the business cycle, that is, as a factor of instability. The theory of Kalecki and others who identify the business cycle with fluctuations in fixed investment will not be impaired in this way.

Measurement of technical progress

As soon as the subject of technology is introduced, some unpleasant questions arise. How is technical progress to be measured? Where is the frontier demarcation line to be drawn between what is endogenous and what is exogenous, i.e. where, at which stage of the metamorphosis from abstract idea to concrete production process, does technology enter the space of relations which we choose to define as endogenous? The metamorphosis is quite complicated: It starts in the field of pure science, basic research, goes on to applied research, from there to development from there to the actual commercial production by the pioneer-innovator and ends with the diffusion of the method.

Of course economic factors are at work more or less all along of this process and special studies may deal with all the stages in greater or lesser depth. For macro-economic purposes and at the present stage of our understanding of the process, however, it is advisable that we should include only the last stages in a growth model. That means that we should regard only the investment of the innovator as endogenous and leave all the preceding stages outside even though that means, for example, regarding R&D as exogenous. If we choose this rather conservative and unambitious approach, we can define technical progress by reference to the yearly sum of investments of an innovative character. All other investments would be regarded as related to diffusion. The task of deciding which investment is innovative and which not is thrown on the specialists of technology assessment. Of course one can find improvements of secondary importance in practically every investment. The decision on what is minor and what not will to some extent rest on judgement and common sense, which does not mean that it is arbitrary. The importance of a new process or product will be judged by its consequences, that is, by the scope of diffusion which again can be measured in terms of the volume of investment. The question of measurement is in any case not new but has to be answered by everybody who analyses empirically the course of technological change. We shall take it, then, that as a first approach we can regard the flow of innovative investments as a measure of the impact of the "exogenous" factor technical progress. We may refine this crude concept if it is possible to allocate the diffusion investment which has materialised in the course of the years to the respective innovation which has called it forth. The various innovative investments can then be given their due weight corresponding to their importance in the total development. The investment in the first motor car factory, for example, will only in this way be given its due weight which can of course only be established *ex post*. For innovations which are in an early stage of development, the weight attributed to them will have to be based on guesswork.

The question of measurement of technology has so far been treated mainly on the micro-economic level by engineers. A very sophisticated treatment is due to Devendra Sahal (Sahal 1981) who deals with the development of the locomotive. The engineering studies suggest surprising continuities and regularities of the learning process, but the economists are still far from being able to integrate this into their own concepts or experience.

Technology and economic structure

For the most part technical progress proceeds in very small steps (Sahal). It is a process of learning which by its nature requires time and consists of gradual advance. In the course of this continuous development there occurs, however, from time to time a major advance, a jump as it were. This is normally embodied in a new type of equipment. This discontinuous change or "innovation" is the resulting sum of a large number of preceding steps which lead up to it. Equally, after the first pioneer has built the new equipment, there is a long series of improvements, a process of learning to use the equipment, and a follow-up process of gradual improvements in the product or in the process or in both. It should be noted that the discontinuity in the process of technical advance has not only a scientific-technical but also an economic-social and institutional side. The novelty meets the resistance of established institutions; if it happens to overcome them, it will be more or less disruptive. In fact, the discontinuity is perhaps more important in society than in the development of technical knowledge itself.

Since long-run growth practically always involves technical change and occasional discontinuous jerks it will always involve structural change. This is a pretty large subject and I mention it here only to introduce certain amendments to my treatment of it in *Maturity and Stagnation*. In this book technical change was exemplified by the case of an industry in which innovation is introduced by one firm and subsequently spreads to the other firms in the industry, leading eventually to the elimination of some firms which are too slow to adapt and for whom there is no more room in view of the growth of the innovating firm's capacity.

This analysis, restricted to the pattern of change in a single industry, applies primarily to process innovations; it can be adapted to the case of a new product which is not so radically different that it involves the establishment of an altogether new industry. It does not cover, however, the case of a radically new product which is produced by an entirely new and different industry and is not in very direct competition with the established products or services of other industries. In an indirect way it may sooner or later affect some of the other industries (television versus cinema), it may in some cases even lead to the disappearance of an old industry, but the function of competition in such a new industry will be taken over for the greater part by new entrants which follow on the heel of the innovator, who contribute to the gradual improvement and cheapening of the new product and who bring about in good time the lowering of the profit margin in the same way as in the case of process innovation in a single industry I treated before.

If one considers the emergence of new and the disappearance of old industries, this suggests a rather simple interpretation of maturity: a new industry will experience a phase of expansion while the circle of buyers and users of the new product widens up to a practical maximum. After that is reached, growth of the output declines to the level of replacement demand. There is saturation. So, even without considering the case where the product goes entirely out of use, we have a general pattern of maturity as long as we consider individual industries only. The protagonists of the "long wave" have tried to use this pattern to explain maturity for the economy as a whole. For this purpose one has to assume either the existence of a dominant industry or technique which, when it matures, drags the whole economy down in its own decline. Or else one has to assume that innovations transforming the whole economy appear in swarms so as to synchronise the life cycle of quite a number of industries which grow and decline *unisono*.

This generalisation, in so far as one may be willing to accept it, only leads to further questions about the reasons for dominance or clustering of innovations. What is certainly true is that this type of maturity is relevant for the structural crises of important industries which become especially tragic when they are concentrated in certain regions.

The question which concerns us here is whether the pattern of aggressive competition which I used in *Maturity and Stagnation* to describe the impact of process innovations on a single industry is still relevant in these cases of major product innovation. The answer is that all product innovations in due course lead to a succession of improvements of the production method as a natural consequence of the process of learning which proceeds as production goes on. Product innovation is followed by process innovation and a cheapening of the product which in turn permits the full exploitation of a potential market (Freeman 1982). This means that the picture which I drew of the role of aggressive competition in an industry is in principle relevant for all cases of product innovation, too. The reduction of the extra profits created by the innovation to a normal level depends on the aggressive competition of firms which are struggling for room in the market to match their capacity. The accent, however, is now strongly on the role of the new entrants which I neglected in my book.

The cycle

What do we expect of a theory of the cycle, what is it good for? There are economists who see not sense in it at all because every cycle is different, and the historical individuality precludes any generalisations. According to another opinion, diametrically opposed to the first, the theory ought to demonstrate the instability of capitalism under all circumstances, that is, also in the absence of exogenous disturbances. But in the world as it is, and with respect to a theory which, realistically speaking, can only contain a part of this world, there exist these exogenous disturbances; for practical purposes instability can only mean that the system is unable to cope with them adequately.

A necessary condition for macroeconomic change – trend or cycle – is that the disturbances and the corresponding reactions in the small do not offset each other so as to permit stability of the whole system but rather tend to go to a large extent in the same direction. They are unlike a self-regulating system either because the individual movements reinforce each other (imitation) or because they all respond to a common signal, for example, the rate of interest.

In my opinion, trend and cycle are to be treated from the point of view of the following "research program" (in the sense of Lakatos): the macroeconomic system is like a machine which works up and transforms the disturbances which are fed into it from the outside in the course of time. This approach is dictated by a dominating practical interest in economic policy: We want to know how the system reacts to various measures or events and how the daily or monthly movements of the *Konjunktur* (state or tendency of trade) have come about in each concrete case. This preoccupation with the practical aims of the theory is the reason why I cannot be convinced by Goodwin's insistence on a non-linear treatment of the cycle. The response of the system to disturbances is, I hope, adequately dealt with by linear approximations. This is true also for the long-term development which is only the result of an accumulation of short-term changes.

This leads to the question of the unity of trend and cycle. Unfortunately very often independent and separate theories have been produced for the one and the other even by those authors who intended to arrive at a unified theory. The failure stems probably from the mathematical formulation which is so much easier if you have one equation for each, independent of each other. But in reality the trend component and the cyclical component are determined at the same time and are parts of the same process, separated only artificially by statistical or analytic exogenous and endogenous elements in the determination of the trend. This combination seems to me essential for the following reason: it is accepted that innovations stimulate growth, but it is not easy to believe that these exogenous technological factors would in themselves explain the rate of growth. The speed with which the economic consequences of an innovation work out could hardly be determined by the innovation as such or by mere technological facts; it is plausible that it should be affected by the general economic conditions such as, for example, availability of finance, of management, skills, of excess capacity in traditional industries, of the climate of business expectations, etc. I am not able to formalize this but I shall try to throw out a hint in this direction. Supposing we could put an estimate on the total gross investment potential which would be directly and indirectly called forth in the course of time by a certain innovation. We could imagine that this potential is gradually worked off in accordance with an exponential function $R = R_o e^{-rt}$. The speed with which the exogenous stimulus is used up (given by r) depends on endogenous macroeconomic developments. It will be determined by the trend cum cycle equation, in particular by the integral term which contains long-term memory. The complement to the above mentioned potential will be the total capital stock built up in the course of time in connection with the innovation: $R_0 (1 - e^{-rt})$.

The influence of the long-term memory may involve either a positive or a negative feedback. In the first case it will generate a trend component which will, however, die out unless it is again stimulated by outside influence. If the long-term memory involves a negative feedback, it will create a long wave and no trend at all.

We may consider an example of a positive feedback. It seems plausible that not only the current flow of retained profits (included in Kalecki's trade cycle equation) but also the stock of those retained profits accumulated in the past, in so far as it has not been invested, should be relevant for the investment decisions.

These disposable funds represent lending of the firm. At the same time we have also to consider the firm's debts as relevant for its investment decisions. Both elements together make up the firm's net indebtedness which should be seen in relation to its equity capital. We find that the long-term memory is here fully expressed in a stock figure which results from an integration of past flows. The present net indebtedness will be positively influenced by past growth rate, and in addition, of course by government deficits and foreign balance in the past years.

Other positive feedbacks may come from the past growth rate, from the long-term rate of capacity utilisation, from the potential of innovations which is somehow existent immediately behind the scene. An example of a negative feedback is the stock of accumulated capital. We shall consider this now in detail.

Excess capacity in the long run

In the course of the business cycle, accumulation is always frustrated, because after a time excess capacity appears which depresses investment activity to negative net levels so that at the end of a "pure business cycle" we are back to where we started from: the resulting net investment is zero. How is it that the long-run accumulation escapes this fate and succeeds in building up a stock of real capital? What makes the mechanism which frustrates the build-up of a capital stock in the short run non-operative in the long run? In my opinion, this is due to a difference in the working of distribution in the short and in the long run. In the short run, the distribution structure is in a sense fixed because of the inflexibility of the mark-up which throws the whole weight of adjustment on the utilisation of capacity which is extremely flexible. In the long run, however, reaction patterns appear which need some time to work out and which as they do can affect the mark-up and the competitive situation of the industry. The long-run response to excess capacity is aggressive competition either by some of the existing producers or by new entrants which may not be discouraged by the industry's overcapacity if they have special advantages as compared to the old producers, such as new technical methods. Another influence can come from the side of labour. If the price of the product is constrained by foreign competition in an open market, the mark-up may be subjected to squeezing by the action of unions or by scarcity of labour.

The danger of appearance of excess capacity which we assume is almost always threatening accumulation arises generally from the fact that technical progress tends to increase the mark-up and therefore shifts distribution in favour of profits. This at the same time tends to create excess capacity.

The relation between a "normal" mark-up and a "normal" long-run capacity utilisation which will be underlying the argument can be described as follows. It is supposed that with a normal (customary) long-run utilisation the mark-up has to be just large enough to yield a profit rate (or rather rate of retained profits) which is sufficient to finance the given growth rate, taking into account borrowing to an extent which will not change the existing relative indebtedness. There is thus a "warranted" rate of retained profits which in turn is determined by a given growth rate – that is the rate of growth which has been ruling so far and which gives rise to the question whether it can continue and under which conditions its continuation is either assured or endangered.

If the "natural" tendency of the system to produce a shift towards profits is counteracted by aggressive competition then there will be two results.

There will be an increase in the real wage and the consequence will be that a certain number of producers – those with the most outdated methods and equipment – will be eliminated. This will be a factor which contributes to the reduction in overcapacity.

Second, owing to the shift to labour the effective demand will increase and that should in principle be a strong force making for the reestablishment of "normal" rates of utilisation. The second factor may be considered the major one, but the first factor will have a considerable role to play in the structural changes due to the maturity of old industries.

The result of these considerations seems to indicate not only that distribution is the element which accounts for the difference in behaviour in short and long run, but also that the continuation of the growth process depends essentially on the action of certain correctives to the tendency of technical progress which tends to shift income towards profits; correctives, either in form of aggressive competition or in form of pressure from labour (in an open economy) will be necessary in order to prevent the appearance of continuing overcapacity which would frustrate the further accumulation. Thus distribution turns out to be a most important element in the explanation of the normal growth process.

This does not mean that the essential role of the exogenous factor as it was described before, is in any way modified.

Acknowledgements

This chapter was found among the late Josef Steindl's papers by Alois Guger (Wifo, Vienna) who made it available with some editorial amendments, in particular, he added some subtitles and the list of references. The chapter, apparently written in 1988 and still considered as preliminary by the author, is the most recent version of a series of manuscripts on this long-lasting theme of Josef Steindl. Professor Kazimierz Laski has also read the chapter and recommended publication. Valuable editorial suggestions by Claudio Milazzo are to be acknowlegded.

References

Abramovitz, M. (1950) *Inventories and Business Cycles*, New York: National Bureau of Economic Research.

Freeman, C., Clark, J. and Soete, L. (1982) *Unemployment and Technical Innovation*, London: Francis Pinter.

Goodwin, R. M. (1953) "The Problem of Trend and Cycle", *Yorkshire Bulletin of Economic and Social Research*; reprinted in R.M. Goodwin, *Essays in Economic Dynamics*, London: Macmillan, 1982.

Kalecki, M. (1943) *Studies in Economic Dynamics*, London: Allen & Unwin.

Kalecki, M. (1954) *Theory of Economic Dynamics*, London: Allen & Unwin.

Kalecki, M. (1962) *"Observations on the Theory of Growth"*, *Economic Journal*, March.

Kalecki, M. (1968) "Trend and the Business Cycle Reconsidered", *Economic Journal*, June.

Lakatos, I. (1978) "Falsification and the Methodology of Scientific Research Programmes", in I. Lakatos and A. Musgrave (eds), *Criticism and the Growth of Knowledge*, London: Cambridge University Press.

Sahal, D. (ed.) (1981) *Pattern of Technological Innovation*, Reading, MA: Addison-Wesley.

Steindl, J. (1952) *Maturity and Stagnation in American Capitalism*, Oxford University Institute of Statistics, Monograph No. 4, Oxford: Basil Blackwell.

Index